SMALL BUSINESS AND ENTREPRENEURSHIP

SMALL BUSINESS AND ENTREPRENEURSHIP

S. Anil Kumar
Professor & Head
Dept. of Commerce and Management
NMKRV College for Women, Bangalore

I.K. International Publishing House Pvt. Ltd.
NEW DELHI • BANGALORE

Published by

I.K. Publishing House Pvt. Ltd.
S-25, Green Park Extension, Uphaar Cinema Market
New Delhi - 110 016 (India)
E-mail : ik_in@vsnl.net

ISBN 978-81-906942-3-0

10 9 8 7 6 5 4 3 2

Published by Krishan Makhijani for I.K. Publishing House Pvt. Ltd. S-25, Green Park Extension, Uphaar Cinema Market, New Delhi - 110 016 and Printed by Rekha Printers Pvt. Ltd., Okhla Industrial Area, Phase II, New Delhi - 110 020.

Preface

It is easy to start a small scale enterprise but difficult to make them survive. It is more so in the context of ever increasing competition in business brought by liberalization, globalization and privatization of the Indian economy. Therefore, knowledge of entrepreneurship and creation of small business carefully is of paramount importance to survive.

Entrepreneurship is presently the most effective method for bridging the gap between science and marketplace, creating new enterprises and bringing new products and services to the market. These entrepreneurial activities significantly affect the economy of country by building the economic base and providing jobs.

The present book is primarily designed to serve as a textbook for those studying entrepreneurship and small Industry business at graduate and postgraduate levels in Management, Commerce, Engineering disciplines. It is also intended to be of value to professionals aspiring to become entrepreneurs and also to the existing entrepreneur.

This book is divided into Part A and Part B.

Part A: Entrepreneurship: It contains:

1. Concept of Entrepreneurship.
2. Entrepreneur.
3. Entrepreneurial Competency.
4. Development of Entrepreneurial Competency and Motivation

Part B: Small Business: It Contains:

5. Small Scale Industries.
6. Enterprise Creation.
7. Business Plan.
8. Implementation of the Project (Support Agencies)
9. Industrial Estates
10. Sickness in Small-scale Industries.
11. Business Crisis.
12. International Entrepreneurial Opportunities.

Being student friendly is the unique feature of this book. The subject matter has been presented systematically in 12 chapters, which will enable the reader to master the topics without any additional guidance.

This book covers the theoretical aspects, case studies, proformas and profiles of entrepreneurs, questionnaires, skill development exercises and questions.

Complete care has been taken to make the book error free. However, mistakes might have crept inadvertently. Readers finding any errors are requested to bring it to my notice, for enabling me to rectify them in future editions.

My acknowledgements are also due to Dr. S.C. Poornima Anil Kumar, without her support and sacrifice this work would not have been completed.

Finally, I acknowledge the Almighty who has blessed me with the knowledge, required for writing this book.

S. Anil Kumar

Contents

Preface v
Syllabus xiii

PART A: ENTREPRENEURSHIP

1. Concept of Entrepreneurship

1.1 Introduction 3
1.2 Definitions 4
1.3 Group Entrepreneurship 5
1.4 Social Entrepreneurship 6
1.5 Enterprise 6
1.6 Types of Enterprises 6
1.7 Need and Importance of Entrepreneurship 8
1.8 India's Potentiality for the Growth of Entrepreneurship 12
1.9 Categories of Entrepreneurship 13
1.10 Entrepreneurship in the New Indian Economy 13
1.11 Entrepreneurship Process of New Venture Process 14
1.12 Entrepreneurship Development 16
1.13 Importance or Objectives of Entrepreneurship Development 17
1.14 Process of Entrepreneurship Development 18
1.15 Impact of Government Policies on Entrepreneurship Development Movement in India 19
1.16 Entrepreneurship Development Programme (EDP) 20
1.17 Measure to Boost the EDP in India 21
1.18 Intrapreneurship 23
Case Studies 25

2. Entrepreneur **32**

2.1 Introduction 32
2.2 Concept of Entrepreneur 33
2.3 Definitions 34
2.4 Importance of an Entrepreneur 35
2.5 Benefits of being an Entrepreneur 35
2.6 Problems of being an Entrepreneur 36
2.7 Qualities of an Entrepreneur 36
2.8 Characteristics or Traits of an Entrepreneur 39
2.9 Functions of an Entrepreneur 41
2.10 Types of Entrepreneur 43
2.11 Women Entrepreneurs 47
2.12 Classification of Women Entrepreneurs in India 48
2.13 Development of Women Entrepreneurs in India 50
2.14 Problems of Women Entrepreneurs 51
2.15 Promotion of Women Entrepreneurs 54
2.16 Intrapreneur 55
Case studies 57

3. Entrepreneurial Competencies **73**

3.1 Meaning 73
3.2 Components of Entrepreneurial Competencies 73
3.3 Entrepreneurial Competency 76
3.4 Types of Competencies or Competency Requirements for an Entrepreneur 77
3.5 Tools for Assessment of Competencies 85

4. Development Entrepreneurial Competency and Motivation **103**

4.1 Introduction 103
4.2 Entrepreneurship Motivation Training (EMT) 104
4.3 Objectives of EMT 104
4.4 EMT Related Activities 104
4.5 Components of EMT 105
Annexures 105

PART B: SMALL BUSINESS

5. Small Scale Industries **139**

5.1 Introduction 139
5.2 Definition of Small-Scale Industries 140
5.3 Investment Limits for Small-Scale Industries 143
5.4 Objective of Promotion of Small-Scale Sector 145
5.5 Advantages of Promotion of Small-Scale Industries 146
5.6 Deficiencies in Small-Scale Industries 148
5.7 Importance and Role of SSI 150
5.8 Problems Faced by SSI 152
5.9 Steps to be taken to Solve the Problems 158
5.10 Strategies of Solve Problems of SSI 158
5.11 Government Policies to SSI 164
5.12 Government Assistance and Concessions for SSIs 167
5.13 Recent Govt. Action 175
5.14 Organizational Form or Ownership Pattern 178

6. Enterprise Creation **184**

6.1 Starting a Small Industry 184
6.2 Entrepreneurial Function or Process of Starting a New Venture Based on Personal Competencies 185
6.3 Entrepreneurial Function or Process 186
6.4 Requirements to Start a Business Venture 190
6.5 Feasibility of the Project 199
6.6 Business Incubators 200
Annexures 202

7. Business Plan **219**

7.1 Introduction 219
7.2 Meaning 219
7.3 Benefits of a Business Plan or a Project Report 220
7.4 When the Business Plan is to be Prepared? 222
7.5 How Long should the Business Plan be? 222
7.6 Composition of a Business Plan or Detailed Project Report 223

7.7 Guidelines or Steps for the Preparation of a Business Plan 224
7.8 Common Pitfalls or Common Errors in the Preparation of a Business Plan 237
7.9 Precautions 239
Annexure 240

8. Implementation of the Project (Support Agencies) 255

8.1 Introduction 255
8.2 Under the Government System 258
8.3 Financial Assistance 273
8.4 Outside the Government System 284
8.5 Sources of Finance 287
8.6 Financial Incentive for SSI & Tax Concessions 290
8.7 Assistance for Obtaining Raw Material 293

9. Industrial Estates 297

9.1 Introduction 297
9.2 Definitions 298
9.3 Objectives of Industrial Estates 298
9.4 Factors to be Considered while Establishing Industrial Estates in India 299
9.5 Types of Industrial Estates 300
9.6 Reasons for Failure of Industrial Estates 302
Case Studies 303

10. Sickness in SSI 314

10.1 Introduction 314
10.2 Definitions 315
10.3 Symptoms of Industrial Sickness 316
10.4 Factors Affecting Sickness or Causes of Sickness 317
10.5 Consequences of Industrial Sickness 320
10.6 Supportive Measures from Government 321
10.7 Preventive and Remedial Measures of Sickness 322

11. Business Crisis: How to Overcome Them **326**

11.1 Meaning 326
11.2 Types of Business Crisis 327

12. International Entrepreneurial Opportunities **336**

12.1 Introduction 336
12.2 Meaning 336
12.3 Benefits of International Business Opportunities 337
12.4 Modes of International Business Opportunities 338
12.5 Export Procedures 345
12.6 Import Procedures 350
12.7 Financing International Business 351
12.8 International Finance 358
Annexures 364

References **375**
Index **377**

Syllabus

OBJECTIVE

To motivate and boost the morale on entrepreneurship among students.

Unit–1 **10 hours**

Entrepreneurs: Concept and evolution—Importance and relevance of the entrepreneur – Characteristics, Function, Types and role of entrepreneurs.

Unit–2 **10 hours**

Entrepreneurship: The evolution of entrepreneurship—meaning and perspective, relationship between'3E', namely, entrepreneur, entrepreneurship and enterprise, growth of entrepreneurship in India, Role of entrepreneurial development programme, Intrapreneurship.

Unit–3 **10 hours**

Women Entrepreneurs—Importance of Women Entrepreneurs, Characteristics of Successful Women Entrepreneurs. Entrepreneur culture, creativity and Innovation. Functions, growth and problems of Women Entrepreneurs. Women recent trends. Recent Trends of Women Entrepreneurs in India.

Unit–4 **10 hours**

Small Scale Industries: Meaning and concept, Types-SSI, Tiny, Ancillary Cottage, product range, capital investment, ownership pattern – Importance and role of SSI in Indian economy, Problems and solutions SSI and Policies governing SSI.

Unit–5 **15 hours**

Enterprise Setup: Factors and steps to start SSE—Business opportunities, environment for opportunities, selection based on personal competencies. Project identification, Project selection, Project report content and formulation of a project report location, clearance and, permit. Licensing and registration procedure. Business Plan.

Unit–6 **5 hours**

Financial and non-financial institutions—SFCs, SIDBI, Commercial Banks, and KSFDC, Non-financial Institutions—DIC, SISI, EDI, SIDO AWAKE, TECKSOK and KVIC.

SKILL DEVELOPMENT

1. Industrial visit and report.
2. Preparation of a project report to start a SSI Unit.
3. Successful stories of entrepreneurs in the region.
4. Group-wise presentation to develop individuality and leadership quality.
5. Preparing a letter to the concerned authority seeking licence to the SS Unit, You propose to start.
6. Preparation of a business plan.
7. A report on the survey of SSI units in the region where college is located.
8. Chart showing financial assistance available to SSI along with rates of interest.
9. Chart showing tax concessions to SSI both direct and indirect.

BOOKS FOR REFERENCE

1. Dr. S. Anil Kumar, Small Business and Entrepreneurship, I.K. International, New Delhi.
2. Udai Pareek and T.V. Rao, Developing Entrepreneurship.
3. S.V.S. Sharma, Developing Entrepreneurship, Issues and Problems.
4. Srivastava, A Practical Guide to Industrial Entrepreneurs.
5. Government of India, Report of the Committee on Development of Small and Medium Entrepreneurs, 1975.

6. Bharusali, Entrepreneur Development.
7. Vasanth Desai, Management of Small Scale Industry.
8. Vasanth Desai, Problems and Prospects of Small Scale Industry.
9. C.S.V. Murthy, Entrepreneurial Development.
10. Entrepreneurial Development—Anil Kumar, S.C. Poornima, Minni K. Abraham. Jayashree K. New Age International Publisher, New Delhi.

PART A
ENTREPRENEURSHIP

1

Concept of Entrepreneurship

STRUCTURE

1.1 Introduction
1.2 Definitions
1.3 Group Entrepreneurship (GE)
1.4 Social Entrepreneurship
1.5 Enterprise
1.6 Types of Enterprises
1.7 Need and Importance of Entrepreneurship
1.8 India's Potential for the Growth of Entrepreneurship
1.9 Categories of Entrepreneurship
1.10 Entrepreneurship in the New Indian Economy
1.11 Entrepreneurial Process or New Venture Process
1.12 Entrepreneurship Development
1.13 Importance or Objectives of Entrepreneurship Development
1.14 Process of Entrepreneurship Development
1.15 Impact of Government Policies on Entrepreneurship Development Movement in India
1.16 Entrepreneurship Development Programme
1.17 Measures to Boost the EDP in India
1.18 Intrapreneurship

1.1 INTRODUCTION

Entrepreneurship constitutes the driving force of today's market based economy. It is one of the four main economic factors, namely, land, labour, capital and organisation. Entrepreneurship can be a very powerful factor in changing the business environment of a country and its entire industrial sector.

Entrepreneurship is presently the most effective method for bridging the gap between science and the marketplace, creating new enterprises and bringing new products and services to the market. These entrepreneurial activities significantly affect the economy of an area by building the economic base and providing jobs.

Entrepreneurship means different things to different people and can be viewed from different conceptual perspectives. However, in spite of the differences, there are some common aspects, like risk taking, creativity, independence and rewards. These commonalities will continue to be the driving force behind the notion of entrepreneurship.

Schumpeter described entrepreneurship as a process and entrepreneurs as innovators who use the process to break the existing system of production and organisation through new combinations of resources and new methods of production and trade.

1.2 DEFINITIONS

1. According to Cole "Entrepreneurship is the purposeful activity of an individual or a group of associated individuals undertaken to initiate, maintain and make profit by production or distribution of economic goods and services".
2. According to Higgins "Entrepreneurship means the function of foreseeing investment and production opportunities, organizing an enterprise to undertake a new production process, raising capital, hiring labour, arranging the supply of raw materials, finding site, introducing a new technique, discovering new resources or raw materials and selecting top managers for day-to-day operations of the enterprise".
3. According to Robert Ronstalt, "Entrepreneurship is a dynamic process of creating incremental wealth. This wealth is created by individuals who assume the major risks in terms of equity, time and/or career commitment of providing value for some product or services. The product or services itself may or may not be new or unique but value must somehow be infused by the entrepreneur by securing and allocating the necessary skills and resources."
4. According to Jeffrey. A. Timmons, Entrepreneurship is:
   a) The ability to create and build a vision from practically nothing, fundamentally it is a human, creative act.

b) It is the application of energy for initiating and building an enterprise or organization, rather than just watching analyzing.
c) The vision makes entrepreneur to take calculated risk both personal and financial, and to do everything possible to reduce the chances of failure.
d) The ability to build an entrepreneurial or venture dream to complement your own skills and talents.
e) It is the knack for sensing an opportunity where others see contradiction and confusion.
f) It is possessing the know-how to find, marshal and control resources.

The above definitions highlight risk bearing, innovating and resource organizing aspects and an individual or group of people achieve goal through production or distribution of products or services.

5. According to Joseph Schumpeter the concept of entrepreneurship includes all those business persons, company directions or even manages of big or small enterprises who carry out innovative functions."

To conclude entrepreneurship is the ability to make something out of nothing.

1.3 GROUP ENTREPRENEURSHIP (GE)

"Group entrepreneurship is found in a group of people tied together by a common bond because they live in a village, engaged in the same profession or share an economic interest. This group engaged in a common productive activity and is able to market the product in such a manner that it sets a fair price which in turn enables it to make a living in the village throughout the year."

There are many unorganised, sometimes informal, groups of artisans, tribal communities or various self-help groups, etc., which could be prepared to act entrepreneurially as a group and reap the benefits of competitive cooperation. This necessitates developing the whole group as an entrepreneur instead of grooming a few of them as individual entrepreneurs, who in the long run may find it difficult to sustain their enterprises owing to a variety of reasons.

1.4 SOCIAL ENTREPRENEURSHIP

The prospects of widespread practice of social entrepreneurship as a global phenomenon for social innovations and addressing complex problems plaguing the contemporary world has elevated the status of entrepreneurial and business management skills to a higher, nobler level. Social entrepreneurs have something in common with business entrepreneurs, but there are some significant differences between these two groups. Their dreams, visions and mission are different, their methods can also be different. The social entrepreneurs measure their success primarily in terms of social value creation, rather than profit. In spite of the positive features of social entrepreneurship, there are very few successful practitioners in this field in countries like India.

Thus, the distinguishing features of social entrepreneurs that can set them apart from their counterparts in business field are:

(a) Their passion for specific social causes and their vision, mission and guiding values which propel them in their work, and
(b) Range of their skills in social as well as business sectors.

The well-managed social venture can trigger sustainable development process in the communities to a certain extent.

The term "sustainable development" is generally defined as "the development that meets the needs of the present generation without compromising the ability of future generations to meet their own needs". Sustainable development embodies the vision of an equitable and prosperous world where environmental and social-cultural resources are also cared for and enriched.

1.5 ENTERPRISE

It means an organisation or an activity or a place where a business takes place to earn profit. Enterprises are based on the type of activities the entrepreneurs perform.

1.6 TYPES OF ENTERPRISES

Enterprises are classified on the basis of: 1) nature of entrepreneurial activities, 2) their size, 3) the level of technology used, and 4) their location.

1. **On the basis of nature of activity:** Based on the nature of entrepreneurial activities, enterprises are broadly classified into three categories. They are as follows:
   a) Industry
   b) Trade and Business
   c) Services
   a) ***Industry Enterprises :*** Industry enterprises deal with manufacturing and processing.
   b) ***Trade and Business Enterprises :*** These enterprises deal with distribution, purchase and sale of goods and services.
   c) ***Service Enterprises :*** Enterprises which provide different types of services ranging from tours and travel, entertainment, information, health, insurance, hotel, consultancy, etc.
2. **On the basis of size:** The next significant way of categorization is based on the size of the enterprises. They are grouped as:
   a) Micro-enterprises
   b) Small-scale industries
   c) Medium enterprises
   d) Large industry

This classification varies in terms of investment, employment and scale of productivity and operation. The first generation entrepreneurs, in proportionately very large numbers, find entry to an entrepreneurship career through micro-enterprises and small-scale industries. Over a period of time, they vertically grow as medium and large enterprises.

3. **On the basis of technology used:** Enterprises can also be categorized as
   a) Hi-tech or knowledge based ventures
   b) Low-tech ventures
4. **On the basis of location:** In terms of location, the enterprises can be classified into :
   a) Rural industries
   b) Urban industries

Thus, whatever may be the name and category, entrepreneurship in last few decades is experiencing rapid horizontal and vertical spread in terms of service, processing, rural micro, small and medium enterprises on one side and hi-tech scientific and knowledge based service enterprises on the other side in urban areas.

1.7 NEED AND IMPORTANCE OF ENTREPRENEURSHIP

Many countries are presently in the process of successfully developing or restricting their economies. Countries like Japan, Malaysia, Korea, Thailand, France and US in which the encouragement of small business or enterprise development contributes to the successful growth of an economy. Many countries which held a negative view of capitalism have now recognized the necessity of small business, entrepreneurship and business management skills in order to promote economic development and employment.

There is a paradigm shift in our development policies since 1990. Our economy is in for a second transition from planned economic growth to liberalization, privatization and globalization. The first transition was from colonial, underdeveloped to planned economic growth with social justice. During the first phase of transition, Government itself played entrepreneurial role and also supported the growth of entrepreneurship in the private sector. The thesis of developing entrepreneurship has found its birth with Mc.Clelland's achieving society. It gained the partner momentum and the status of practical applicability in India.

The relevance of entrepreneurship and need for the socio-economic development of a country is for the following reasons.

1. Increase in National Production

Due to globalization, it is necessary to produce goods and services at a competitive costs by increasing the production. At the same time entrepreneurs need to focus their attention on exports and simultaneously plan for producing goods and services that will substitute our imports. This helps the nation in conserving foreign exchange. Manufacturing of leather goods, gems and jewellery, handicraft, textiles and garments, etc. has tremendous opportunities in export generation. By encouraging more and more entrepreneurs there will be an overall increase in the production and the productivity for both internal and external markets.

2. Balanced Regional Development

There is a tendency on the part of the entrepreneurs to start enterprises in and around big cities due to the facilities available in urban areas. This creates an imbalance in the growth of urban and rural areas due to migration of rural manpower, heavy financial burden on the Government for providing bank and essential commodities like housing, water, transport, power, etc. for the migrated population. In order to balance the growth of rural and urban areas, there is a need for encouragement of entrepreneurs to start ventures in the rural areas to increase the industrial growth.

3. Dispersal of Economic Power

For the equitable distribution of wealth and weakening the monopoly of big business houses, an attempt should be made to promote more competent entrepreneurs for the disposal of economic power in the country.

4. Reinvestment of Profits

Entrepreneurs should be encouraged to invest or reinvest the capital or profit for better productivity and for the welfare of the community from which the profit is generated.

5. Solving Unemployment and Underemployment

Unemployment is a major socio-economic problem in India. To overcome this problem there is a need to design the programmes to promote the entrepreneurs who can set up small industries or enterprises. Small-scale industries have the potential to generate employment five times more than that of large establishments for the same amount of capital investment.

Underemployment can be seen in large establishments. This has resulted in frustration and job dissatisfaction among qualified and experienced technical personnel. Therefore, the Government has introduced self-employment programme for the educated unemployed technologists. To mention a few, Prime Minister's "Rozgar Yojana", Priyadarshini Scheme of Bank of India (for women), Kalyani Yojana of Central Bank of India (for women), Mahila Udyam Nidhi Yojana, Refinancing scheme of small Industrial Development Bank of India (IDBI) for small and rural entrepreneurs, etc.

6. Harnessing Youth Vigour

Unemployment is a major problem in India. Fifty-eight per cent of India's population represents total workforce, among them 43 per cent of them are unemployed which represents nearly 25 million educated youth with full of vigour to work. This may be dangerous to the society because in the absence of opportunities to engage in productive activities, they become frustrated and use their energy to violent and other destructive activities.

One effective way of harnessing the youth vigour is by entrepreneurial motivation to educated youth by providing them an opportunity for self-employment. This will provide an opportunity to earn their livelihood and channelise their energy to productive activities. The Government has to introduce several programmes for self-employment.

Benefits of harnessing youth vigour to entrepreneurial motivation is as follows:

a) It provides an opportunity for self-employment.
b) It provides an opportunity to earn their livelihood.
c) It channelises the unemployed youth towards productive activities.
d) It helps in developing self-confidence.
e) It enables to reduce the rate of unemployment.
f) A challenging entrepreneurial pursuit leads to "entrepreneurialisation of the society".

7. Encouragement for Micro, Small and Medium Enterprises

India, in the past four decades, has taken up several programmes for micro, small and medium enterprises development to provide assistance for benefiting youth, women, minorities, and socially, economically weaker sections of society.

The Government of India through its new policy of small industries 1991, has announced a policy package for the promotion of small, tiny and village industries. The primary objective of the policy is to impart more vitality and growth impetus to the small sector.

Entrepreneurship is needed to encourage micro, small and medium enterprises for the following reasons.

a) They are suitable for the Indian economy which is short of capital and labour intensive. In India small enterprises provided 140 lakh of net jobs created with 23 lakh small units in 1993-94.
b) They contribute approximately 35 to 40 per cent of direct exports. The economy needs business which brings in foreign currencies through exports of manufactured goods and services.
c) They have a higher per unit output of capital investment and per unit of energy used.
d) They invest out of necessity, a major portion of their profits and thus help in increasing the national production.
e) They are more flexible and innovative than large firms.
f) They may reduce economic and regional disparities and thus foster social stability and help in dispersal of economic power.
g) They may better serve small local markets in solving problems of unemployment and underemployment.
h) They may be less damaging to the environment.
i) They help in harnessing youth vigour.

8. Innovation/Invention of Products

The role of entrepreneurship in economic development involves more than just increasing per capita output and income. It involves initiating and constituting change in the structure of business and society. This change is accompanied by growth and increased output, which allows more wealth to be divided by the entrepreneurs. One theory of economic growth depicts innovation as a key, not only in developing new products or service for market but also in stimulating investment interest in the new ventures being created. This new investment works on both the demand and supply side of the growth equations. The new capital created expands the capacity for growth (supply side) and resultant new spending utilizes the new capacity and output (demand side).

9. For Socio-economic Gain or Growth

The entrepreneurs are unique and valuable assets to an economy. For the development of entrepreneurship, Government play an important role. In this direction Government of India is evincing lot of interest in the entrepreneurship development programmes for socio-economic gain or growth. This depends on the importance of entrepreneurship in all the sectors of the economy like agriculture, trade, infrastructure or service sector, etc.

10. Optimizing Natural Resources

The entrepreneurship helps in utilizing the locally available raw materials, talent, and other material resources to a maximum extent.

11. For Industrial Development

Encouragement of entrepreneurship by the Government in all the sectors leads to overall industrial development of the country.

12. Development of Women as a Special Need Group

Out of the total number of self-employed persons, women account for five per cent. The majority of the self-employed women are engaged in the unorganised sector like handicraft, handloom, cottage industries and agriculture. It is estimated that among the small-scale entrepreneurs, nearly nine percent are women. If this trend continues, women's participation is likely to increase to twenty per cent of the total small-scale sector units.

1.8 INDIA'S POTENTIAL FOR THE GROWTH OF ENTREPRENEURSHIP

India being the second highest populated country in the world has tremendous potential in creating and developing the effective and competitive entrepreneurs. India possesses the following factors essential for the growth of entrepreneurship.

1. A large domestic market of about 300 million people middle and high level of income and another 700 million people whose purchasing power is gradually increasing.

2. A high saving rate over 25%
3. An extensive financial sector
4. Availability of cheap and skilled human resources
5. A very good network of technical and management institutes of high international standards.
6. Various incentive schemes of self-employment having been formulated by the Government of India.
7. Number of economic reforms have been planned by the Govt. of India in terms of liberalization of Indian industry, globalization of market, allowing the multinational companies to invest in India.

1.9 CATEGORIES OF ENTREPRENEURSHIP

In India we can see the following categories of entrepreneurship:

1. Unemployed youth who are economically not so sound.
2. Unemployed person with good financial background.
3. Experienced and trained persons aspiring to set up their own enterprises.
4. Industrialists/businessmen/self-employed persons who are planning expansion/diversification in their existing enterprises.

1.10 ENTREPRENEURSHIP IN THE NEW INDIAN ECONOMY

The revolution currently taking place in India, which began with IT boom, will have a bright future. Every child in India now want to become a software engineer. It has taken root in the mindset of the young generations which will now be much more likely to take risks in order to reach goals. Does this mean that, thanks to this IT revolution, entrepreneurship has become part of the Indian culture?

It is difficult to answer this question normally, one would say that a country's culture influence entrepreneurship. But it could also be the opposite. Whatever the real answer is, one thing is clear that India is becoming more entrepreneurial. It would perhaps be even more accurate to say that the inherent entrepreneurial spirit has helped many self-employers. Nowadays, we observe that more and more people are looking up to face themselves the challenges which every entrepreneurs has to confront.

Along with IT boom, biotechnology may emerge as a growing sector within next five to ten years. However, really promising sector where India can set a tremendous competitive advantage is definitely 'bioinformatics'.

Entrepreneurship has become an essential resource in the economic growth process both in developing and developed countries. In the former case and in the case of India, entrepreneurship in the small and medium sectors is of crucial importance mainly because, it opens up the path too faster economic growth and facilitates the creation of larger employment, carrier or business opportunities at the same time.

It is difficult to say how far India will be in the next ten years. However, considering the recent developments in IT, biotechnology, telecommunication and other services sector, one can say the entrepreneurship has had the effect of a tremendous accelerator for economic growth and prosperity, unfortunately, only a minority can really benefit from this positive revolution. Hence, the most difficult challenge for the country is to ensure sustainable growth in all sectors, to implement the appropriate reforms, to give a chance to everyone and to build up a social network ensuring that nobody is left behind.

Obviously, this vision may sound too idealistic. But visions and ideals are precisely what drives entrepreneurs and will determine and shape the fate of the country. As Eleanor Roos Evelt once said, "The future belongs to those who believe in the beauty of their dreams."

1.11 ENTREPRENEURIAL PROCESS OR NEW VENTURE PROCESS

To examine the activities involved in entrepreneurship, a number of methods and models attempts to structure the entrepreneurial process or new venture process. We will discuss the entrepreneurial process as a consolidation of diverse in entrepreneurship. Entrepreneurship is viewed as a complex, multidimensional framework that emphasizes the individual or personal, the environment, the sociological, the organization and the venture process. It is the process by which individuals plan, implement and control their entrepreneurial activities.

The specific factors that relate to each of these dimensions is given below:

The individual or personal factors

1. Need for achievement.
2. Locus of control or internal control.
3. Risk taking.
4. Job satisfaction.
5. Previous work experience.
6. Age.
7. Education.
8. Gender.
9. Commitment.
10. Vision.
11. Personal values.

Sociological factors

1. Entrepreneurial parents.
2. Family support.
3. Team building.
4. Role models.

The environmental factors

Scanning of environment is necessary to an entrepreneur for examining the external and internal environment's ability.

1. Venture capital availability.
2. Presence of experienced entrepreneurs.
3. Technically skilled labour entrepreneurs.
4. Accessibility of suppliers.
5. Accessibility of customers or new markets.
6. Government policies.
7. Availability of land or facilities.
8. Accessibility of transportation.
9. Attitude of the area population.
10. Availability of supporting services.
11. Living conditions of people.

12. Prevailing competition.
13. Existence of investors.
14. Support of bankers.
15. Political or legal forces.
16. Technological forces.
17. Socio-cultural forces.

The organization factors

1. Type of organization—sole trader, partnership or company.
2. Culture of the organization.
3. Decision of products.
4. Strategies.

The process

1. Locating a business opportunity.
2. Converting ideas into reality.
3. Developing business plan (market research).
4. Accumulating resources.
5. Marketing products and services. (developing marketing concept).
6. Producing the product.
7. Building an organization or growth or development.

1.12 ENTREPRENEURSHIP DEVELOPMENT

Introduction

Entrepreneurship development has been recognized widely as the key to economic development and human welfare. Entrepreneurial development is essential for industrialization and for eradicating unemployment and poverty. Experience of developed and developing countries clearly show that it is possible to develop entrepreneurship through planned efforts. The myth that entrepreneurs are born not made, no longer holds good. Therefore, in recent years, both Government and private agencies have initiated strategies and programmes for developing entrepreneurial skills among people. A large number of schemes have been formulated for developing entrepreneurship self-employment among different target groups. Training has been the common component of most of these schemes.

Attempts have been made to provide the necessary support and services to train entrepreneurs. The successful entrepreneurs can be exposed to formal and informal training or education process from which they have learnt many things which helped them to be successful as entrepreneurs. Thus, formal or informal entrepreneurship development programmes are very much needed. Considering changes taking place in business world and pattern of occupation, majority of Indians will not have proper informal exposure to develop their entrepreneurship. In that case formal entrepreneurship development programmes are inevitable. In addition to that the nature of entrepreneurship development will not be identical for all entrepreneurs.

In India, the system of service has been developed to assist people to start their ventures. The service ranges from providing awareness courses to members of the public interested in becoming entrepreneurs to mentoring (personal consistency) assistance which include how to start a venture and how to service and prosper once a venture is set up.

1.13 IMPORTANCE OR OBJECTIVES OF ENTREPRENEURSHIP DEVELOPMENT

Following are the important objectives:

1. To analyse the environmental set-up relating to small industry and small business.
2. To select the product and project.
3. To develop and strengthen entrepreneurial qualities.
4. To understand procedure of small-scale industries.
5. To develop wide vision about the business.
6. To develop passion for integrity and honesty.
7. To understand the need of entrepreneurial discipline.
8. To understand feasible design to meet the specific needs of the entrepreneurs.
9. To analyse active investment of finance.
10. To help in accelerating industrial development by enlarging the supply of entrepreneurs.
11. To help in assessing industrial development of rural and less developed areas where local entrepreneurship is not readily available and to which entrepreneurs from nearby cities and towns are not easily attached.

12. To help in enlarging the small and medium enterprise sector which offers better potential for employment generation and wider dispersal of industrial ownership.
13. To help in providing productive self-employment to a number of educated and low educated young men and women coming out of schools and colleges.
14. To help in improving performance of small industries by enlarging the supply of carefully selected and trained, 'well-rounded' entrepreneurs.
15. To help in diversifying sources of entrepreneurship and thereby promoting dispersal or business ownership.
16. The overall objective of entrepreneurship development is the supply of entrepreneurs for industrial development.

1.14 PROCESS OF ENTREPRENEURSHIP DEVELOPMENT

The process of entrepreneurship development among individuals consists of three phases:

1. Stimulating.
2. Supporting.
3. Sustaining.

These are shown in the below figure.

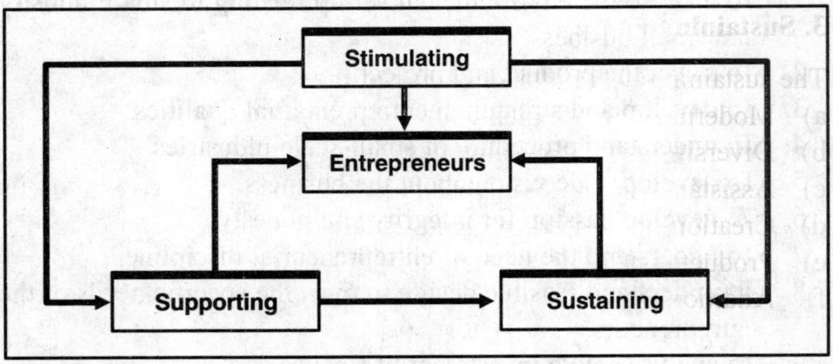

Fig. 1.1. Process of Entrepreneurship Development.

1. Stimulating Phase

Stimulating phase includes some of the following typical functions:

a) Entrepreneurial awareness.
b) Entrepreneurial motivation.

c) Planned publicity for entrepreneurial opportunities.
d) Identification of potential entrepreneurs.
e) Information on project planning and implementation.
f) Assistance in product or services identification and market survey.
g) Assistance in preparation of business plan project report.
h) Help in development of new products or processes.
i) Counselling.

2. Supporting Phase

The supporting phase includes some of the following functions:

a) Assistance in registration of a unit.
b) Assistance in obtaining finance.
c) Help in getting land, workshop, building, power, water, etc.
d) Help in obtaining various permissions and licences.
e) Guidance in selection, procurement, erection and commissioning of plant and equipment.
f) Supply of scarce raw materials.
g) Grant of incentives and subsidies.
h) Assistance in marketing.
i) Provision of management consultancy.

3. Sustaining Phase

The sustaining phase includes some of the following functions:

a) Modernization of units.
b) Diversification, expansion or product substitution.
c) Assistance in improving business and profitability.
d) Creation of need based common facility centre.
e) Product standardization and testing services.
f) Additional finances for rehabilitation of units.

1.15 IMPACT OF GOVERNMENT POLICIES ON ENTREPRENEURSHIP DEVELOPMENT MOVEMENT IN INDIA

The Government of India has been planning various schemes and policies to develop the favourable environment for the new entrepreneurs in India from time to time. The present economic reforms declared by the Government has further boosted the entrepreneurship movements in India. Number of govt./private institutions and organizations have come to the forefront to give the practical shape to this movement. The results of these economic reforms are very encouraging. The impact of which on entrepreneurship is enumerated below:

1. Liberalization of Indian industry has given a big boost to new entrepreneurs by simplifying various rules and procedures for setting up new units.
2. With the arrival of multinational companies, the productivity will increase. The competitive quality product will come into the market on a large scale. Hence, there will be requirement of more units in the trading and servicing sectors.
3. By globalization of business, there are bright chances for Indian entrepreneurs to expand their business in the international market.
4. By permitting the private sector parallel to public sector will create more opportunities to develop new entrepreneurs.
5. In order to compete the multinational companies in the domestic market, the local entrepreneurs specially in the small and medium industries will have to adopt in the small and medium industries the new concept of consortium for their survival.
6. Multinational companies will require a large number of ancillary units for their operations which in turn will provide the opportunity to the new entrepreneurs to set up their ancillary units.
7. By winding up some of the sick public sector undertakings, there will be problem of rehabilitation of skilled and unskilled labour force. Incentives given through self-employment schemes may solve this problem up to certain extent.

1.16 ENTREPRENEURSHIP DEVELOPMENT PROGRAMME

The entrepreneurship development programme is designed to promote small enterprises by tapping the latent talents of potential entrepreneurs through training. The Entrepreneurship Development Institute of India (EDII) and National Institute of Entrepreneurship and Small Business Development (NIESBD) play an important role in training the prospective entrepreneurs.

Entrepreneurship development programme emphasizes more on operational aspects than academic training to meet the specific need of participants. The EDP trains the participants to set up an enterprise and tailors its techniques and strategies depending on the environment in which he operates the business.

Process of entrepreneurship development programme

1. Selection of prospective entrepreneurs/participants.
2. Creation of infrastructure for training programme.
3. Designing of techniques for training.
4. Selection and commencement of training programme or process.
5. Post-training survey.
6. Strategies to make entrepreneurship development more effective.

1.17 MEASURES TO BOOST THE ENTREPRENEURSHIP DEVELOPMENT PROGRAMME IN INDIA

Government of India has made an excellent attempt through various reforms and schemes to boost the development of new entrepreneurship but there is always scope for further improvement. The following measures have to be taken to boost the entrepreneurship programme in India.

1. Creating the Awareness of Entrepreneurship at Grass Roots Level

In order to shift the trend from wage employment to self-employment the individual will have to be groomed at an early age by creating the awareness of self-employment and by incorporating the vocational subjects in educational system starting from primary education only. This system should be followed very religiously in the true spirit of its reality.

2. Entrepreneurship Development Training Programme by Government / Private Institutions

a) **Entrepreneurship Motivation Programme :** This programme is required to create the awareness among the people in general and providing guidelines to the interested individuals for setting up the new business units in particular.

b) **Special Programme :** There may be the need of planning special programmes, separately for different types of entrepreneurs, for example, the technician entrepreneur is comfortable with the problems relating to production, designing and technology but he may not be comfortable in the area of market, finance, etc. Hence, this category of entrepreneurs need to undergo special training in the area of market, finance, etc. However, the persons having trading business background find difficulty in the area of production and technology, these persons need to be trained in technology and production.

c) **Guidance for trading and servicing business :** The persons interested in setting up trading/service unit should be imparted training separately from the individuals as mentioned in the above paragraph. A special training programme is required to be made and more emphasis should be given to cover the subject on marketing of services.

d) **Follow up Action :** Institutions/organizations conducting the entrepreneurship programme should have a system to monitor the progress of their students in all the stages of business life cycle and provide them the guidance as and when asked for.

3. Further Simplifying the Loan Procedure

In spite of various reforms being incorporated by the Govt. to set up the new units, still there are number of formalities required by the entrepreneur to undergo before getting the loans. These formalities need a fresh look which should be reduced to the bare minimum requirements of the bank so that minimum time, after the project has been finalized, is taken to bring it in operational stage. The loan procedure should be streamlined so that entrepreneur does not experience harassment before setting up his new enterprise.

4. Practical Outlook of Special Schemes

The schemes like Prime Minister Rozgar Yozna (PMRY) and District Rural Industrial Project (DRIP) should be executed in true spirit of their organization. A special independent and competitive authority should be assigned to implement these programmes. A very deliberate effort is required to select the suitable entrepreneur under these schemes. The selection should be made after the candidates have been imparted the awareness training on entrepreneurship. The Govt. and private institutes should be assigned the task of imparting the entrepreneurship awareness programme. However, special training programme should be planned immediately after selection.

5. Marketing Oriented Entrepreneurship

Till date more emphasis is given to technically qualified persons for the development of the entrepreneurship. However, there is need in the present context to develop the marketing oriented entrepreneurship.

Thus, the economic reforms of the Indian Govt. has given a new term to the development of new entrepreneurship. The globalization and opening up the economy and the liberalization policy has widened the scope of entrepreneurship in the domestic market as well as in the international market.

1.18 INTRAPRENEURSHIP

In recent years the subject of intrapreneurship has been popularized. The major thrust of intrapreneurship is to develop the entrepreneurial spirit within organizational boundaries, thus, allowing an atmosphere of 'innovation to prosper'. The new 'corporate revolution' represents an appreciation for and a desire to develop intrapreneurs within the corporate structure.

Intrapreneurship is most strongly reflected in entrepreneurial activities as well as in top management orientations in organizations. These entrepreneurial endeavours consist of the following four key elements:

1. New business venturing
2. Innovativeness
3. Self-renewal and
4. Proactiveness

1. New Business Venturing or Corporate Venturing

It refers to the creation of new business within an existing organisation. These entrepreneurship activities consist of creating something new of value either by redefining the company's current products or services, by developing new markets, etc.

2. Innovativeness

Organizational innovativeness refers to product and service innovation with an emphasis on development and innovation in technology. It includes new product development, product improvements and new production methods and procedures.

3. Self-renewal

Self-renewal reflect the transformation of organizations through the renewal of the key ideas on which they are built. It has strategic and organizational change connotations and includes a redefinition of the business concept, reorganization and the introduction of system wide changes to increase innovation.

4. Proactiveness

Proactiveness includes initiative and risk taking, as well as competitive aggressiveness and boldness. A proactive organisation is inclined to take risks by conducting experiments and bold and aggressive in pursuing opportunities, organizations with such a proactive spirit attempt to lead rather than follow competitors in such key business areas as the introduction of new products or service, operating technologies and administrative techniques.

ANNEXURE–I: CASE STUDIES

Following are some of the success stories of small-scale industries assisted by KSFC, Bangalore.

CASE 1

Success Story of M/s. Lakshmi Embroidery Computerised Works, Bangalore-560 040 Prop. Smt. Jyothi Balakrishna: Outstanding Business Woman

Beginning her career in 1986 with a single-head manual embroidery machine in a small shop. Smt. Jyothi Balakrishna is currently the proprietor of Lakshmi Embroidery Computerized Works in Bangalore, having a turnover of Rs. 1.26 crore. As a result of hard work, determination and innovative ideas, the unit has attained an important position in the embroidery industry.

The unit was established in 1989 with 10 manual machines to produce in bulk for exports. Smt. Jyothi Balakrishna installed 70 more machines during the 1990s that led to considerable growth of Lakshmi Embroidery Computerized Works. She upgraded the unit with a new technology–CNC computerized embroidery machines—imported from Japan. She took financial assistance from Karnataka State Financial Corporation to expand the unit.

The promoter availed financial assistance of Rs. 59.80 lakhs to the unit M/s. Lakshmi Embroidery Computerized Works during 1996 and 1998 and she repaid the amount promptly and closed the account. She started another unit, M/s. J.B. Creations, a partnership concern and availed loan of Rs. 57.00 lakhs during 2002 from Karnataka State Financial Corporation under TBMF scheme and has been repaying regularly to the Corporation.

Growing at an average annual rate of more than 31 per cent, Lakshmi Embroidery Computerized Works today owns 120 head computerized embroidery machines. It employs 120 people and has the capacity to produce more than 20,000 metres of embroidered fabric per month. With the help of in-house design and development and R&D facilities at Lakshmi Embroidery, a wide range of products are being produced to cater to the requirements of high fashion embroidery fabrics in international market.

Smt. Jyothi Balakrishna is committed to quality and good service. Her company has adopted quality parametres at various stages of operations. This has ensured faster communication, state-of-the-art facilities, efficiency, quality and timely delivery of innovative designs at competitive rates.

Smt. Jyothi Balakrishna's vision is to grow into a leading exporter of fabric made-ups, consistently outperform expectations and to continue to deliver quality products to her customers.

The outstanding Business Woman Award 2004 was presented by PHDCCI, New Delhi, to Smt. Jyothi Balakrishna in recognition of her outstanding achievement as a business woman. The PHDCCI Awards of Excellence is instituted to recognosce Indian businesses, entrepreneurs and individuals for their outstanding achievements/ contributions in selected areas and to promote corporate and individual initiatives in economic, social, educational and cultural areas. Smt. Jyothi Balakrishna was selected under the 'AWARD EXCLUSIVELY FOR WOMEN". The other recipients for PHDCCI awards—2004 were "BRAND EQUITY AWARD" to CMD for I-Flex Solutions Ltd., "GOOD CORPORATE CITIZEN AWARD" to CMD of HPCL, "ETHICS IS GOOD BUSINESS AWARD" to CMD of L&T Ltd.

QUESTION

What factors, in your opinion, helped Smt. Jyothi Balakrishna to become an outstanding business women?

CASE 2

M/S. STANDARDS INTERNATIONAL PRECISION ENGINEERING PVT. LTD.

A-169, 4th Cross, Peenya 1st Stage, Bangalore - 58.
e-mail : standint_india@yahoo.com

Standards International Precision Engineering (P) Ltd., known as Standards International (SI), is essentially an electromechanical engineering consultancy organisation with special expertise in translating any new process technology innovations into precise engineering module that is from laboratory model to commercial manufacturing model, incorporating specific graded norms and requirements at each level.

Sri Ashok G. Shanbag, Managing Director of SI is a mechanical engineer graduate from REC, Suratkal. He served with M/s. Tata Consultancy Engineering, Mumbai, M/s. Toyo Engineering India Ltd., Mumbai, posted in Kuwait, M/s. Petroleum Development, Sultanate of Oman. With this rich experience in industrial line, he started his own industry during 1993 in Bangalore with financial assistance of Rs. 5.00 lakh from Karnataka State Financial Corporation essentially as an electromechanical engineering consultancy organisation with special expertise in translating any new process technology innovations into precise engineering module, i.e., from laboratory model to commercial manufacturing model, incorporating specific graded norms and requirements at each level. The promoter has in-depth knowledge of design and project engineering, manufacturing, site execution, installation and commissioning of varieties of projects such as petrochemical, biotech, chemical, food and offshore-engineering.

The promoter has so far accomplished several major projects for leading food and beverages, pharmaceutical, biotech, dairy, chemical, gas, fertilizer, electrical/electronic, aircraft and petrochemical, industries in India and abroad. Few of the companies for which Standards International has executed projects are: M/s. Hindustan Lever Ltd., M/s. Ruchi Soya Industries Ltd., Mangalore, M/s. Pathalgang, Indore, M/s. Param Industries Ltd., Indore, M/s. Nikhil Refineries Ltd., Hyderabad, M/s. Bidco Oil Refineries Ltd., Kenya, Tanzania, Uganda, M/s. Ceylon Speciality Fats Ltd., Colombo, M/s. Bhaskar Global Pvt. Ltd., Sri Lanka, M/s. Cherubium Pte. Ltd., Sri Lanka, M/s. Unilever

Ceylon Ltd., Sri Lanka, M/s. Naratha Agro Pte, Ltd., Sri Lanka, M/s. East Coast Oil & Fats Ltd., Dar-Es-Salaam, Tanzania.

Karnataka State Financial Corporation has so far sanctioned Rs. 181.10 lakhs to the unit since 1994 and the unit has a good track record. The unit employs well qualified engineers and the company's administration, production and other operations are controlled and monitored by the Executive Director of the company Mrs. Sumitra A.G. Shanbhag. The unit had made a turnover of Rs. 10.00 lakhs during its first year of operation and reached Rs. 1.03 crore during 2000 when they received a major order from Biocon India Ltd. During 2005-06 its turnover reached Rs. 10.38 crores.

QUESTION

What is the secret of success of M/s Standard International Precision Engineering Pvt. Ltd.?

CASE 3

SUCCESS STORY OF M/S. TECHNO SPARK GRANITES (P) LTD., KAVALBYRASANDRA, R.T. NAGAR POST, BANGALORE

M/s. Techno Spark Granites (P) Ltd., was established in the year 1990 with the financial assistance from KSFC. Sri M. Suresh and Smt. Surekha Suresh are the directors of the company. The company situated at No. 1341, Kavalbyrasandra, R.T. Nagar Post, Near Dr. Ambedkar Medical College, Bangalore is engaged in the manufacture of polished granited slabs and industrial granite slabs.

The Managing Director of the company Sri M. Suresh has vast experience of over 15 years in this line of business. The company has availed 6 loans from the Corporation aggregating to Rs. 115.60 lakhs for acquisition of highly advanced machines and equipment like auto polishing machine, heavy duty cast iron body vertical sawing machine, 30 tonne capacity 12 metre. Double grinder box type Gantry crane, etc. for manufacturing products to international standards.

M/s. Techno Spark Granites (P) Ltd., unique in its area of operation in the sense it is the only full-fledged industrial granite manufacturer in India. With their entrepreneurial skills, the promoters of the company continue to dominate the industrial granite systems market. The company specialises mainly in granite pickling tanks for steel cold rolling mills, anti-corrosive chemical tanks from granite slabs for chemical, fertilizer and pharmaceutical industries, industrial granite surface plates, polished monuments and markers, pharmaceutical rollers and pans, polished granite slabs and titles and tailor-made granite furniture and anti-corrosive granite tiles for steel, pharmaceutical and chemical industries.

The company is supplying industrial granites to all the major steel mills in India. They have also executed many overseas projects at Maracco, South Korea, Dhaka, Malaysia. The company has qualified and experienced engineers, marketing executives, etc. It has provided employment to more than 75 people which includes engineers skilled and unskilled labourers.

The company has started with a turnover of just Rs. 46.40 lakhs during its first year of operation in 1994-95 and achieved a turnover of more than Rs. 650.00 lakhs during 2004-05 and is expected to reach Rs. 750.00 lakhs during 2005-06.

M/s. Techno Spark Granite (P) Ltd., has recently bagged "CAPEXIL's Certificate of Merit for the year 2004-05" award given under SSI category in recognition of their export achievement in granite tiles. This award is sponsored by the Ministry of Commerce and Industry, Government of India. The award was presented to Sri M. Suresh, Managing Director on 0.8.10.2005 by the Hon'ble Union Finance Minister Sri P. Chidambaram and Sri E.V.K.S. Elangovan. Hon'ble Union Minister of State for Commerce and Industry.

QUESTION

List out the secret of success Techno Spark Granites (P) Ltd.

EXERCISES

Section A

1. Define 'Entrepreneurship'.
2. Define 'Group entrepreneurship'.
3. What do you mean by 'Social entrepreneurship'?
4. What do you mean by 'Sustainable development'?
5. What do you mean by an 'enterprise'?
6. Mention the categories of entrepreneurship.
7. What do you mean by entrepreneurship development?
8. What do you mean by entrepreneurship development programme?
9. What do you mean by "intrapreneurship"?

Section B

1. Discuss the different types of enterprises.
2. Discuss the potential for the growth of entrepreneurship in India.
3. Write a note on entrepreneurship in the new Indian economy.
4. What is the impact to government policies on entrepreneurship development movement in India?
5. What are the processes of entrepreneurship development programme?

Section C

1. Discuss the importance of entrepreneurship for the socio-economic development of a country.
2. Explain the entrepreneurial process.
3. Explain the important objectives of entrepreneurship development.
4. Discuss the process of entrepreneurship development among individuals.
5. Discuss the measures to boost the entrepreneurship development programme in India.

SKILL DEVELOPMENT

1. Visit a successful small-scale industry and find out the secret of success and write a success story of any one entrepreneur.
2. Meet a successful intrapreneur in any organisation. Find out his entrepreneurial competency and prepare a report.
3. Collect the success stories like Nirma.

2

Entrepreneur

STRUCTURE

2.1 Introduction
2.2 Concept of Entrepreneur
2.3 Definitions
2.4 Importance of an Entrepreneur
2.5 Benefits of being an Entrepreneur
2.6 Problems of being an Entrepreneur
2.7 Qualities of an Entrepreneur
2.8 Characteristics or Traits of an Entrepreneur
2.9 Functions of an Entrepreneur
2.10 Types of an Entrepreneur
2.11 Women Entrepreneurs
2.12 Classification of Women Entrepreneurs in India
2.13 Development of Women Entrepreneurs in India
2.14 Problems of Women Entrepreneurs
2.15 Promotion of Women Entrepreneurs
2.16 Intrapreneur

2.1 INTRODUCTION

It is the entrepreneur who powers the process of economic development. The strength of an economy is in one way the strength of the entrepreneur class in the society. Entrepreneurship must acquire new management skills to succeed because mere mercantile entrepreneurship may not survive in this competitive world.

Entrepreneur density, innovative propensity and managerial ability determine the character, strength and future of economic development. Anyone who wants to become an entrepreneur can become one. All he or she has to do is keep an open mind, search, understand and analyse the implications of changes all round. A systematic search for changes will throw up many valuable opportunities.

The success of an entrepreneur depends on the intelligence, imagination and strength of purpose of the individual. Converting vision into reality is more about hard work than good luck. Jamshedji Tata, Jamunalal Bajaj, Laxmanrao Kirloskar, G.D. Birla, Dhirubhai Ambani, Lakshmi Mittal, Narayana Murthy, Azim Premji, Kiran Mazumdar-Shaw are some of the Indian entrepreneurs, who have proved their entrepreneurial abilities.

2.2 CONCEPT OF ENTREPRENEUR

The dictionary tells us that an entrepreneur is "a person who undertakes an enterprise or business, with chance of profit or loss" and adds that an enterprise is "an undertaking, especially a bold or difficult one". An entrepreneur is someone who sees life as a blank canvas waiting to be painted on; someone who greets the dawn as an opportunity not an obligation; someone whose mind never stops looking for the relationship between resources and needs; someone to whom the creation of products, services, wealth are noble and exciting causes.

The word "entrepreneur" is derived from the French verb *entrepredre*. It means 'to undertake'. In the early 16th century, the Frenchmen who organized and led military expeditions were referred as 'entrepreneur'. In the early 18th century French economist Richard Cantillo used the term entrepreneur to business. Since then the word entrepreneur means one who takes the risk of starting a new organization or service to society.

In recent years the entrepreneurs have been doing so many things that is necessary to broaden this definition. Today an entrepreneur is a developer who recognizes and seizes opportunities, converts those opportunities into workable/marketable ideas, adds value through time, effort, money or skills; assumes the risks of the competitive market place to implement these ideas; and realizes the rewards from these efforts. In other words an "EN – TRE – PRE – NEUR" is an individual who creates, develops and manages a business venture with personal risk for potential profit.

Entrepreneurs are "free thinkers" which implies a combination of a large element of creativity coupled with experience, the knowledge of economic, social, psychological and demographic trends, plus the experience base for comparison and being comfortable with new technology and changes.

Entrepreneurs can have high status in society as leaders of industry and of the nation. It is necessary to create employment and contribute to the growth of the economic wealth of a country.

2.3 DEFINITIONS

1. According to J.B. Say, "An entrepreneur is an economic agent who unites all means of production, land of one, the labour of another and the capital of yet another, and thus produces a product. By selling the product in the market he pays rent of land, wages to labour, interest on capital and what remains is his profit". Thus, an entrepreneur is an organizer who combines various factors of production to produce a socially viable product.
2. According to Joseph Schumpeter, "An entrepreneur in an advanced economy is an individual who introduces something new in the economy—a method of production not yet tested by experience in the branch of manufacture concerned, a product with which consumers are not yet familiar, new source of raw material or of new markets and the like". The functions of an entrepreneurship according to Schumpeter are:
   a) Introduction of a new product.
   b) Introduction of methods of production.
   c) Developing new markets and finding fresh source of raw materials.
   d) Making changes.
3. According to Cantillon "An entrepreneur is an agent who buys factors of production at certain prices in order to combine them into a product with a view to selling it at uncertain prices in future".
4. According to Peter. F. Drucker, an entrepreneur is "one who always searches for change, responds to it and exploits it as an opportunity". Innovation is the specific tool of entrepreneurs, the means by which they exploit change as an opportunity for a different business or service.
5. According to Francis. A. Walker, "the true entrepreneur is one who is endowed with more than average capacities in the task of organizing and coordinating the various other factors of production".

To conclude an entrepreneur is the person who bears risk, unites various factors of production, to exploit the perceived opportunities in order to evoke demand, creates employment and contributes to the economic wealth of a country.

Entrepreneurism

The term entrepreneurism can be defind as "the art and science of doing entrepreneurial things".

2.4 IMPORTANCE OF AN ENTREPRENEUR

1. He acts as the engine of economic growth of a country.
2. He is risk-taker, who takes advantage of opportunities to acquire and use scare resources in new ways or develop new ways of thinking.
3. He brings in overall changes through innovation for maximum social good.
4. He combines entrepreneurial drive with leadership and innovativeness.
5. He activates the development of backward areas, rural areas and tribal areas.
6. He plays an important role in the creation of employment opportunities, improvement in the standard of living of weaker sections of the society.
7. He is treated as a pillar of industrial strength i.e., people who constantly challenge the existing mode of carrying business operations or gainful activity.
8. He can inspire younger generation (would-be entrepreneurs) because, they are often treated as achievement oriented individuals driven to seek challenges and achieve something new.
9. He is the "economic functions". He envisages new opportunities, new techniques, new line of production, new products and who muster together effectively the finance management, labour and material management to make the ball roll.

2.5 BENEFITS OF BEING AN ENTREPRENEUR

The following are the benefits of being an entrepreneur :

1. There is scope for innovation and creativity. The entrepreneurship provides an opportunity for self-expression and the realization of one's passion for doing something new and different.
2. He can make his own decisions and act on them.
3. There are numerous opportunities for self-development.
4. Yields immense satisfaction and pleasure for more than what one can set in a job because he works on his own.
5. He can generate employment for others as an employer.
6. Monetary rewards can be more than commensurate with one's capacity and capabilities.
7. He can make significant contribution to the development of the country.
8. He can be an achiever, realize his goals and prove one's achievements to the world.
9. He can be doubly fulfilled. He realizes both goals, that of individual states as well as of contribution to society, benefiting from one's own competence and experience.
10. He can be independent.

2.6 PROBLEMS OF BEING AN ENTREPRENEUR

Dispite the various benefits, an entrepreneur has to face the following problems:

1. He should be prepared to sacrifice his family for his business. Not in the sense that he has to stay away from family, but he has to put his business first for initial 10 years of its existence.
2. He should be prepared to forgo regular income. There may be fluctuation in income or sometime he may incur loss due to competition, government policies, etc.
3. The entrepreneur has to manage the stress in the initial stages of the business. The stress could be individual stress, organisational stress, group stress and environmental stress.
4. Managing time is a crucial factor for an entrepreneur. He cannot enjoy time as enjoyed by employed persons. He has to manage the time effectively.

2.7 QUALITIES OF AN ENTREPRENEUR

The essential qualities of an entrepreneur is not very different from the qualities required to achieve success in everything in this world. There are some, however, that are needed more abundantly if an entrepreneur wants to succeed with his business. They are:

1. **Courage :** An entrepreneur must have courage. In the early stages of every business he runs into a bad patch. It may last a long time. For example, the projected sales are not being met, overheads are running ahead of budget, the spare cash is running out, etc. Therefore, courage is described as 'grace under pressure'.
2. **Judgement :** An entrepreneur need brains but not as much as people think. More important than conventional brain is 'judgement'. Judgement about what people want, what they will pay for it, how many will want it, how to reach them to tell them about it, etc.
3. **Determination :** Determination is sometimes described as 'fixedness of purpose'. Determination is for the optimist, not for the pessimist. For instance, as any doctor can tell you, recovery is part nursing, part determination. So is business, good management (nursing) will get you a long way, if there is determination.
4. **Man of action :** An entrepreneur must be a 'man of action' who gets his hands dirty, know an how to delegate, but when necessary, himself does what needs to be done.
5. **Goal oriented :** An entrepreneur must be goal oriented and respond to corporate rewards and recognition.
6. **Highly motivated :** An entrepreneur must be highly self-motivated individual who take risks to achieve goals.
7. **Highly creative :** An entrepreneur must have high degree of creativity, innovation, imagination and integration.
8. **Result oriented :** An entrepreneur must be result oriented. He must work hard in turn for personal and financial rewards.
9. **Responsibility :** An entrepreneur must accept responsibility with enthusiasm and endurance.
10. **Self-confidence :** An entrepreneur must have self-confidence and dedication.
11. **Perseverance :** High on the list of qualities of an entrepreneur is perseverance. The poet Robert Burns said : "whether doing, suffering or forbearing you may do miracles by persevering."
12. An entrepreneurs must be both thinker and doer, planner and worker.

13. **Attributes and skills :** An entrepreneur must have a number of attributes and skills in order to properly plan his/her enterprise and make it successful during the initial stages of bussiness. These are :
    a) Knowing about himself, that is, the attributes of entrepreneur
    b) Assessment of business ideas.
    c) Having skill to operate the business
    d) Having the technical skill to produce the goods and provide services that are offered to the customers.

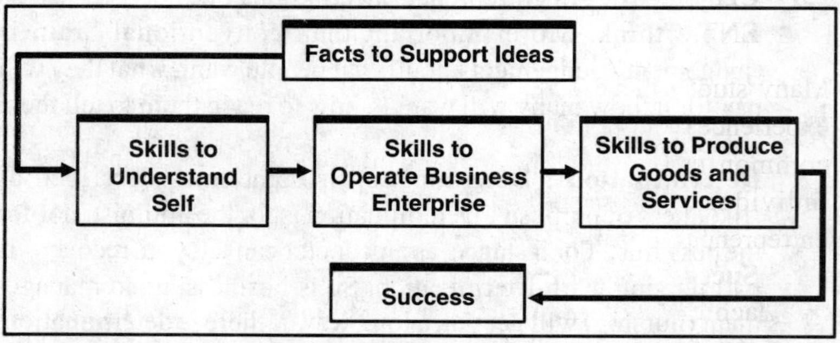

***Fig 2.1:** Attributes and skills for an entrepreneur*

14. **Technically competent :** Entrepreneurs must be technically sound and competent to produce the product.
15. **Ability to communicate :** Effective communication is important for a successful entrepreneur for smooth and productive working within the enterprise and outside the enterprise for good image of the business.
16. **Ability to have human relations :** An entrepreneur must have good relationship with employees, customers, suppliers, creditors and the general public with a sense of humour for the success of his business.
17. **Other qualities :** Entrepreneurs must have other personality traits contributing to the success of an enterprise such as emotional stability, consideration, tactfulness, etc.

Thus, there are number of ways in which different people have achieved success. But there is indeed no single full proof formula to be successful. Circumstances and factors leading to success could be quite varying in various cases. The intention of including numerous qualities which can help in making an entrepreneurial efforts a success is not to emphasize that an entrepreneur must possess all these qualities. In fact, he need not necessarily require all A to Z qualities and personal traits. In other words, the qualities required may differ in different situations. An entrepreneur must therefore try to possess the kind of qualities required for success in the kind of business he operates.

2.8 CHARACTERISTICS OR TRAITS OF AN ENTREPRENEUR

Many studies have investigated the personality, behaviour and life experience of self-employed individuals and their results have shown common characteristics or traits, that are often found in these individuals. Essential characteristics or personal traits of an entrepreneur are as follows:

1. **Success and Achievement :** The entrepreneur is determined to achieve high goals in business. This achievement motive strengthens him to overcome the obstacles, suppress anxieties, and repair misfortunes to run a successful business.
2. **Risk Bearer :** An entrepreneur accepts risk. He selects a moderate risk situation, rather than gambling or avoiding risk. He understands and manages risk.
3. **Opportunity Explorer :** An entrepreneur identifies opportunities. He seizes opportunity and converts them into realistic achievable goals.
4. **Perseverance :** An entrepreneur makes extreme efforts and works hard till the goal is successfully accomplished. They are deterred by uncertainties, risks and difficulties coming in the way of achieving the ultimate goal.
5. **Facing Uncertainty :** Achievement oriented people tend to tackle an unfamiliar but interesting situation. They go ahead with solutions for the problems even without the guidelines.
6. **Feedback :** An entrepreneur likes to have prompt and immediate feedback of his performance.
7. **Independence :** An entrepreneur likes to be his own master and wants to be responsible for his own decision. An entrepreneur is a job giver and not a job seeker.

8. **Flexibility :** An entrepreneur makes decision based on the prevailing situations. Successful entrepreneurs do not hesitate in revising their decision. An entrepreneur is a person with open minds and not rigid.
9. **Planner :** An entrepreneur frames realistic business plans and follows them rigorously to achieve the objectives in a stipulated time limit.
10. **Self-confidence :** An entrepreneur directs his abilities towards the accomplishment of goals with the help of his strengths and weaknesses.
11. **Motivator :** An entrepreneur influences and initiates people and makes them think in his way and act accordingly.
12. **Stress Taker :** An entrepreneur as a focal point will make many right decisions which may involve lot of physical and emotional stress. He keeps cool under a lot of tension while making decisions.
13. **Initiative and Responsive :** An effective entrepreneurs actively seeks and takes initiative. He has been viewed as an independent and highly self-reliant innovator. He willingly puts himself in situations where he is personally responsible for the success or failure of the operation. He likes to take the initiative in solving a problem or filling a vacuum, where no leadership exists. He also likes situations where his personal impact on problems can be measured. This is the action oriented nature of an entrepreneur.
14. **Internal Focus of Control :** An entrepreneur believes that his accomplishments and focus are within his own control. A successful entrepreneur believe in himself.
15. **Integrity and Reliability :** An entrepreneur's integrity and reliability are crucial factors to success. He believes that these two attributes establish good personal and business relationships among investors, partners, customers and creditors.
16. **Creativity and Innovativeness :** Creativity is an exclusively inherited characteristic of an entrepreneur. "Creativity" is the generation of ideas that results in the improved efficiency and effectiveness of a system.
17. **Quick Learners :** An effective entrepreneur is often described as a quick learner. He will have strong desire to know well and improve his performance.

18. **Tolerance :** A successful entrepreneur has the ability to face setbacks, surprises and stress. He is not disappointed, discouraged or depressed by a failure.
19. **Vision :** An entrepreneur will have a vision or foresight of what his firm should be after few years.
20. **Team Building :** Even though the entrepreneur desires for independence and autonomy, he prefers to build a strong entrepreneurial team for the venture's growth and development.
21. **High Energy Level :** A successful entrepreneur will have high level of energy to handle the extraordinary workloads and stress. He fine-tunes his energy levels by carefully monitoring his food habits, exercise, routines, etc.

2.9 FUNCTIONS OF AN ENTREPRENEUR

An entrepreneur performs all the necessary functions which are essential from the point of view of management of an enterprise. The functions can be broadly classified into:

1. Primary functions
2. Other functions
3. Functions for developing or underdeveloped countries.

I. Primary Function

The primary function of an entrepreneur is as follows:

1. Planning

Planning is an indispensable function of an entrepreneur determining the objectives to be achieved and the course of action to be followed to achieve them. It is the first step in the direction of setting up of an enterprise. Following are the planning processes involved in the setting up of an enterprise.

1. Generation of ideas
2. Scanning the ideas generated.
3. Determination of form of organisation (i.e., sole trading, partnership or company)
4. Capital requirement
5. Selection of capital resources.
6. Selection of location.

7. Selection of product or product line.
8. Study of labour force availability
9. Analysis of market and adoption of suitable marketing strategy.
10. Study of Government regulations, rules and policies of both centre and state.
11. Fulfilling the requirements of Government rules and regulations.

2. Organizing

Organizing involves identification and grouping two activities to be performed. Organizing can be viewed as a bridge connecting the conceptual ideas developed in creating and planning to the specific means for accomplishing these ideas. Therefore, an entrepreneur organizes the basic requirements like land, labour and capital during the promotion stage and at the performance stage. It all depends on the organisational network employed and monitored by the entrepreneur.

3. Decision Making

According to Aruther H. Cole an entrepreneur has to take the following decisions:

1. Decision on objectives of the enterprise.
2. Decision on procurement of machinery, materials men, money and market.
3. Decision on marketing strategy for the product.
4. Decision on public relations with public authorities and society at large.

4. Management

Management refers to managing the venture at the beginning and also managing the day-to-day operations. For example, managing, raw material, labour, machinery, money, etc.

5. Innovation

Innovation is an exclusively inherited characteristic of an entrepreneur. According to Schumpeter, innovation may occur in any one of the following forms.

1. Launching of a new product in the market
2. Introduction of a new technology in the production.
3. Creation of new markets.
4. Discovery of new and better source of raw material.
5. Creation of monopoly or breaking up monopoly.

6. Risk Taking

The entrepreneur takes calculated chances in creating and running a venture.

II. Other Functions

Besides the above mentioned functions, the entrepreneur has to perform many other activities at the later stage. They are as follows:

1. Diversification of production.
2. Expansion of the enterprise.
3. Maintaining cordial employer-employee relations.
4. Tackling of labour problems.
5. Coordination with outside agencies.

III. Functions for Developing or Underdeveloped Countries

The functions of an entrepreneur with reference to underdeveloped countries has been provided by Kilby is as follows:

1. Management of scarce resources.
2. Dealing with public bureaucracy (concession, licences, taxes).
3. Acquiring and overseeing assembly of the factory.
4. Industrial designing and engineering.
5. Marketing of product and responding to competition.
6. Perception of market opportunities (novel or initiatives).
7. Financial and production management.
8. Management of customers and supplies relations.

2.10 TYPES OF ENTREPRENEURS

Following is the classification of entrepreneurs on the basis of personal and other considerations:

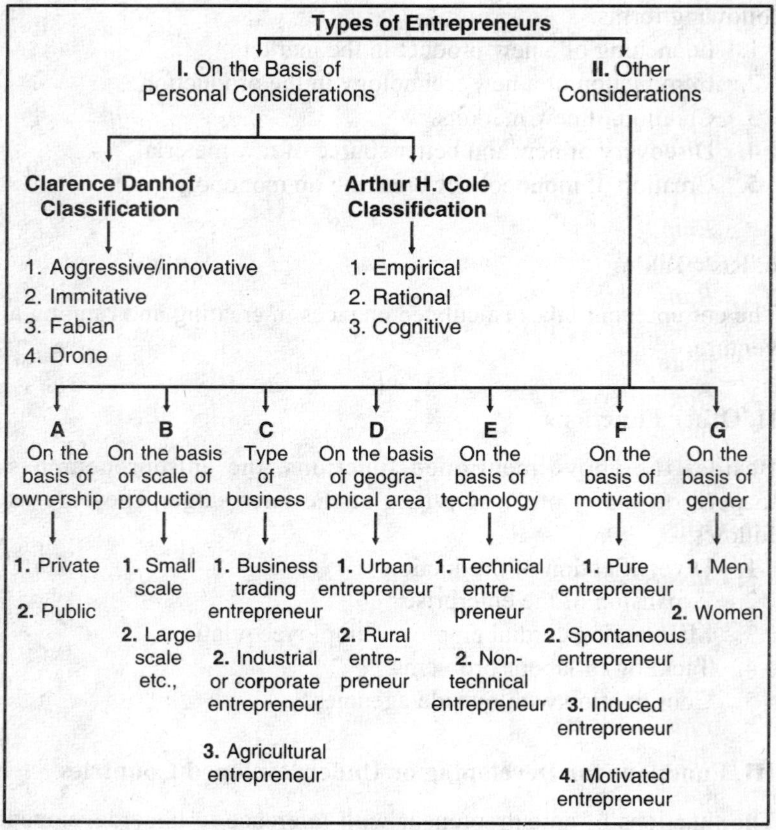

Fig. 2.2. Types of Entrepreneurs

I. On the Basis of Personal Considerations

A. Clarence Danhof Classification

Clarence Danhof classifies entrepreneurs into four types:

1. ***Innovative :*** An innovative entrepreneur is one who assembles, synthesizes information and introduces new combination of factors of production.
2. ***Imitative :*** Imitative entrepreneur is also known as adoptive entrepreneur. He simply adopts successful innovation introduced by other innovators.
3. ***Fabian :*** The Fabian entrepreneur is timid and cautious. He imitates other innovations only if he is certain that failure to do so may damage his business.

4. ***Drone :*** His entrepreneurial activity may be restricted to just one or two innovations. He refuses to adopt changes in production even at the risk of reduces returns.

B. Arthur H. Cole Classification

Arthur H.Cole classifies entrepreneurs as

1. ***Empirical :*** He is an entrepreneur who hardly introduces anything revolutionary and follows the principle of rule of thumb.
2. ***Rational :*** The rational entrepreneur is well informed about the general economic conditions and introduces changes which look more revolutionary.
3. ***Cognitive :*** Cognitive entrepreneur is well informed, draws upon the advice and services of experts and introduces changes that reflect complete break from the existing scheme of enterprise.

II. Other Considerations

A. Classification on the basis of ownership

1. ***Private*:** Private entrepreneur is motivated by profit and it would not enter those sectors of economy in which prospects of monetary rewards are not very bright.
2. ***Public*:** In the underdeveloped countries Government will take the initiative to share enterprises.

B. Classification Based on the Scale of Production

1. ***Small-scale :*** This classification is specially popular in the underdeveloped countries. Small entrepreneurs does not possess the necessary talents and resources to initiate large-scale production and introduce revolutionary technological changes.
2. ***Large-scale :*** In the developed countries most entrepreneurs deal with large-scale enterprises. They possess the financial and necessary enterprise to initiate and introduce new technical changes. The result is the developed countries are able to sustain and develop a high-level of technical progress.

C. Classification on the Basis of Type of Business

1. **Trading entrepreneur :** A trading entrepreneur is one who

undertakes buying and selling activity or trading activity in the channel of distribution process. He is not concerned with manufacturing activity. Trading entrepreneur could be a retailer, a wholeseller or a distributer.

2. **Industrial entrepreneur :** An industrial entrepreneur is one who undertakes manufacturing activity i.e., converting raw materials into finished goods.
3. **Agricultural entrepreneur :** An agricultural entrepreneur is one who undertakes agricultural activities like raising and marketing of agricultural produce and other agriculture related activities.
4. **Services entrepreneur :** A service entrepreneur is one who engage himself in service activities like tourism and travel, hotel, hospital, consultancy service, accounting and taxation, etc.

D. Classification on the Basis of Geographical Area

1. **Urban entrepreneurs:** An urban entrepreneur is one who establishes his business in urban areas (i.e., in cities). He could be in trading a industrial or service entrepreneur of any age and gender.
2. **Rural entrepreneur:** A rural entrepreneur is one who undertakes business activity in the rural area (i.e., villages).

E. Classification on the Basis of Technology

1. **Technical entrepreneur:** A technical entrepreneur is one who has technical knowledge or expertise, craftsmanship, technical know-how, and who can develop a new or improved quality product. Example: Automobile production, biotechnology products, and so on.
2. **Non-technical Entrepreneur:** A non-technical entrepreneur is one who is not specialized in technical aspects of the product. He is concerned with other business activities like marketing and distribution.

F. Classification on the Basis of Motivation

1. **Pure Entrepreneurs:** A pure entrepreneur is one who undertakes an entrepreneurial activity for his personal satisfaction and status to gain economic rewards.

2. **Spontaneous Entrepreneur :** A entrepreneur who establishes the business out of his natural talent with strong conviction and confidence in their ability.
3. **Induced Entrepreneur :** Entrepreneur who starts an enterprise to avail some benefits from the government, like financial, non-financial and technical assistance and concessions.
4. **Motivated Entrepreneur :** Motivated entrepreneur is one who is motivated through an entrepreneurial motivation training. He is trained to achieve, improve self-confidence, communicate and success in business.

G. Classification on the Basis of Gender

1. **Men entrepreneur :** Majority of the entrepreneurs are men. They have the natural ability to start and sustain the business.
2. **Women entrepreneur :** An entrepreneur who initiates, organizes, and operates a business entrepreneur as a woman. Woman takes the lead and organizes the business or industry and provides employment to others.

2.11 WOMEN ENTREPRENEURS

Introduction

Women entrepreneurship in India is still at nascent stage. Women are often heavily discriminated against in many countries including India. In some situations this may actually encourage women to start then own ventures because they may not secure employment or rise in pay and leadership within their current employment. In other situations, certain crafts may not be socially acceptable for women. There is a great struggle for equality in many countries which is usually test identified as the equal opportunity for the job skill a position and the same pay.

Education and awareness programmes have encouraged women entrepreneurs. Women have set up establishments to manufacture solar cookers in Gujarat, small foundries in Maharashtra and TV capacitors in Orissa. These are non-traditional industrial units. Women also engage themselves in the traditional sectors of embroidery, lace, toys, doll making, mat-weaving and the production of fancy-cum-utility articles. Some women employ technicians and managerial personnel, since they do not have the requisite technical and professional know-how. Government organizations help in preparing project reports and setting finance training.

Of late, a few organizations have been set up especially in the NGO sector to provide support and assistance to women entrepreneurs and bring about attitudinal change in them. These include organizations such as Indian Council of Women Entrepreneurs, Association of Women Entrepreneurs of Karnataka (AWK) and Self-Employed Women's Association (SEWA). Organized efforts have provided the much needed attitudinal and skill training.

Definition

Women entrepreneurs may be defined as women or a group of women who initiates, organizes and operates a business enterprise. Women are expected to innovate, initiate or adopt an economic activity to be called women entrepreneurs.

2.12 CLASSIFICATION OF WOMEN ENTREPRENEURS IN INDIA

The proposed classification recognizes four types of entrepreneurs, which have been tentatively known as young achiever entrepreneurs, block factor entrepreneurs, family-driven entrepreneurs and financial need entrepreneurs.

1. Young Achiever Entrepreneurs

Since they typically start enterprises at the age of 25 or so, directly out of college, by the time they are 30 (if they survived) they could go in for the second round of entrepreneurship and by 45 could emerge in charge of growing businesses.

2. Block Factor Entrepreneurs

Entrepreneurs of this type opted for business either because they could not get promotions fast enough, because of low satisfaction in their jobs (glass ceiling factors), or because they could not get jobs commensurate with their skills, due to late entry into the workforce for gender reasons (mommy track compulsions).

They could be early drifters who end up self-employed, because of lack of suitable opportunities in the workplace. They are most likely to persist in business until they reach the success-disengage stage given their low-commitment to entrepreneurial ideals. They either choose to spend more time on family and home related activities, keeping their businesses small and stable, or opt out and join the formal workforce if that offers a better equilibrium in terms of their personal, financial, family and community related goals. Lack of resources at the start-up stage often locks them into low potential ventures and firms that would typically exhibit a low growth potential.

3. Family-Driven Entrepreneurs

For these entrepreneurs, business choices and decisions are substantially influenced by family considerations. Business comes after family and is run more like a hobby for self-fulfilment. Given a strong relational support structure, entrepreneurs in this group would typically start ventures in the 35-40 age group when work-home conflicts have tapered off. Once again, a low commitment to entrepreneurial ideals would see the enterprise being run as hobby by largely home-based women entrepreneurs and the business would rest at a success-disengage level. In certain cases, especially where the women come from family business backgrounds and if the relational support base can provide enough finance and personnel to support growth, the firm may move further up the stages of growth. However, this would depend on the synergy possible with the mainline family business, and at this stage the woman is likely to be aided substantially by others in the network.

4. Financial Need/Additional Income-Driven Entrepreneurs

For these women, entrepreneurship is a necessity, not a choice. They could be resource-poor because they are from low income group or because they have experienced a trauma—the death of husband or a divorce, which reduces their monetary status. Given the high importance of conventionally defined gender roles in this segment, women who start their business in their middle age would carry high levels of work-home conflict through the initial subsistence and survival stages of their business. Given also their resource-poor status, low relational support base and their general unpreparedness of entrepreneurship, the likelihood of their being locked into low potential ventures would be great. Once their firms achieve success, these entrepreneurs would most likely disengage and opt for small and stable business. Their financial need levels may also make them more risk averse and these entrepreneurs would be more likely to keep the enterprise running so as to provide for their needs or at best to keep the enterprise alive until the next generation can take over.

2.13 DEVELOPMENT OF WOMEN ENTREPRENEURS IN INDIA

As per the 1981 census, women constitute forty eight per cent of the total population. The women workforce constitutes only the twenty-eight per cent of the female population. Out of the total number of self-employed persons women account for only five percent. The majority of the self-employed women are engaged in the unorganized sector like handicrafts, handloom, cottage industries and agriculture.

The Seventh Five-Year Plan has covered the integration of women in economic development. In this regard the plan document has suggested the following:

1. To consider women as specific target groups in developmental programmes.
2. To diversify vocational training facilities for women to suit their varied needs and skills
3. To encourage appropriate technologies, equipment and practices for reducing their drudgery and increasing their efficiency and productivity.
4. To provide marketing assistance at the state level.
5. To increase women's participation in decision making.

The Eighth Five-Year Plan gave due importance to the development of the small sector. The number of small-scale units were expected to increase from one and half million to two and half million during 1992 to 1997. It is estimated among the small-scale entrepreneurs, nearly nine per cent would be women. If this trend is maintained women's participation is likely to increase to twenty percent of the total small-scale sector units.

The new industrial policy has stressed the importance of entrepreneurship among women. The policy has the strategy for the holistic development of women. This will help to develop their personality and to improve their economic and social conditions. This policy has redefined "women units" as units in which they had a majority share holding arid management control.

The New Industrial Policy has also stressed the need for conducting special entrepreneurship development programmes for women with a view to develop entrepreneurship among women. The policy has given the following recommendations :

1. Conduct product and process-oriented courses to enable women to start small-scale industries.
2. The objective of small courses should be to give representation to women in the small industry for their upliftment of their economic and social states.

Thus, development of women entrepreneurship should form an integral part of socioeconomic developmental efforts.

2.14 PROBLEMS OF WOMEN ENTREPRENEURS

In the man dominated society, the greatest deterrent to women entrepreneurs is that they are women. The problems faced specially by the women entrepreneurs are as follows.

1. Lack of Encouragement from Financial Institutions

Financial institutions are sometimes doubtful of women entrepreneurs' entrepreneurial abilities. The bankers consider women loaners are higher risk than men loaners.

2. Lack of Financial Resources

Women entrepreneurs suffer from inadequate financial resources both long-term and working capital. Due to negative attitude of financial institutions and male members, about the capabilities of women, they are forced to rely on their own savings and loaners from family friends. This leads to failure of enterprise due to insufficient financial resources.

3. Low Mobility

Women entrepreneurs generally face the problem to travel from one place to another for business purposes.

4. Family Commitments

In India it is regarded as commitment or responsibility of the women to look after the children and other members of the family. It is difficult for the women entrepreneurs to strike a balance between business and home. Therefore, the success depends on the support given by the family.

5. Social Attitudes

In a men dominated society, despite constitutional equality, women do not get equal treatment. There is widespread discrimination against women. This attitude prevents women entrepreneurs from becoming successful and independent entrepreneurs.

6. Lack of Education

In India literacy among women is very low. Due to this women are unaware of the latest technological development, basic accounting and market trends. This may lead to failure of business.

7. Personal Problems

Many women entrepreneurs lack the necessary initiative, suffer inferiority complex and are easily disheartened by failure.

8. Low need for Achievement

Many studies have shown that women have preconceived notions about their role in life and this inhibits achievement. Women may not set goals (other than marriage) for themselves. It is partly due to their several role conflicts.

9. Over-Dependence

Most of the women entrepreneurs are seen to undertake purely as a subcontractor (i.e., ancillary unit) on raw materials, or manufacture items that are usually used by large-scale units. This leads to dependence on large-scale industries. The success or failure of women entrepreneurs depends on the success or failure of large-scale industries.

10. Lack of Raw Materials

The majority of the women are engaged in the unorganized sector like handicrafts, handloom and cottage-based industries. For these sectors there is inadequate availability of raw materials.

11. Stiff Competition

Women entrepreneurs in the unorganized sector face intense competition from organized sector and male entrepreneurs in terms of quality and price of the product.

12. Lack of Training

A woman entrepreneur from middle class starts her first entrepreneurial venture in her late thirties or early forties due to her commitments towards children. Therefore, her biggest problem is the lack of sufficient business training and this weakness is all the more glaring in the case of rural entrepreneurs who are uneducated.

Thus, in addition to the above, the women entrepreneurs also face other problems faced by small-scale sector.

Due to social structure which is often culturally driven, women have different training needs when it comes to entrepreneurship and self-employment that helps to gain confidence.

13. Marketing Problems

Access to market is more difficult than access to finance. Access to market pose a very big challenge to entrepreneurs. Women entrepreneurs with adequate experience continue to face the problem of marketing their products.

14. High Cost of Production

The profitability, development and expansion depends on the cost of production.

High cost of production due to problem of material, labour, infrastructure, human resource, etc. hinders the efficiency, development and expansion of an enterprise. Women entrepreneurs also face the same problem.

15. Lack of Information

Women entrepreneurs sometimes are not aware of technological developments and other information on subsidies and concessions available to them in respect of getting loan or getting industrial sheds, or raw materials, etc.

16. Lack of Self-confidence

The element of risk is very high in business. The women entrepreneurs hesitate to take risk. The risk bearing ability is comparatively lower than men.

2.15 PROMOTION OF WOMEN ENTREPRENEURS

The future of small-scale industry depends very much on the entry of women and their participation. So, promotion of women entrepreneurs should become an integral part for the women development as well as economic growth.

Steps for Promotion

Following steps to be taken to promote women entrepreneurs in India.

1. An environment should be prepared to enable their participation.
2. Women should be motivated to come out of their traditional occupation for accepting more challenging and economic activities.
3. Funding agencies to be sympathetic towards women entrepreneurs.
4. Banks and other financial institutions must provide credit to women entrepreneurs on both priority basis and concessional terms.
5. Simplify the procedure of licensing and Government regulations to start a new business enterprise for women entrepreneurs.
6. Motivate new women entrepreneurs into this field through audio-visual media.
7. The promotional and regulatory agencies should also be motivated to be considerate, understanding and helpful towards women entrepreneurs.

8. The State Government should formulate programmes to assist women entrepreneurs by providing them with the initial stage of setting up an enterprise.

2.16 INTRAPRENEUR

Corporate entrepreneurs are known as intrapreneurs. The term is used to describe the process whereby big companies set out to encourage entrepreneurial characteristics in their own managers.

The term intrapreneur refer to an enterprising person within the boundaries of his job in an organisation. He is an entrepreneur who catches hold of a new idea for a product, service or process and work to bring his vision to fruition within the framework of the organisation. For example, Mr. Subrotrio Batchi of Mind Tree Consulting Company (co-founder) when he was working for WIPRO.

Intrapreneurs are not necessarily the inventors of new products or services but are the persons who can turn ideas into profitable realities. They are the people behind a product or service. They are the team builders with a commitment and strong drive to see their ideas become a reality.

In other words, an intrapreneur works for others as a paid employee and uses all his entrepreneurial skills for growth of the company. Thus, an intrapreneur is a person having all the qualities of an entrepreneur but not having a business of his own.

Intrapreneurial Leadership Characteristics

Within the overall corporate environment, certain individual characteristics have been identified that constitute a successful intrapreneur. These include the following:

1. Understanding the environment.
2. Being visionary and flexible
3. Creating management options.
4. Encouraging teamwork
5. Encouraging open discussion
6. Building a coalition of supporters
7. Persistence

2.17 AN ENTREPRENEUR AND AN INTRAPRENEUR: A COMPARISON

Point of Distinction	Entrepreneur	Intrapreneur
1. Qualities	An innovative, risk taker, high achiever etc.	Person having all the qualities and characters of an entrepreneur
2. Goal Management	An entrepreneur starts a venture by setting up a new enterprise for his personal gratification	But the main aim of a intrapreneur is to render his service in an enterprise already set up by someone
3. Status	An entrepreneur is the owner of enterprise.	Works for others as a paid employee
4. Risk	An entrepreneur bears all risks and uncertainty involved in the enterprise.	Does not bear all the risk involved in the enterprise (moderate risk taker)
5. Rewards	Entrepreneur for his risk bearing role he receives profits. It is only uncertain and irregular but can at times be negative	Which is fixed and regular income can never be negative.
6. Innovation	As an innovator he is called chage agent who introduces goods and services to meet changing needs of the customer.	An intrapreneur executes the plans of the entrepreneur. Thus, intrapreneur translates the ideas into practice.

ANNEXURE–I

PROFILES OF SUCCESSFUL ENTREPRENEURS

CASE 1

1. N.R. Narayana Murthy

N.R. Narayana Murthy, Chairman and CEO of Infosys Technologies Ltd., is one man who has fructified middle-class Indians' dreams. It is not exactly a rags-to-riches story but, Murthy came from a middle-class background. He is the son of a teacher, a member of a large family of eight children (three brothers and five sisters). Like an ordinary middle-class boy, he studied well and qualified for the prestigious IIT. He could not afford it and therefore, went to NIE, Mysore—a local college for a degree in electrical engineering. Murthy completed his postgraduation in electrical engineering at IIT Kanpur in 1969 and took up a job. The only thing is, he did seemingly the very same things, but obviously differently. He always took risks.

First, he pursued a career in computer science when there were not too many jobs in this field. The Indian industry/business was very much into mortar-and-bricks business and had just about started appreciating the role of computers. The second risk that he undertook was to turn down attractive offers from large companies such as Telco, HMT, ECIL and Air India; instead, he joined as a systems programmer at IIM Ahmedabad. IIMA was in the process of installing a Hewlett-Packard minicomputer and was forging ahead to become the second business school after Stanford to have a time-sharing operating system. The thrill of such a pioneering job thus gave him a great learning opportunity and was the main reason that Murthy joined the team at IIMA under J.G. Krishnayya, Professor of Information Systems. Murthy received a salary of Rs 800 a month. He feels 'It was the best decision of my life. There were many 20-hour work days but Murthy loved being a pioneer, of working at the cutting-edge of computer technology those days.

Then came a chance from Sesa, a French software company, to build an operating system to handle air cargo at the Charles de Gaulle airport in Paris. What is worth noting is that at around the same time, he had received scholarships to pursue a Ph.D. in the USA and Israel. But, Murthy did not take these soft options. He instead, went to Paris, which also meant mastering another language—French.

After the successful execution of this project, Murthy did not take the next flight back home. He donated most of his earnings, keeping only $ 450 with him and spent almost a year on the road from Western Europe to Eastern Europe to Kabul in Afghanistan. Kabul to Amritsar was the only route on which he took a plane before coming over to Pune in 1974 to join his mentor, Professor Krishnayya.

A little later, Murthy took up a job in Patni Computer Systems (PCS) a Mumbai-based firm, after some time he was somewhat frustrated with the work at SRI (getting the usual bureaucratic treatment of seldom implementing sincere suggestions).

At PCS he was head of the software group and it was here that he met some of his would-be founder-partners of Infosys. He quit the job and started his software service firm along with his partners. This was the firm which was to become the giant that Infosys is today. Out of his six founder-partners, three were rookies—PCS was the first job for Nandan M. Nilekani, S. Gopalakrishnan and Ashok Arora. Only K. Dinesh (NGEF, Bangalore), N.S. Raghavan (Union Carbide) and S.D. Shibulal (BEST, Mumbai) had some prior experience elsewhere. Not that all these had any money. They were all from middle class backgrounds and pooled in Rs. 10,000 capital borrowed from their better-halves. Infosys Consultants was born in July 1981 in one bedroom of a two-bedroom apartment in Pune.

The incidents surrounding the life of this unusual 'middle class' businessman do not end here. The first ten years after 1981 were quite tough for Murthy and his team. 'It tooks us one year to get a telephone; it tooks us two years to get a licence to import a computer; ... stupidity was the order of the day then'. Says Murthy. Murthy stuck it out through thick and thin. In 1990, his partners thought of selling the company. But, Murthy differed and even offered to buy his partners out. Murthy always tooks risks and it always seems to have paid off.

Look at the more recent development. Most Indian companies, throughout these 50 plus years of Independence have shown a tremendous resistance to set up shop abroad. There has always been this foreign-phobia for which there are many reasons. Most reasons do look genuine as usual. In such a milieu, Murhty did the unthinkable. If Dhirubhai Ambani went to the Indian people with his famous equity issues, Narayans Murthy went to the USA itself and listed his company on the NASDAQ National Market. Some others later, followed suit.

He is one of the India's top-most businessmen but he has a rather simple lifestyle. But, behind these externalities he is a man as sharp as one could get in the whole wide world. He appears to have a highly developed intuition that tells him to do the right things at the right time. Or, perhaps, it is just the way he looks at circumstances as they are presented to him. 'Leadership is about making what seems impossible, possible'. Early in his business career, he realized that the Indian economy was fettered by rules, regulations and licences. He, therefore, quickly changed the major thrust of his business to the export of services abroad. Even now, most of Infosys' business is from foreign contracts/assignments. Murthy and Infosys is the originator of the very successful concept of Offshore Software Development emulated subsequently by several other IT companies.

Today there are about 100 of his 'team-members' at Infosys who are rupee billionaires, and about 2000 who are rupee millionaires. It is said that Murthy's chauffeur is a 'crorepati' and several waiters in the Infosys canteen are at least millionaires. One may call it 'sharing wealth' or 'sharing stakes'; but, it is indeed a great management concept, if not an idealized philosophical philanthropy.

'Leadership' is about creating a vision, communicating that vision to one's followers, and exhorting them to move towards that vision', says Murthy.

Murthy's goal in life was clear; India got its extraordinary visionary, entrepreneurial businessman-leader who would take the country's business to places, a beacon of light for all the new entrepreneurial talent in the country. The world got a businessman for a role-model—a businessman who believed in sharing wealth with his employees (rather, 'co-workers' or 'co-owners'), in giving the shareholders all that they would normally ask for and more, a businessman who truly believes in business being conducted ethically. Murthy believes in enduring qualities in personal and corporate life.

A man cut of a truly different mould, who has shown the Indians that a whole world of opportunities exist in the wide world outside India, the man who has shown the world that an Indian can do wonders in the world of business, who has shown the entire world that business can be and should be conducted with a human touch and enduring human values, Narayana Murthy is truly a trailblazer. To count his success in terms of the growth of Infosys and its market capitalization would be to present an extremely truncated view of the worth and message of this visionary corporate leader of the 21st century.

QUESTION

Go through the case and list the major entrepreneurial competence you find in Narayana Murthy.

CASE 2

Kiran Mazumdar-Shaw

Kiran Mazumdar-Shaw at 47 is the Chairman and Managing Director of India's biggest biotechnology venture. The Biocon India Group. For the past 20-odd years she has been leading in the biotech industry.

Kiran was brought up in Bangalore where she studied Science with an eye on a career in medicine. When she could not procure a seat in a medical college. She studied for her bachelor's degree in biological sciences and topped the batch in Bangalore University.

Accomplishing the most unusual is another of her characteristic. Kiran completed a postgraduate course in brewery technology from Australia and became a brew master. During her search for a job, she stumbled upon the opportunity to start an enzyme manufacturing unit for an Irish company. The 'explorer' within her took charge and she did all that she could to excel in the business. The results are there for all of us to see the Biocon group of industries that started in a garage is today the largest biotech company in India. It is not the size that matters in this case. There may be so many other soap, toiletries and cosmetics companies that are much bigger. It is the leadership of Biocon Group in the new and very promising area of biotechnology that is extremely significant. It has the potential to give a totally new direction to Indian industry, economy and to the world's industry at large. This truly is creative work in setting up a steel industry in India, Kiran Mazumdar-Shaw's contribution to Indian industry is similarly heroic.

Kiran has chosen to do business in virgin field, leading the biotech revolution in India from the forefront. Until recently and the dawn of the new millennium, very few in India and even in the world were aware of the potential of biotechnology. It was like a dark tunnel. However, Kiran recognized the inherent potential and worked relentlessly with a dedicated band of people whom she selected and developed. Talking about the Biocon Group's achievement in terms of its growth rate, turnover, the number of scientists working for the group and its total manpower would only divert attention from her singular task of pioneering leadership in an area hitherto unexplored by Indian business.

Kiran has that ability to spot an opportunity miles away, a kind of telescopic vision. So far, it was infotech that India saw its vast potential, now it is biotech. With the advent of the human genome project, it now appears that biotech will soon match Infotech as one of the two most promising industries in India. Much of this is now possible, thanks to the foundation laid by Kiran.

She is such an exemplary leader and has achieved such heights of success in her endeavours that to draw attention to the fact that she is a woman in a largely male-dominated business and industry may risk one speaking about things that are insignificant.

To sum it up, Kiran Mazumdar-Shaw can be rightly called a great entrepreneur of our times. A creative mind par excellence, combined with a keen organizing capacity, she has given this country an entirely new area to develop and scope to compete in the international arena. India has the capacity to produce hundreds of thousands of researchers in biology, geneticists, biochemical engineers, agricultural and food scientists and environmentalists.

Thanks to the vision and leadership of Kiran Mazumdar-Shaw, Karnataka, from where the Biocon Group operates, has now formed a Biotechnology Vision Group with Kiran as its Chairperson. There is also a Biotechnology Development Council, with Kiran as one of its members. The Council will develop norms to set up biotech companies, represent trade and interact with government departments. Kiran Mazumdar-Shaw will advise the government on policy initiatives. A Centre for Human Genetics is being set up in Bangalore with leading scientists and policymakers on its governing board. An institute of agro-biotechnology is to be set up in Dharwad. The spark set off 20 years ago by an electric Kiran has now become a fire to augment the engine of growth in India.

Yes, today if some starry-eyed entrepreneurial aspirant were to ask for heroes and role models, Kiran Mazumdar-Shaw should definitely figure at the top of the list.

QUESTION

Examine the true qualities in Kiran Mazumadar-Shaw–a successful Entrepreneur.

CASE 3

Dr Verghese Kurien

It is not an easy task to describe Dr Verghese Kurien, 80, founder Chairman of the National Dairy Development Board (NDDB) and also founder Chairman of Gujarat Cooperative Milk Marketing Federation, popularly known for his utterly butterly delicious 'Amul'. He is a businessman par excellence but it would be quite a narrow classification for a man whose achievements go far beyond the realm of business as we know it. He is an excellent businessman, a highly successful Chief Executive, an institution builder, a social reformer and a socio-economic revolutionary. All these caps fit perfectly on this man with the Midas touch. Dr Kurien himself joked about his multifaceted personality at the entrance and said, 'Everyone else is in a suit. They won't let me in!' They honoured him with the Lifetime Achievement Award. The only other person who got this award was Dhirubhai Ambani, a towering figure in the business scenario.

Dr Kurein is much more than a businessman. He is a part of our Indian history. Although he calls himself 'Doodhwalla from Anand' (milkman from Anand) in jest, 'Doodh' has been only a vehicle for this revolutionary. His life is a study as to how business can start a social revolution.

Speaking about his achievements in dairying alone, these are phenomenal. Two days before the dawn of 1950, when he was requested to join the Kaira District Cooperative Milk Producers' Union, now better known by its trade name AMUL (Anand Milk Union Limited), milk collection was to the tune of a few thousand litres a day. Today, there are 180 'Anands' in India handling close to 16 million litres of milk a day. The sales of AMUL now exceed Rs 3,000 crore. The GCMMF has 19 dairy plants with a total milk handling capacity of over 6.7 million litres per day. GCMMF has produced similar and associated movements all over India and even in the neighbouring countries of Sri Lanka and Bangladesh. But speaking of Gujarat alone, there are 2.2 million milk producers who are members of the Village Cooperative Societies in 10,675 villages with 12 District Unions federated with the GCMMF. The revolution in the production of milk, or the White Revolution has reached 96,206 villages all over India covering 180 District Unions and 15 state federations with a total membership of 10.7 million milk producers/farmers handling about one-third of the nation's marketable surplus milk. This is a tremendous achievement even in simple 'milk' terms.

Tremendous, because it directly touches the lives of more than 10 million Indians everyday, every morning and evening. Indirectly, it would touch at least as many families, which means about 50 million Indians. The total impacts much more than this. One commodity, milk, making a difference to the lives of such a large section of our population is indeed remarkable. This population is the segment where the difference matters most, the segment of marginal farmers and that of rural women. When this is taken into consideration, Verghese Kurien's achievement has received international acclaim. The World Bank made an evaluation of operation flood and in its report published in 1998, it said, 'The overall expansion of dairy industry from the early 1970s has been comparable to the more widely recognized Green Revolution crops of wheat and rice'. Operation Flood is unusual. In that it is a single-commodity 'integrated development project'. For those landless people who already own a milch animal or who have been able to purchase one, it has been a boon. In the villages of Gujarat they now say, 'Jene ghar kalli, tene ghar roj Deewali' (one who has a black animal (a buffalo) at home, has Deewali festival celebrations in his house everyday).

Also, in collaboration with NGOs, more than 10,000 women's dairy cooperative societies have been established in India. The social impact of such societies has been dramatic since they are exclusively managed by women and empower the rural womenfolk. These have given rise to an army off self-confident and talented leaders. As women earn a higher income and achieve a financial freedom never known before and as they understand the world around them, they encourage better education for their children, ask for better healthcare and avail family planning facilities. 'If a female buffalo can have good health, why can't we'—it is a simple logical extension. The understanding of a buffalo's reproductive cycle, which is essential for AI (Artificial Insemination), provides them with a compulsory tutorial on the possibilities of family planning. Preventive vaccination of cattle has led to a greater acceptance of vaccination in mothers and children. The World Bank reports that 'with more than 6,000 women's cooperative societies and upwards of 3,00,000 active members Operation Flood provides an example of a large-scale programme redesign to address gender issues'.

When women take up dairying, they give up coolie work; this creates additional jobs for the poorer men folk in the rural areas. So, Kurien's baby, Operation Flood has been a major employment generating project as well. Additional milk income also means that children need not go to work and they can instead, attend school. The impact is particularly significant in the case of girl children. So, we have villages with women and men who have somewhat higher incomes and more attendance in schools. Kurien has, therefore, also generated an educational project as the outcome of Operation Flood.

Kurien calls the village cooperative societies, his schools and universities for learning what democracy is, how to make it work, how to sustain it and to achieve the good of a large number of people. He explains, 'The basic philosophy of the Anand pattern is to combine India's greatest asset, the power of its people, with professional management, in a vertically integrated cooperative structure that establishes a direct linkage between those who produce the milk and those who consume it, either at milk or milk products, eliminating all the middlemen. This structure transfers to the producer the largest share of the consumer's rupee. It supports production by exposing farmers to modernity. By placing the farmer in command, as owner of his cooperative it involves him/her in the process of development. The democratic form of the cooperative provides an underpinning for democracy in the country through a foundation of democratic institutions right down to the village level.

Of course, the Anand pattern is more than a description of structures and activities. It is based on certain values, techniques and ideals. These are the values and principles that are important for the resurgence of our country or, for that matter, of poor people anywhere in the world.

There is the other kind of education. When Prime Minister Lal Bahadur Shastri inaugurated the cattle feed factory at Kanjari on 31 October 1964, he insisted on spending the previous night at a village near Anand. Shastri strolled through Ajarpura, the village and asked all men and women of all castes and religions various questions. 'You are a Harijan. If a high-caste Brahmin comes to supply milk to the society, where will you stand ? he asked. 'If I come in before the Brahmin, I will stand ahead of him in the line. If I come in after him, I will stand behind him'. Replied the Harijan villager. The Prime

Minister was impressed. A simple-looking village cooperative; but, how effective it had been in levelling caste differences !

No one would be happier than Kurien that the saplings he planted and nurtured have taken such a beautiful shape. But, he doesn't take credit for it. 'It was Tribhuvandas Patel, a freedom fighter who had been jailed many times in our struggle for Independence, a leader of men, a man of wisdom, unrelenting, stern and puritanical integrity, who made Amul, not I. I only helped him. I owe a great deal to Shri Tribhuvandas, our nation and our farmers. He was my guru, he says in all humility. 'the farmer is my boss. I have 10 million bosses. I have to satisfy them or I will be fired, he adds.

Kurien is also very quick to acknowledge that this was an accident, a happy accident, because in 1949 when he came to Anand, he got the release orders from his job at the Government Creamery in Anand, he was all set and eager to pack off to Mumbai. But Tribhuvandas Patel, the then Chairman of Kaira District Cooperatie Milk Producers' Union, a freedom fighter and an associate of Sardar Vallabhbhai Patel, with whom Kurien had developed neighbourly friendship, requested him to stay on in Anand for some more time and help him put his cooperative society's dairy equipment together. Kurien decided to stay back for a few more days, stayed there forever and the rest that happened is now history. He initially thought that he was only helping a friend set up. A small dairy, but slowly he imbibed the spirit behind the dairy and the cooperative society that his guru Tribhuvandas had started. From an engineer he bloomed into a fighter for a larger cause, the cause of poor farmer.

Despite the huge success that his projects and programmes achieved, for Kurien, the task is far from complete. Nothing for him is 'enough'. What is the definition of "enough"? he asks and adds, 'Today we produce "enough" cereals in India, we produce "enough" milk and "enough" fruits and vegetables. What it means is because 40 per cent of our population cannot afford to buy most of the commodities that they need, there is enough to go around between those who can afford to buy what is available. And that is not enough!".

It is an imperative for Kurien's programmes to be educational. His basic belief is that true development is the development of man. Kurien the educationist, it's the Founder-Chairman of the Institute of Rural Management (IRMA) and has been on he board of Indian Institutes of Management at Ahmedabad and Bangalore. He is very fond of telling students and teachers form these premier institutions that 'the richness of life comes, not from a fat pay slip, but from placing one's talents at the service of those who genuinely need them. 'Kurien's life is in itself a book that one could learn from.

QUESTIONS

1. List the major entrepreneurial competency you find in Dr Verghese Kurien
2. Go through the case and bring out the factors making Amul a success story.

CASE 4

Azim Premji

He was born in an industrialist's family and inherited Wipro from his father. But these facts did not make his climb to his present position any easier. He had to take over his father's business when he was barely 20 years old and studying Electrical Engineering at Stanford University in the USA. He was in the final year of the degree programme when the calamity struck, his father, 52-year-old Mohammed Hashan Premji, passed away on 11 August 1966 and young Azim had to rush to Mumbai and take up the responsibility of heading Wipro which his father had set up in 1947 at the dawn of independence. Shortly after he took over the leadership of the company, some shareholders demanded that the company, be sold to the highest bidder. They were unwilling to trust a 21-year-old to run it! Azim was determined to prove himself and took to the serious business of industry-building when college goers his age were enjoying the carefree, joyous campus life.

When Azim Premji took over the Western India Vegetable Products Limited in 1966 (later the name changed to Wipro), it was a small company with Rs 4 crore in sales. Its only business was production of Sunflower-brand of 'vanaspati' (hydrogenated cooking oil) at a plant located in Amalner, 400 km from Mumbai. The sales of the Wipro group today have crossed Rs 3,000 crore with more than 85 per cent of the revenue comes from its Information Technology business, both domestic and global. From an income of Rs 4 crore to over Rs 3,000 crore, from manufacturing and distributing 'vanaspati' to providing computer software services, and from being a seller of product locally to being a leading exporter of this country, Premji has brought in a change of Himalayan proportions on multiple fronts for Wipro and for the entire country.

Software services today constitute 13 per cent of India's total exports. It is a sea change, literally, for a country that sold mostly basic and low-tech goods abroad—goods such as agricultural produce, minerals and base metals. Azim Premiji and Wipro have been one of the prime movers in this change. More important than the change in complexion and the quantitative rise in exports is the change that has come over in the mindset of our people, young people who are confidently stalking shores abroad and/or are opening their own small computer set-ups Azim and his genre of business leaders have given India's young generation new hope and a new vision, and the 'fourth eye'. Front-stage in the band of visionary leaders who charted unknown and hostile territory, Azim is showing the route to a new world of opportunities.

There is an air of informality in the Wipro offices where every person is equally important. Unlike the traditional Indian business houses and offices in American or West European companies (where an uncomfortable tinge of superiority pervades the atmosphere) Wipro is different. A company that has 65 per cent of its revenue coming from sales to the developed world, particularly the USA, it seems to truly believe in the dignity of labour. For instance, Azim Premji's secretary appears quite friendly a lady living next-door. Azim's motto is efficiency which does not need to be proclaimed from the roof-tops—it will be proved in your results. This is Wipro's fundamental belief shared by one and all in the organization.

Azim Premji and synonymously, Wipro has placed enormous faith in 'efficiency'. 'Value for money' is an important commitment from Wipro. Its promise to the customer is:

'With utmost respect to **Human values,**
We promise to serve our
Customer with Integrity,
Through a variety of **Innovative,**
Value for Money, products and services,
By **Applying Thought,** day after day.

Value for money is the bottom line, the base of enduring success in business, which few businessmen truly understand. Constantly improve or even to maintain the same level of value for money for the customer. Azim Premji's success in any branch of business can be understood in the light of this 'mantra'. From 1966 to 1975 his main business was that of hydrogenated vegetable oil, 'vanaspati'; he made good in that line of business despite the fact that he had to face major giants such as Hindustan Lever and Godrej by applying thought. He departed from the prevalent business norms and approached the consumers directly. He did this by providing 'vanaspati' in smaller packages convenient for the consumer and by developing brand recognition. Since, he now sold directly to the retailers instead of the middlemen, he improved the profit margins considerably. Amongst the giants in that line of products, he carved out his own special niche.

A chance encounter with M.S. Rao brought out the engineer in Azim Premji and Wipro Fluid Power was set up in 1975 to manufacture hydraulic and pneumatic cylinders. The 'vanaspati' business, however, continued.

During the 1970s particularly the later half of the 70s India saw the exit of many multinationals such as IBM because of the central government's anti-MNC policies. With IBM gone, many business houses saw an opportunity to fill in the vacuum. Some of the big names during those days were ORG Systems, DCM Data Products and Hindustan Computer (HCL). Wipro had never been into information technology earlier.

But Azim Premji, the astute businessman and marketer that he is, sensed a major opportunity and entered the new business. Interestingly, he did things, again, contrary to prevalent business norms. He sought managers who did not know computers but could adapt to quickly-changing technology. One manager was from the refrigeration industry while another was form truck manufacturing. The wipro 'mantra' for competitiveness is and was; value for money' by 'applying thought'. This is what he did he gave better value for money and won the war of competition. The computer industry was in the nascent stage in India and the customers needed to be guided at every step as the computer was a new tool. Premji understood this need and provided intensive service support for his high-quality products. Wipro was very successful in the domestic and overseas market. During the later half of the 1980s, Wipro did big business with Russia in Personal Computer (PC) sales, and that of dot matrix printers under the rupee trade.

When software services exports boomed in the 1990s Wipro went slow on hardware sales as the socialist world's market dried up. The company decided to go full gear on information technology services. It was another turning point in the history of the company. Wipro gave better value for money in this sector and successfully became one of the major leaders in this business from India. Azim Premji channelled the R&D talent. Wipro had nurtured in the computer business, into a software lab that could provide expertise in areas such ass telecommunications and other complex but more profitable projects. He believes in quick technological adaptability to changing market environment and customer needs.

Azim Premji has boldly taken many risky turns in business. His boldness emanates from his unshakeable belief in his 'mantra'and the understanding of his customers. He says, 'People come first. We respect our customers as individuals; (and) recognize that they have different needs.

He thoroughly understood and practised 'customer focus' much before it became the popular jargon in management seminars. In his words, 'we believe that it is the customer who really has the choice to grant us the future'. That is the secret of his success.

Values that Premji and his team at Wipro abide by are integrity, personal commitment, determination and hard work. The distinguishing features of Wipro services and products are quality, speed and experts, which have their source in the organisation's values.

QUESTION

What factors in your opinion, helped Mr. Azim Premji to become a successful entrepreneur?

EXERCISE

Section A

1. Who is an entrepreneur?
2. Define an entrepreneur.
3. Mention any four benefits of being an entrepreneur.
4. Mention any four crises of being an entrepreneur.
5. Mention any four qualities of an entrepreneur.
6. Mention any four characteristics of an entrepreneur.
7. Mention any four functions of an entrepreneur.
8. Who is imitative entrepreneur?
9. Who is an innovative entrepreneur?
10. Who is a Fabian entrepreneur?
11. Who is a Drone entrepreneur?
12. Who is a women entrepreneur?
13. Mention any four problems of women entrepreneur.
14. What is entrepreneurship?

15. Who is a "pure entrepreneur"?
16. Who is a "spontaneous entrepreneur"?
17. Who is an "induced entrepreneur"?
18. Who is a "motivated entrepreneur"?
19. Who is an "intrapreneur"?
20. Mention the Intrapreneurial leadership characteristics.

Section B

21. What are the benefits of being an entrepreneur?
22. Distinguish an entrepreneur and an intrapreneur.
23. What steps are taken to solve the problems of women entrepreneurs?

Section C

24. Discuss the problems of being an entrepreneur.
25. Discuss the qualities of an entrepreneur.
26. Explain the characteristics of an entrepreneur.
27. Explain the functions of an entrepreneurs.
28. Explain different types of entrepreneurs
29. Discuss the problems of women entrepreneurs.

SKILL DEVELOPMENT / PRACTICAL EXERCISES

1. Conduct an interview of a successful entrepreneur in your city. Find out the qualities, benefits of being an entrepreneur, problems faced by him and his functions to become a successful entrepreneur.
2. Prepare a brief report based on the observations made during the interview.
3. Collect the profiles of successful entrepreneurs and analyse the reasons for success.

3

Entrepreneurial Competency

STRUCTURE

3.1 Meaning
3.2 Components of Entrepreneurial Competencies
3.3 Entrepreneurial Competency
3.4 Types of Competencies or Competency Requirements for an Entrepreneur
3.5 Tools for Assessment of Competencies

3.1 MEANING

Competence is a characteristic of a person, which results in effective and/or superior performance in a job. Competence is an underlying characteristic of a person, that is, it may be motive/traits/skills or aspect of one's self-image or a body of knowledge which one uses. The existence of these characteristics may or may not be known to the person. In this sense, the characteristic may be unconscious aspect of the person. In simple terms, a competence is a combination of a body of knowledge, soft skills and cluster of appropriate motives/ traits, an individual possesses to perform a given task effectively and efficiently.

3.2 COMPONENTS OF ENTREPRENEURIAL COMPETENCIES

In order to understand more about competencies, let us understand the meaning of knowledge, skills, traits and motives which form among various components of entrepreneurial competencies.

1. Knowledge

Knowledge means collection of information and retention of facts that an individual stores in some parts of his brain. But this alone will not enable one to actually swim unless one has something more than the knowledge for performing a task. Let us take for example swimming, one could be in a position to describe how to swim which would mean that one possesses knowledge of swimming. In real life situation, one may find various examples wherein people possessing adequate knowledge have failed while performing the task. Therefore, besides knowledge, an individual should have skills to translate the knowledge into action.

2. Skill

Skill is the ability to demonstrate a system and sequence of behaviour that are functionally related to in attaining a performance or goal. Using a skill is not a single action. Since a skill is the ability to demonstrate a system and sequence of behaviour, it must result in something observable, something that someone in the person's environment can 'see'. For example, planning ability is a skill. People who have this skill can identify sequence of action to be taken to accomplish a specific objective. They can identify potential obstacles to those actions. People with this skill can identify sources of help in avoiding obstacles or overcoming them when they interfere with the action sequence. Going by the example of knowledge of swimming, if one has to be in a position to swim, one needs to have the skill too. Knowledge could be acquired by reading, listening, visuals, etc. while the skill can be acquired only through practice, which enables the individual to demonstrate the system and sequence of behaviour that are functionally related to performing a task.

To achieve corporate excellence in the dynamic future, managers must learn to transcend the past with the new age skills like:

1. Creative sight
2. Sensitivity
3. Vision
4. Versatility
5. Focus
6. Patience

The first two skills help to forge a strong foundation for excellence because insight forms successful strategies and sensitivity helps build strong cultures. Vision and patience help to integrate the skills. While vision helps to invent an excellent future, patience allows to take the necessary time to implement it successfully.

3. Motive and Traits

A **motive** is a recurrent concern for a goal or condition appearing in fantasy, which drives, directs and selects behaviour of the individual. Motive includes thoughts related to a particular goal. For example, people who think about improving their own performances and competing against a standard of excellence are said to have 'Achievement Motivation'. When people with a high achievement motivation encounter a situation in which their performance can be measured and a goal can be stated, their achievement motivation is aroused. Once aroused the motivated thoughts direct and select their behaviour, that is they will choose to do things that help them get feedback on their performance and engage in activities that may result in improved performance.

Coming back to the example of swimming, the knowledge on how to swim followed by practice which could help an individual to acquire skills in swimming would lead to the individual acquiring capability to swim. But then this does not lead him to become the best swimmer within a given reference group. The individual's urge to do better and better leading to a desire to become the best swimmer could be termed as a concern for excellence, in other words achievement motivation. It is this concern which would help the individual to constantly practice swimming, look out for ways and means of increasing the speed thereby ultimately increasing the possibility of becoming a good swimmer.

A **trait** is a disposal or a characteristic way in which a person responds to an equivalent set of stimuli. A trait includes thoughts and psychomotor activities related to a general category of events. For example, people who believe themselves to be in control of their future are said to have the trait of efficacy. When people with this trait encounter problems or issues in any aspect of life take initiative to resolve the problem or understand the issue. They do not wait for someone else to do it nor expect that luck will take care of it. The thought pattern and resultant behaviour occur in response to any of events, which allow the trait to be expressed.

4. Hard and Soft Skills

The task could be that of a manager, a supervisor or an entrepreneur, one aspect that leads to effective performance is the 'hard skill' of the performer. Hard skills, mean those related to given profession and acquired, generally through academic education as also through hands-on experience in performing a task. Taking the example of a 'design engineering' engaged in designing gears as that apart of a complex machine, the technical knowledge/skills of designing is the hard skills that would contribute to his performance. However, between a successful design engineer and not so successful one, the difference could be in terms of 'soft skills'. The soft skill competencies that contribute to success of a design engineer in this illustration could be problem solving approach, tendency to gather information from various sources so as to perform the task effectively and the like. Such soft skill competencies are functionally interchangeable. For example, someone who possesses problem solving skill—a soft skill competence can apply it in any situation other than one's profession. Thus, soft skills are generally inherent in an individual or are developed by him consciously or unconsciously, for example, communication skills interpersonal skills and entrepreneurial competencies, etc.

Thus, to perform any given task including that of launching an industrial venture and managing it successfully, a person needs a set of knowledge, skills, motives and traits which could be together labelled as competencies.

3.3 ENTREPRENEURIAL COMPETENCY

Entrepreneurial competencies are defined as underlying characteristics such as generic and specific knowledge, motives, traits, self-images, social roles and skills which result in birth of a venture, its survival, and /or growth. Entrepreneurial competencies are obviously carried by individuals—the entrepreneurs who begin or transform organizations and who add value through their organizing of resources and opportunities.

The best way to understand what it takes to perform a task effectively is to find out what good performers actually do, how they approach a given situation and compare the same with what average performers do. Job competencies assistance is based on the following premises. (Assumptions)

1. In every job some people perform more effectively than others. These people also approach their jobs differently.
2. These differences in approach relate directly to specific characteristics that are often absent or weak in average performers.

The approach towards job competency involves the following factors:

1. Determining performance standards i.e., factors indicating top performers and using this information to identify superior performers.
2. Analyzing performer characteristic and behaviour.
3. Developing the top performer in return of observable behaviourally specific characteristics and deriving validated competency model that directly relates to critical aspects of the job.

3.4 TYPES OF COMPETENCIES OR COMPETENCY REQUIREMENTS FOR AN ENTREPRENEUR

The competencies may be classified into the following categories:

1. Personal entrepreneurial competencies
2. Venture initiation and success competencies
   a) Enterprise launching competencies
   b) Enterprise management competencies

1. Personal Entrepreneurial Competencies

It is the personal characteristic of an individual who possesses to perform the task effectively and efficiently. Personal entrepreneurial competencies include the following:

a) Initiative

Persons with high initiative takes action that goes beyond job requirements or demand of the situation. They do things before being asked or forced to do things and acts to extend the business into new areas products or services. This results in the tendency to work one's ideas and decide on the line of action appropriate for them to take.

b) Sees and acts on Opportunities

Entrepreneurial person looks for and takes action on opportunities. They seize unusual opportunities to obtain financing equipment, land, work, space or assistance.

c) Persistence

Entrepreneurial persons take repeated and different actions to overcome obstacle. They take action in the phase of significant obstacles. This competency requires a lot of confidence which comes automatically by taking care in setting the goal.

d) Information Seeking

Entrepreneurial persons take action on their own to get information, to reach objectives and clarify problems. They do personal research on how to provide a product or service. They seek information or ask questions to clarify what is wanted or needed. They personally undertake research and use contacts or information networks to obtain useful information.

e) Concern for High Quality of Work

Entrepreneurial persons act to do things that meet or beat existing standards of excellence. They have a desire to produce work with high quality and compare their own work with others.

f) Commitment to Work Contract

Entrepreneurial persons place the highest priority for getting a job completed. They make a personal sacrifices or take extraordinary effort to complete a job. They accept full responsibility for problems in completing a job for others and express concern for satisfying the customer.

g) Efficiency Orientation

Entrepreneurial persons look for or find ways to do things faster or with fewer resources or at a lower cost. They use information or business tools to improve efficiency.

h) Systematic Planning

Entrepreneurial persons develop and use the logical step by step plans to reach goals. They plan by breaking a large task into sub-tasks and develop plans, then, anticipate obstacles and evaluate alternatives. They take a logical and systematic approach to activities.

i) Problem Solving

Entrepreneurial persons identify new and potentially unique ideas to reach goals. They generate new ideas or innovative solutions to solve problems and they take alternative strategies to solve the problems.

j) Self-confidence

Entrepreneurs with this competency will have a strong belief in self and in their own abilities. They express confidence in their own ability to complete a task or meet a challenge. They stick to their own judgement while taking decisions.

k) Assertiveness

Entrepreneurs with this competency vindicate the claim to assert their own rights on others. Sometimes they confront problems with others directly. They demand recognition and disciplines those failing to perform as expected. They assert own competence, reliability or other personal or company's qualities. They also assert strong confidence in own company's or organization's products or services.

l) Persuasion

Entrepreneurs with this competency successfully pursue others to perform the activities effectively and efficiently. They will have the ability to convince others to buy products or services or to get finance or convince to do something else that he would like that person to do.

m) Use of Influence Strategies

Entrepreneurs with this competency influence the environment comprising individuals and institutions, for mobilizing resources, organizing production and selling goods and services to develop business contacts. They have a strong desire to influence others and have the ability to present themselves in the convincing way to others. They aiso have the tendency to find out ways and means to influence others.

n) Monitoring

Entrepreneurs with this competency normally monitor or supervise all the activities of the concern to ensure that the work is completed by maintaining good quality.

o) Concern for Employee Welfare

Entrepreneurs with this competency take action to improve the welfare of employees and take positive action in response of employee's **personal concerns.**

2. Venture Initiation and Success Competencies

In addition to personal competencies, the entrepreneur must also possess the competencies required to launch the enterprise and for its growth and survival.

The competencies is necessary to launch a venture or implement a business idea or plan may be conceived as "base line" for most studies of entrepreneurship and highly effective entrepreneurs are those who go beyond launch into organizational growth and survival. Therefore, it is further divided in two categories of competencies. These are:

A. Enterprise launch competencies.
B. Enterprise management competencies.

A. Enterprise Launch Competencies

Enterprise launch competencies includes the following competencies:

1. Competency to understand the nature of business

a) To analyse the personal advantage of owning a small business.
b) To analyse the personal risks of owning a small business.
c) To analyse how to maximize the opportunities and minimize the risks of owning a business.

2. Competency to determine the potential as an entrepreneur

a) To consider the personal qualification and abilities needed to manage own business.
b) To evaluate the own potentials for decision-making, problem-solving and creativity.
c) To determine own potential for management, planning, operations, personnel and public relations.

3. Competency to develop a business plan

a) To identify how a business plan helps the entrepreneur.
b) To recognize how a business plan should be organized.
c) To identify and use the mechanisms for developing a business plan.

4. Competency to obtain technical assistance

a) To prepare for using technical assistance.

b) To select professional consultants.
c) To work effectively with consultants.

5. Competency to choose the type of ownership

a) To analyse the type of ownership of business.
b) To follow the steps necessary to file for ownership of the business.
c) To define policies and procedures for a successful multi-owner.

6. Competency to plan the market strategy

a) To use goods classification and life cycle analysis as planning tools for marketing.
b) To develop and modify marketing mixes for a business.
c) To use decision-making tools that aid in evaluating marketing activities.
d) To evaluate operations to improve decision-making about marketing.

7. Competency to locate the business

a) To analyse customer transportation, access, parking and so forth, i.e. relative to alternative site locations.
b) To complete a location feasibility study for the business.
c) To determine the cost of renovating or improving a site for the business.
d) To prepare an occupancy contract for the business.

8. Competency to finance the business:

a) To describe the source of information available to help in estimating the financing necessary to start a new business.
b) To determine the finance necessary to start a new business.
c) To prepare a project profit and loss statement and a projected cash flow statement for the new business.
d) To prepare a loan application package.

9. Competency to deal with the business

a) To determine the need for legal assistance.
b) To select the provisions that is desired in the lease.
c) To prepare sales contract (such as credit sales or long-term sales) that may be utilized in the contracts.
d) To evaluate contracts.
e) To determine the need for protection of ideas and intentions.

10. Competency to comply with government regulations

a) To appraise the effects of various regulations on the business operations.
b) To acquire the information necessary to comply with the various rules and regulations affecting the business.
c) To develop policies for the business to comply with the Government rules and regulations.

B. Enterprise Management Competencies

1. Competency to manage the business

a) To plan goals and objectives for the business.
b) To develop a diagram showing the organizational structure for the business.
c) To establish control practices and procedures for the business.

2. Competency to manage human resources

a) To write a job description for a position in the business.
b) To develop a training programme outline for employees.
c) To develop a list of personnel for employees in the business.
d) To develop an outline for an employee evaluation system.
e) To plan a corrective interview with an employee concerning a selected problem.

3. Competency to promote the business

a) To create a long-term promotional plan.
b) To describe the techniques used to prepare advertising and promotion.

c) To analyse competitive promotional activities.
d) To evaluate promotional effectiveness.
e) To plan a community relations programme.

4. Competency to manage sales efforts

a) To develop a sales plan for the business.
b) To develop policies and procedures for serving the customers.
c) To develop a plan for training and motivating sales people.

5. Competency to keep business records

a) To determine who will keep the books for the business and how they will be maintained.
b) To describe double-entry book keeping.
c) Select the types of journals and ledgers that you will use in the business.
d) To identify the types of records that will be used in the business to record sales, cash receipts, cash disbursements, accounts receivable, accounts payable, payroll, petty cash, inventory, budgets and other items.
e) To evaluate the business records.
f) To identify how a micro-computer may be used to keep the business records.

6. Competency to manage the finances

a) To explain the importance of cash flow management.
b) To identify financial control procedures.
c) To describe how to find cash flow patterns.
d) To analyse trouble spots in financial management.
e) To describe how to prepare an owner's equity financial statement.
f) To analyse financial management ratios applicable to a small business.
g) To identify the components of breakeven point problem.
h) To review microcomputer application for financial management.

7. Competency to manage customer credit and collection

a) To analyse the legal rights and recourse of credit guarantors.
b) To develop a series of credit collection reminders and follow-up activities.

c) To develop various credit and collection policies.
d) To prepare a credit promotions plan.
e) To discuss information, resources and systems that apply to credit and collection procedures.

8. Competency to protect the business

a) To prepare policies for the firm that will help minimize losses due to employee theft, vendor theft, bad cheques, shoplifting, robbery, injury or product liability.
b) To determine the kinds, amounts and costs of insurance needed by the firm.

3.5 TOOLS FOR ASSESSMENT OF COMPETENCIES

Entrepreneurship demands certain characteristics or traits, skills and qualities in an individual to become an entrepreneur. Before venturing to take up self-employment, one has to make a self-assessment of himself/herself to know whether he/she has the required traits.

Many psychological and behavioural tests have been developed and validated both in India and abroad. At the end of this chapter you will find annexure 1 to 5 which gives some of the assessment questionnaires and their assessment methodology as samples.

ANNEXURE–I

"Entrepreneurial Qualities Assessment Quiz"

Time 10 Minutes

This quiz is designed to determine the latent qualities in you. Read each question and respond by indicating 'T' for true or 'F' for false. Give your immediate reaction. Be completely honest, so that the quiz will really be useful to you. Complete the quiz in one siting and be free from distractions.

		True/False
1.	When faced with a problem, I always find a new way of overcoming it.	________
2.	When a decision has to be made, I can make it easily even though I am not sure of the outcome.	________
3.	I have a strong need for social interaction.	________
4.	After learning how to do something right the first time, I don't change my approach.	________
5.	I have a plan of where I want to be financially ten years from now.	________
6.	When I am placed in a new situation at work I quickly sort out what needs to be done.	________
7.	I see potential problems as challenges.	________
8.	Constantly having to deal with problems wears me down.	________
9.	I revise my goals time to time in the light of changing situations.	________
10.	It is important for me to know that I have a dependable income.	________
11.	When I am dealing with a problem, I tend to get struck easily.	________
12.	If I were laid off, I know I could find some other source of income.	________
13.	I thrive on the challenge of solving different problems.	________
14.	I don't enjoy being directed by others.	
15.	I take courses on how to improve what I do.	________
16.	Once I've met a challenge I am usually satisfied, and don't need to look for other project.	________

17. I normally start off my day with a list of things to do. ________
18. I don't enjoy working alone. ________
19. The fear of losing my job causes me great apprehension. ________
20. I am not good at dealing with a multitude of problems at the same time. ________
21. I consider myself to be very resourceful in tight situations. ________
22. I usually have a plan of action before starting a project. ________
23. I am good at finding creative ways of solving problems. ________
24. The idea of being my own boss appeals to me. ________
25. At times, I don't feel completely comfortable with myself. ________
26. I worry about what will happen if my plans do not work out. ________
27. When I came up against unexpected obstacles, I prefer not to continue. ________
28. I have a strong desire to improve myself in everything I do. ________
29. I read books on how to achieve success.
30. I need to keep taking on challenges and feeling myself. ________
31. I think of a glass or being half-empty rather than half-full. ________
32. I get disappointed when things do not go my way.
33. I believe in the saying "If anything can go wrong, it will". ________
34. My friends would call me an optimist. ________
35. I always look at the bright side of the life. ________

Scoring

Dimensions	
Innovation	1 (T), 4(F), 5(T), 21(T)
Tolerance to Uncertainty	2(T), 6(T), 10(F), 12(T), 19(F)

Desire for Independence	3(F), 14(T), 18(F), 24(T), 25(F)
Continuous Goal Setting	15(T), 9(T), 16(F), 17(T), 20(T)
Persistent Problem Solving	7(T), 18(F), 13(T), 22(F), 23(T)
Achievement Oriented	26(F), 27(F), 28(F), 29(T), 30(T)
Positive Outlook	31(F), 32(T), 33(F), 34(T), 35(T)

The Result

The score obtained may help to understand one's position and status on different qualities. This creates disequilibrium or tension that enhances the score further to be more entrepreneurial.

ANNEXURE – II

"Entrepreneurial Competencies Test"

Self Rating Questionnaire

Your Name ________________________________

Address ________________________________

Date ________________________________

Instructions

1. This questionnaire consists of 70 brief statements. Read each statement and decide how well it describes you. Be honest about yourself. Remember, no one does, everything very well, nor is it even good to do everything very well.
2. Select one of the numbers below to indicate how well the statement describes you:
   - 5 = Very well
   - 4 = Well
   - 3 = Somewhat
   - 2 = Very little
   - 1 = Not at all

1. Write the number you select on the line to the right of each statement. Here is an example: *I remain calm in stressful situations.*

   The person who responded to the item about wrote "2" indicating that the statement described him very little.
2. Some statements may be similar but no two are exactly alike.
3. Please answer all questions.
   1. I look for things that used to done. ________
   2. I like challenges and new opportunities. ________
   3. When faced with a difficult problem, I spend a lot of time trying to find a solution. ________
   4. When starting a new task of project, I gather a great deal of information. ________
   5. It bothers me when things are not done very well. ________
   6. I give much effort to my work. ________
   7. I find ways to do things faster. ________

8. I plan large projects by dividing it into smaller tasks. ________
9. I think unusual solutions to the problems. ________
10. I feel confident that I will succeed at whatever I try to do. ________
11. I tell others when they have not performed as expected. ________
12. I get others to support my recommendations. ________
13. I develop strategies to influence others. ________
14. No matter who I'm talking to, I'm a good listener. ________
15. I do things that need to be done before being asked to by others. ________
16. I prefer activities that I know well and with which I am comfortable. ________
17. I try several times to get people to do what I would like them to do. ________
18. I seek the advice of people who know a lot about the problems or tasks I am working on. ________
19. It is important to meet to do a high quality job. ________
20. I work long hours and make personal sacrifices to complete jobs on time. ________
21. I am not good at using my time well. ________
22. I think about the advantages and disadvantages of different ways of accomplishing things. ________
23. I think of many new ideas. ________
24. I change my mind if others disagree strongly with me. ________
25. If I am angry or upset with someone, I tell that person. ________
26. I convince others of my ideas. ________
27. I do not spend much time on thinking about how to influence others. ________
28. I feel resentful when I do not get my way. ________
29. I do things before it is clear that they must be done. ________
30. I notice opportunities to do new things. ________
31. When something gets in the way of what I am trying to do, I keep on trying to accomplish what I want. ________

32. I take action without seeking information. ________
33. My own work is better than that of other people I work with. ________
34. I do whatever it takes to complete a job. ________
35. It bothers me when my time is wasted. ________
36. I try to think of all the problems I may encounter and plan what to do if each problem occurs. ________
37. Once I have selected an approach to solving a problem, I do not change that approach. ________
38. When trying something difficult or challenging, I feel confident that I will succeed. ________
39. It is difficult for me to order people to do things.
40. I get others to see how I will be able to accomplish what I set out to do. ________
41. I get important people to help me accomplish my goals. ________
42. In the past, I have had failures. ________
43. I take action before it is clear that I must. ________
44. I try things that are very new and different from what I have done before. ________
45. When faced with a major difficulty, I quickly go on to other things. ________
46. When working on a project for someone, I ask many questions to be sure I understand what that person wants. ________
47. When something I have been working on is satisfactory, I do not spend extra time trying to make it better. ________
48. When I am doing a job for someone, I make a special effort to make sure that person is satisfied with my work. ________
49. I find ways to do things for less cost. ________
50. I deal with problems as they arise, rather than spend time trying to anticipate them. ________
51. I think of many ways to solve problems. ________
52. I do things that are risky. ________

ANNEXURE–III

"Assessing Entrepreneurial Qualities and Competencies"

"Where am I?" "Where to go" are relevant questions in the process of becoming entrepreneurial. While the first question is related to the assessment of oneself, the second one focusses more on strategies to develop oneself, it is possible to draw certain inferences based on a simple test given in this section. The test if implemented on oneself, introspection can be done to draw meaningful inferences.

Note: Any inferences drawn on the basis of these tests must be discussed thoroughly for better understanding.

TEST 1

"Motivation"

Your Motivational Profile

For each of the following 15 statements, circle the number that most closely agrees with how you feel. Consider your answers in the context your current job or past work experience.

	Strongly disagree				Strongly agree
1. I try very hard to improve on my past performance at work.	1	2	3	4	5
2. I enjoy competition and winning.	1	2	3	4	5
3. I often find myself talking those around me about non-work matters.	1	2	3	4	5
4. I enjoy a difficult challenge.	1	2	3	4	5
5. I enjoy bringing in change.	1	2	3	4	5
6. I want to be like brothers.	1	2	3	4	5
7. I want to know I am progressing as I complete task.	1	2	3	4	5
8. I confront people who do things I disagree with.	1	2	3	4	5
9. I tend to build close relationships with co-workers.	1	2	3	4	5
10. I enjoy setting and achieving realistic goals.	1	2	3	4	5
11. I enjoy influencing other people to get my way.	1	2	3	4	5

12. I enjoy belonging to groups and organizations.	1	2	3	4	5
13. I enjoy the satisfaction of completing a different task.	1	2	3	4	5
14. I often work to gain more control over the events around me.	1	2	3	4	5
15. I enjoy working with others more than working alone.	1	2	3	4	5

Scoring of Motivational Profile

To determine your dominant needs—and what motivates you—place the number 1 through 5 that represents your score for each statement next to the number for that statement.

Achievement	Power	Affiliation
1. ________	2. ________	3. ________
4. ________	5. ________	6. ________
7. ________	8. ________	9. ________
10. ________	11. ________	12. ________
13. ________	14. ________	15. ________
Total ________	________	________

Result Analysis

On the basis of score obtained in three categories of motivation, it may be inferred that which is the dominant motivational category present in oneself. Accordingly, the strategies for concerned motivation development can be planned.

ANNEXURE – IV

"Achievements Motivation Test"

Time 10 Minutes

There are sets of eleven statements against which answers are given. You are expected to choose one amongst the alternatives and tick mark against them.

1. To succeed in life, one needs.
   a) money
   b) friends
   c) self-confidence
   d) good luck
   e) skill
2. If there is a good demand, it requires _______ to earn in business
   a) proper instruction
   b) quality product
   c) intensive and good advertisements
   d) capacity to store goods
   e) own control over market
3. My main aim in running industry should be
   a) to keep workers happy
   b) to earn good profit
   c) to improve quality of products
   d) to remain undisturbed by strikes and unrest
   e) to work hard
4. To continue progress, it requires
   a) hard work
   b) new and progressive ideas
   c) honesty and trustworthiness
   d) education
   e) work systematically and thoughtfully
5. The person became a successful industrialist because he
   a) knew how to maintain relations
   b) has dependable friends and relatives
   c) has vision and enterprising nature
   d) market fluctuations were favourable to him
   e) gentle person and a good business person

6. The person is successful because he
   a) is highly educated
   b) knows value of time and makes plans accordingly
   c) has tact to get work done by others
   d) has large group of known people
   e) has sufficient assets/wealth
7. The person was unsuccessful because
   a) friends/acquaintances did not cooperate
   b) he did not learn from failures
   c) is extravagant
   d) planning was defective
   e) was a good and gentle person
8. I want to start a new business because:
   a) I should earn
   b) I would be popular in society
   c) I want to do something new
   d) The state wishes that we should do something
   e) I want to serve my caste and society
9. Slow economic progress of the country is because of
   a) Faulty policies of the government
   b) Lack of good facilities
   c) Lack of our own venture
   d) Labour unrest
   e) Lack of increasing opportunities
10. I will face difficulties in my work then
    a) I will leave it and will start a new work
    b) I will take advice of known and proper person
    c) I will think why it happened, and then again will work with new enthusiasm
    d) I will blame my colleagues
11. If business fails or there is a loss then
    a) I shall try to pay less tax reduce the loss
    b) I will accept it with sportsmanship and try again
    c) I will sell goods at cheaper price, so that everything is sold out
    d) I will join with somebody in partnership
    e) I will try to find out who is responsible for the failure.

Scoring Manuals for Sentence Completion Test

One of the alternatives given against each statement is the right answer indicating the presence of achievement motivation. The right answer is indicated in the parentheses of each statement. The score need to be calculated on the basis of number of right answer obtained by a person.

1. To succeed in life, one needs
   Self-confidence (c)
2. If there is a good demand, it requires:
   Quality product to earn in business (b)
3. My main aim in running industry should be:
   to earn good profit (b)
4. To continue progress, it requires:
   New and progressive ideas (b)
5. The person became a successful industrialist because he:
   has vision and entrepreneurial nature (c)
6. The person is successful because he:
   knows value of time and makes plans accordingly (b)
7. The person was unsuccessful because:
   he did not learn from failure (b)
8. I want to start new business because:
   I should earn (a)
9. Slow economic progress of country is because of
   Lack of our own ventures (c)
10. If will face difficulties in my work, then:
    I will take advice of known and proper persons (b)
11. If business fails or there is loss then

    I will accept it with sportsmanship and try again (b)

Make a total of the statements tick marked in the answer sheet by the applicant.

ANNEXURE – V

"Entrepreneur Self-assessment Profile Guide"

Instructions

The 48 questions have been grouped into three categories: personal background, behaviour patterns, and lifestyle. Each question addresses specific areas that relate to entrepreneurs; these areas are noted in the parenthesis following each question. The answers you see here are what studies show to be the responses commonly given by small business owners. You will want to compare your answers from the survey to what is shown here for similarities and conflicts.

Personal Background

1. Has someone in your family shared the experience of starting a business with you? (family training) ________ ________
2. Do you get sick often? (attitude, energy health) ________ ________
3. Have you ever been fired from a job? (displacement experience) ________ ________
4. Did you participate in school activities or sports? (need to achieve) ________ ________
5. Were you a very good student? (average is common) ________ ________
6. Were you the first-born child?
7. Was your father mostly present during your early life at home? (early responsibility) ________ ________
8. Were you expected to do odd jobs at home before ten years of age? (early experience) ________ ________

Behaviour Patterns

9.	Do you worry about what others think of you? (self-confidence, locus of control)	______	______
10.	Do you take risks for the thrill of it? (risk taking, internal locus of control)	______	______
11.	Do you find it easy to get others to do something for you? (leadership)	______	______
12.	Do you believe in organizing your tasks before getting started? (management, goal setting)	______	______
13.	Do you enjoy doing something just to prove that you can ? (achievement oriented)	______	______
14.	Do you find yourself constantly thinking of new ideas? (creative, innovation)	______	______
15.	Do you like to take care of details? (risk oriented)	______	______
16.	Do you believe there should be security in a job? (internal locus of control)	______	______
17.	Will you deliberately seek a direct confrontation to get needed resuts? (determination, assertiveness)	______	______
18.	Do you get bored easily? (impatience, energy)	______	______
19.	Are you sometimes arrogant about your accomplishments? (self-confidence, independence)	______	______
20.	Can you concentrate for extended periods of time on one subject? (perseverance, determination)	______	______

21. Do you, on occasion, need pep talks from others to keep you going? (self-starter, self-control) ________ ________
22. Do you find unexpected energy resources as others to keep you going? (energy, resourcefulness) ________ ________
23. Does personal satisfaction mean more to than having money to spend on yourself? (egoism) ________ ________
24. Have you ever deliberately exceeded your authority at work? (self-confidence, assertiveness) ________ ________
25. Do you try to find the benefits of a bad situation ? (optimism, flexibility) ________ ________
26. Do you blame others when something goes wrong? (personal ability, problem solving) ________ ________
27. Do you enjoy tackling a task without knowing all the potential problems? (resourcefulness, risk taking) ________ ________
28. Do you persist when others tell you it can't be done? (optimism) ________ ________
29. Do you take rejection personally? (flexibility, self-confidence) ________ ________
30. Do you believe that you generally have a lot of good luck that explains your successes? (internal locus of control) ________ ________
31. Do you enjoy being able to make your own decisions on the job? (independence, responsibility) ________ ________

32. Did you wake up happy most of your life? (optimism)	______	______
33. Can you accept failure without admitting defeat? (determination, optimism)	______	______
34. Do you believe that entrepreneurs take a huge risk? (self-confidence, internal control)	______	______
35. Do you believe that entrepreneurs must have advanced college degrees? (resourcefulness, initiative)	______	______
36. Do you strive to use past mistakes as a learning process? (initiative, optimism)	______	______
37. Do you find the answers to problems come to you out of nowhere? (foresight, perceptiveness, persistent)	______	______
38. Do you enjoy finding an answer to a frustrating problem? (tolerance of ambiguity, initiative)	______	______

Lifestyles

39. Do you take risks for the thrill of it? (risk taking, internal locus of control)	______	______
40. Do you prefer to let a friend decide on your social activities? (control, responsibility)	______	______
41. Do you enjoy socializing regularly? (goal oriented, time management)	______	______

42. Are you likely to work long hours to accomplish a goal? (persistence, determination) ________ ________
43. Do you have a savings account and other personal investments? (profit oriented) ________ ________
44. Are you people oriented than goal oriented? (need to achieve) ________ ________
45. Do you prefer to be a longer in your final decision? ________ ________
46. Do your conversations discuss people more than events or ideas? (idea oriented, creativity) ________ ________
47. Do you feel good about yourself in spite of criticism of others? (tolerance of ambiguity, self-confidence) ________ ________
48. Do you sleep as little as possible? (time management, energy) ________ ________

Source: *"Beyond a Dream—An instructor's guide for small business exploration". The National Centre for Research in Vocational Education.*

EXERCISES

Section A

1. What do you mean by competence?
2. What do you mean by 'knowledge'?
3. What do you mean by 'skill'?
4. What do you mean by 'motive'?
5. What do you mean by 'trait'?
6. What do you mean by 'entrepreneurial competencies'?
7. Mention any four personal competencies required by an entrepreneur.
8. Mention any four entreprise launching competencies.
9. Mention any four entreprise management competencies.

Section B

1. Explain in brief the basic components of entrepreneurial competencies.

Section C

1. Explain in brief the different types of competencies required by an entrepreneur.
2. Explain the personal entrepreneurial competencies organized by an entrepreneur.
3. Explain the venture initiation and success competencies required by an entrepreneur.

SKILL DEVELOPMENT/PRACTICAL EXERCISES

1. Make a self-assessment of yourself to know whether you have the required traits to become an entrepreneur.
2. Collect the information through questionnaires to assess the traits of the individual wants to become an entrepreneur.
3. Use the "Entrepreneurial qualities assessment quiz' to know qualities latest with you or with others.
4. Make a competency assessment test using the questionnaire.
5. Collect the profiles of a successful entrepreneurs.
6. Study visit by students to any enterprise of their own choice. With the help of a schedule/questionnaire the students will record observations regarding—the background of entrepreneur, reasons for selecting the entrepreneurial career, starting the enterprise, the type of enterprise, the process of setting this enterprise, products/services, production process, investment made and marketing practices followed, profit or loss, growth and development problems faced, institutions/organizations offered support and entrepreneur's level of satisfaction.
7. Prepare a brief report based on the observations made during study visit to an enterprise.

4

Development of Entrepreneurial Competency and Motivation

STRUCTURE

4.1 Introduction
4.2 Entrepreneurship Motivation Training (EMT)
4.3 Objectives of EMT
4.4 Components of EMT

4.1 INTRODUCTION

Entrepreneurial motivation and competency can be developed through training. But the entrepreneurial motivation and competency through training is a complex process. It is considered the most significant and integrated component of the entire entrepreneurship development programme package. The programme touches the core of the individual motivation, perception and his goal.

David Mc Clelland revealed in his finding that:

a) People can acquire motives and develop through education or training.
b) The newly aroused motives are more likely to influence future thought and action.

Entrepreneurial motivation and competency can be developed through entrepreneur's motivation training. Which is developed by EDI of India which provides entrepreneurship education in India.

4.2 ENTREPRENEURSHIP MOTIVATION TRAINING (EMT)

The entrepreneurial programme, with the entrepreneur as its focus, taps and energizes entrepreneurial potentialities and transforms visions into actions. These programmes are conducted through the entrepreneurial motivation training (EMT) labs. These labs provide entrepreneurs with experimental learning situation which helps them to examine their outlook and attitude towards entrepreneurship and to practice newly learned behaviour. EMT labs are based on the psycho-dynamic theories on personality formation, development and motive among adults.

EMT labs are training centres where the training is given to entrepreneurial motivation to enhance entrepreneurial spirit, competency and recognizing oneself, his creative and innovative potentialities and makes individuals entrepreneurs sensitive to several other dimensions of entrepreneurial personality.

4.3 OBJECTIVES OF ENTREPRENEURSHIP MOTIVATION TRAINING (EMT)

Following are the objectives of entrepreneurship motivation training:

1. To enhance entrepreneurial spirit and improve entrepreneurial competence by emphasizing motivation, planning and cooperative efforts.
2. To help the entrepreneur to examine his own self and relate his image of himself with the environment.
3. To make him aware about his own style of influencing others and on going situations.
4. To enable him to recognize his creative and innovative potentialities.

4.4 EMT RELATED ACTIVITIES

Following are the activities at the EMT for the entrepreneurs:

1. ***Opportunity to analyze:*** Entrepreneurs are given opportunities to analyze their own spontaneous thinking or imagination. The purpose is to help them recognize achievement thinking in its various aspects, so that they can reproduce it in their actions.
2. ***Encourage to evaluate:*** They are encouraged to use the understanding of their own motivation and thinking to evaluate their approach to their work, to set realistic challenging goals for themselves.

3. ***Practice of achievement thinking:*** Entrepreneurs practise achievement thinking by learning to perceive job situations, problems and possibilities in achievement terms. They are encouraged in achievement-related activities in a simulated business situation. Here, they become aware of the relationship between achievement thinking and entrepreneurial action.
4. ***Presentation of cases:*** Cases of successful entrepreneurs are presented to enable the entrepreneur to see the relationship between the successful functioning of a business and achievement thinking and also to understand the origins of entrepreneurial behaviour.
5. ***Opportunity to experience:*** During the course, the entrepreneurs are given opportunity to experience and internalize the characteristics of a successful entrepreneurs.
6. ***Plan for the future:*** The individual is encouraged to write an autobiography, to make plan for his future, to take practical steps and make the commitment necessary to fulfil the personal goals he has set for himself. Personal counselling sessions are arranged for individuals to obtain better self-knowledge, more realistic appraisal of goals and more creative ways to obtain them.
7. ***Examining the relations:*** Entrepreneurs are encouraged to examine their relations with others in the group throughout the course. In small and large groups, they are given opportunities to understand the needs of others and to help them in solving their problems.
8. ***Practice in aiding and supporting:*** Entrepreneurs are given practice in helping and supporting one another in group activities. This activity increases the probability of mutual reinforcement of one another in the future.
9. ***Coping strategies:*** Finally, the entrepreneurs are made to understand various coping strategies arising out of complexity of an entrepreneurial career and are helped to examine their ability to influence others and ongoing situations.

4.5 COMPONENTS OF ENTREPRENEURSHIP MOTIVATION TRAINING (EMT) TO DEVELOP ENTREPRENEURIAL COMPETENCY

The entrepreneurial motivation and competency can be developed through the entrepreneurship motivation-training programme. It comprises the following:

i. Achievement motivation.
ii. Creativity, innovation or invention
iii. Self-efficacy.
iv. Risk taking.
v. Leadership.
vi. Communication and influencing ability.
vii. Planning action.

4.5.1 Achievement Motivation

Introduction: Achievement motivation is one of the most important characteristics of the entrepreneur.

David Mc Clelland has developed the 'Achievement motivational theory'. According to this theory an individual's need for achievement (n *Ach)* refers to the need for personal accomplishment. It is the drive to excel, to a set of standards.

People with high achievement motive like to take calculated risks and want to win. They like to take personal responsibility for solving problems and want to know how well they are doing. High achievers are not motivated by money but instead employ money as a method of keeping sure of their achievements. Such people strive for personal achievement rather than the rewards of success. They want to do something better and more efficiently than it has been done before.

Need for achievement is simply the desire to do well not so much for the sake of social recognition or prestige but for the sake of an inner feeling of personal accomplishment. It is this need for achievement that motivates people to take risk. People with high need for achievement behave in an entrepreneurial way. Need for achievement stimulates the behaviour of a person to be an entrepreneur.

Mc Clelland considers the need for achievement to be most crucial to a nation's economic development. He held that a strong inner spirit in individuals to attain a measurable variable arising from a need, which the individual develops mainly in childhood and seeks to satisfy throughout his life. This 'inner spirit' which he called 'need for achievement' if higher, would produce more energetic entrepreneurs capable of generating rapid economic development. High need for achievement or ambition motivates an entrepreneur to take risks, work hard, find new things, save more, reinvest the savings in industry, and so on.

Definitions

1. According to Mc Clelland, achievement motivation is defined as "Desire to do well, not so much for the sake of social recognition or prestige but to attain an inner feeling of personal accomplishment".
2. According to Atkinson J.W., achievement motivation is defined as "a talent disposition to strive for a particular goal, stage or aim."
3. According to Rogers, E.M and Svenning L., achievement motivation is defined as "social value that emphasizes a desire for excellence in order to attain a sense of personal accomplishment."
4. According to Murry A.H., Achievement motivation is defined as "a desire and effort to accomplish something difficult, to master, manipulate or organize physical objects, human beings or ideas. To do this as rapidly and as independently as possible, to overcome obstacles and attain a high standard. To increase self-regard by the successful exercise of talent.
5. According to Neil Ralph E. and Rogers E.M., achievement motivation is defined as "value installed in the individual through the socialization process, in which individual feels a need for desire to excel in reacting certain goals only for the satisfaction of reaching the goal and not for the goals or ends involved.

Significance of achievement motivation : The following are some of the significance of achievement motivation:

1. Achievement motivation is one of the most important characteristics of the entrepreneur.
2. Achievement motivation is responsible for economic growth of a nation.
3. The *n Ach* is an essential ingredient of entrepreneurship leading to economic development.
4. The *n Ach* in important contributing factor towards entrepreneurial activity.

5. The *n Ach* is a major factor in assessing entrepreneurial awareness and entrepreneurial supply in a social system.
6. The *n Ach* is a psychological characteristic in nature and manipulative through appropriate training programme.
7. The *n Ach* is viewed as an intervention for organizational development.
8. The *n Ach* is found to be significant even for successful managers, executives, salesmen, etc.

Characteristics of Persons with High need for Achievement

Mc Clelland suggests an entrepreneur, the importance of high need for achievement is found dominating one. In his view, the people with high need for achievement are characterized by the following:

1. A person with *n Ach* will have compelling drive to succeed. They strive for personal achievement rather than the rewards of success per se.
2. They have a desire to do something better or more efficiently than it has been done before.
3. They seek situation in which they can attain personal responsibility for finding solutions to problems, in which they can receive rapid feedback on their performance. So, they can tell easily whatever they are improving or not, and in which they can set moderately challenging goals.
4. High achievers are not gamblers, they dislike succeeding by chance. They prefer the challenge of working at a problem and accepting the personal responsibility for success or failure rather than leaving the outcome to chance or actions of others. Importantly, they avoid what they perceive to be very easy or very difficult task. They want to overcome obstacles, but they want to feel that their success (or failure) is due to their own actions.
5. People with high a *n Ach* like to take calculated risks and want to win .
6. High achievers are not motivated by money per se but instead employ money as a method of keeping sure of their achievements.
7. They decide moderate, realistic and attainable goals for them.
8. They need concrete feedback about their performance.

9. A person with high *n Ach*, shows tolerance. He is able to tolerate ambiguity and maintains a sense of accomplishment of every task.
10. A person with high *n Ach* recognizes the importance of inter-personal relationships in achieving objectives. Therefore, he devotes reasonable effort to develop and maintain adequate relations with experts in the field.
11. A person with *n Ach* tends to be active and restless. He likes to take the initiative.
12. A person with *n Ach* tends to be mobile and feasible in terms of ideas and physical action. He is an advertiser and is willing to move anywhere for new venture.
13. A high *n Ach* person tends to be innovative. He generates an ideas, develops it, and brings it into practice.
14. A person with *n Ach* is adventurous. He seeks adventure for personal gain or enjoyment. He is venturesome and enterprising who sets his sight on a new difficult target.

Sources of Development of Achievement Motivation

1. **Parents :** Though we are mainly concerned with achievement motivation as related to entrepreneurship, the parents should know something about the sources of development of achievement motivation. They are :
   a) ***Child Rearing:*** It is very important that the way a child is brought-up or reared, making him/her 'achievement oriented'. The early socialization makes a child independent in his/her thinking, involving him/her in decision-making at home and rearing him/her to take risks on his/her own, makes the child an achiever in life. (It helps not only for the child but also for the community and country in general.)
   b) ***Literature:*** For children, whatever they see, hear or read, influences them and their life. When they grow up, their motivation depends on what they were exposed to in childhood. If they have been exposed to literature in any form in general and will instill in them a desire to be independent, they exhibit a motivation to take own decision to do something worthwhile in life to have a goal and to be an achiever.
   c) ***Family environment:*** The family environment is the most

critical in developing entrepreneurial instinct. Indeed, family support in the individual is education and career is extremely important. In addition, growing up in a family running a business already involves the children in the way of thinking as well as in all the activities of the business.

The importance of family education in Marwari and Gujarati families represents a strong basis for children, who are trained for business and instilled discipline.

2. **SWOT Analysis:** The prospective entrepreneur has to do a SWOT analysis of himself. 'Need to achievement' consists of long term involvement, competition which self-set standards of excellence, competition with others and unique achievement.
3. Developer achievement imagery (thought process) through psychological tools.
4. **Achievement Motivation Training (AMT):** For the development of competitive entrepreneurs, AMT is given to develop the entrepreneurial traits such as need to achieve, risk taking, initiative, etc. The motivation inputs serve to:
   a) Increase the person's need for achievement.
   b) Help entrepreneur to define their goals realistically and work towards their achievement.
   c) Heighten their self-awareness.

Achievement Motivation Training is a crucial dose of behavioural, psychological inputs. It is aimed at crediting self-awareness and self-analysis, making the persons aware of their strengths and weakness, making them positively and realistically and through one-to-one counselling, developing their self-confidence level. The concept and techniques are adopted from the renowned work of professor David Mc Clelland on human motivation.

Tools used

To gain an insight into their own motivation and behaviour, a set of psychological instruments and exercises are used to develop achievement motivation. They are :

1. Ring toss game.
2. Business game.
3. Tower building.

4. Proprietor, supervisor, work game.
5. Father, mother, child game.
6. 'Win as much as you can' game.
7. TAT.
8. Transaction analysis.
9. FIRO-B.

Generating data on a person's natural flow of behaviour in different situations through various exercises helps effective learning through feedback and analysis. The participants need such a help to analyze his personality, his motivation and his behaviour. Simulation exercises providing such feedback in a non-threatening atmosphere help a lot in diagnosing measures to improve his traits.

In AMT, the particular individual gets enough opportunity and help, not only to understand his own behaviour and the underlying motive, but also to internalize the implications of such behaviour. The experience resulting from such efforts towards understanding one's own strengths as well as weaknesses would help to make the participant hopeful about his becoming an entrepreneur.

4.5.2 Creativity

Creativity has been defined in relation to various frames of reference: as a process, as a product and as a set of human characteristics. The dictionary describes creativity as the power or ability to create, to originate, or to produce. In dictionary definitions, creativity carries implications of originality and productivity. In the broad literature that discusses creativity, the term overlaps (and is often used interchangeably) with terms such as 'inventiveness', 'productive thinking and the act of 'discovery'. The literature includes contributions from psychology, philosophy, sociology, anthropology, the history of science and technology, the history of thought, economics, biography and from the specific fields in which creativity plays a conspicuous role, such as the plastic and performing arts, scientific and engineering fields, management and medicine.

In the literature concerned with creativity and creative thinking, the majority of definitions include the criteria of novelty, originality.

"New combinations of ideas and things."

" A new association of existing elements."

"The forming of associative elements into new combinations."

"A response that is novel or at least statistically infrequent."

"The production of an idea, concept, creation or discovery that is new or original to its creator."

Role of Creativity: It is important to recognize the role of creativity in the innovative process. **Creativity** is the generation of ideas that result in the improved efficiency or effectiveness of a system.

Two important aspects of creativity exist i.e., process and people. The process is goal oriented; it is designed to attain solution to a problem. The people are the resources that determine the solution. The process remains the same, but the approach the people use will vary. For example, sometimes they will adapt a solution and at other times they will formulate a highly innovative solution.

The Nature of the Creative Process: Creativity is a process that can be developed and improved. Everyone is creative to some degree. However, as is the case with many abilities and talents (example, athletic, artistic), some individuals have a greater aptitude for creativity than others. Also, some people have been raised and educated in an environment that encouraged them to develop their creativity. They have been thought to think and act creatively. For others, the process is more difficult because they have not been positively reinforced and if they are to be creative, they must learn how to implement the creative process.

Many people incorrectly believe only a genius can be creative. Most people also assume some people are born creative and others are not or only the gifted or highly intelligent person is capable of generating creative ideas and insights. The creative process involves seeing relationship among things others have not seen. The creative process has four commonly agreed **phases** or **steps**. Experts also agree that these phases do not always occur in the same order for every creative activity.

PHASES OR STEPS IN CREATIVE THINKING PROCESS

Following are the four phases of creative thinking process:

Phase 1: Background or Knowledge Accumulation

Successful creations are generally preceded by investigation and information gathering. People practise the creative search for background knowledge in a number of ways. Some of the most useful ways are follows:

1. Read a variety journals of fields.
2. Join professional groups and associations.
3. Attend professional meetings and seminars.
4. Travel to new places.
5. Talk to anyone and everyone about the subject.
6. Scan magazines, news papers and journals for articles related to the subject.
7. Develop a subject library for future reference.
8. Carry a small notebook and recording useful information.
9. Devote time to pursue natural curiosities.

Phase 2: The Incubation Process

Creative individuals allow their subconscious to mull over the tremendous amounts of information they gather during the preparation phase. This incubation process often occurs while they are engaged in activities totally unrelated to the subject or problem. It happens even when they are sleeping. Some of the most helpful steps to induce incubation follows:

1. Engage in routine, "mindless" activities (cutting the grass, painting the house).
2. Exercise regularly.
3. Play (sports, board, games, and puzzles).
4. Think about the project or problem before falling asleep.
5. Meditate or practise self-hypnosis.
6. Sit back and relax on a regular basis.

Phase 3: The Idea Experience

This phase of creative process is often the most exciting. It is when the idea or solution the individual is seeking is discovered. Sometimes referred to as the "eureka factor" this phase is also the one average person incorrectly perceives as the only component of creativity.

As with the incubation process, new and innovative ideas often emerge while the person is busy doing something unrelated to the enterprise, venture or investigation (e.g., taking a shower, driving on an interstate highway leaving through a newspaper). Sometimes the idea appears as a bolt out of the blue. In most cases, however the answer comes to the individual incrementally. Slowly, but surely, the person begins to formulate the solution. Because it is difficult to determine when the incubation process ends and the idea experience phase begins, many people are unaware of moving from phase 2 to phase 3.

In any event here are the ways to speed up the idea experience:

1. Day dream and fantasize about the project.
2. Practise the hobbies.
3. Work in a leisurely environment (e.g., at home instead of the office).
4. Put the problem on the back burner.
5. Keep a notebook at the bedside to record late-night or early-morning ideas.
6. Take breaks while working.

Phase 4: Evaluation and Implementation

This is the most difficult step of a creative endeavour and requires a great courage, self-discipline and perseverance. Successful entrepreneurs can identify ideas that are workable and that have the skills to implement. More important, they do not give up when they run into temporary obstacles. Often they will fail several times before they successfully develop their best ideas. In some cases entrepreneurs will take the idea in an entirely different direction or will discover a new and more workable idea while struggling to implement the original idea. Another important part of this phase is reworking of ideas to put them into final form. Because frequently an idea emerges from phase 3 in rough form, it needs to be modified or tested in order to put it in final shape. Some of the most useful suggestions for carrying out this phase are as follows:

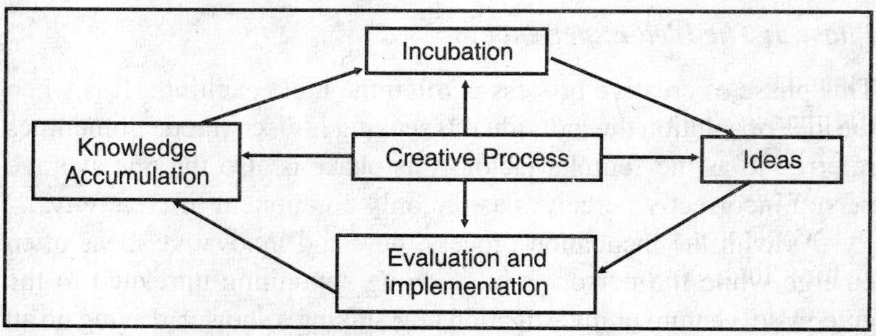

***Fig. 4.1:** Four phases of the creative thinking process.*

1. Increase the energy level with proper exercise, diet and rest.
2. Educate yourself in the business planning process and all facts of business.
3. Test the ideas with knowledgeable people.
4. Take notice of the intuitive hunches and feelings.
5. Educate yourself in the selling process.
6. Learn about organizational policies and practices.
7. Seek advice from others (e.g., friends, experts).
8. View the problems encountered while implementing the ideas as challenges.

Developing the Creativity

You can do a number of things to improve your own creative talents. Of course, as with most processes, the development will be more effective if you regularly practise exercises designed to increase the creative abilities.

Methods of Developing Creativity

a) Recognizing relationships : Creative people see new and different relationships among objects, processes, materials, technologies and people. To improve the creativity, it helps to look for different or unorthodox relationships among the elements and people around you. Creative people have developed a talent for recognizing new and different relationships. These relationships often lead to visions that result in new ideas, products and services. In order to develop the ability to recognize new relationships, the following exercise helps the entrepreneur.

A creative exercise or tools: Analyze and elaborate upon as to how the following pairs relate to each other in a complementary way: nut and bolt, husband and wife, athlete and coach, winning and losing and manager and production workers.

b) Developing a functional perspective: The principle of perceiving helps to develop a functional perspective towards things and people. A creative person tends to view things and people in terms of how they can satisfy his or her needs and help to complete a project. For example, the homemaker who cannot find a screw drive often will use a butter knife to tighten a loose screw. Or the cereal manufacturer will add fruit to his product to create a new product line that appeals to a health-conscious market.

To become more innovative and creative, you need to visualize the complementary relationships to the things and people of the world. You must learn to look at them in terms of how they complement you in the attempts to satisfy your own needs and to complete the projects. You must begin to look at things and people in non-conventional ways and from a different perspective. The following exercise is designed to help you develop a functional perspective.

A creative exercise/tools: Think of and write down all the functions that you can imagine for the following items (spend five minutes on each item):

1. An egotistical staff member.
2. A large pebble.
3. A fallen tree branch.
4. A chair.
5. A computer "whiz kid".
6. An obsessively organized employee.
7. The office "gossip".
8. An old hubcap.
9. A new secretary.
10. An empty roll of masking tape.
11. A yardstick.
12. Your sister, a college theatre major.
13. The office tightwad.
14. An old coat hanger.

c) Using your brains : Ever since split-brain studies were conducted in the 1950s, 1960s, experts on creativity, innovation and self-development have emphasized the importance of developing the skills associated with both hemispheres of the brain.

The **right brain** hemisphere helps an individual understand analogies, imagine things and synthesize information. The **left brain** hemisphere helps the person analyze, verbalize and rational approaches to problem solving.

The creative process involves logical and analytical thinking in the knowledge accumulation, evaluation and implementation stages; it calls for imagination, intuition, analogy conceptualization and synthesizing in the incubation and idea creation stages. So in order to become more creative, it is necessary to practise and develop both right and left hemisphere skills. The following problem solving exercise is designed to demonstrate the effectiveness of combining the skills of both hemispheres when solving problems.

A creative exercise or tools: Assume you have an idea that will save your organization time and money on processing customer complaints. Your supervisor has been extremely busy and has been unwilling to stop and listen to your ideas.

1. Write down all the left-hemisphere-type solutions to this problem you can think of in five minutes.
2. Write down all the right-hemisphere-type solutions to this problem that you can think of in five minutes.
3. Compare these lists and combine the two or more solutions from each list that will result in a unique and innovative way to solve this problem.
4. Repeat the numbers 1, 2 and 3 using a current problem you are facing at work or at home.

d) Eliminating Muddling Mindsets: A number of mental habits block or impede creative thinking. It has been estimated that adults use 2 to 10 per cent of their creative potential. For example, many individuals tend to make quick judgments about new things, people and ideas. Another inclination is to point out the negative components of a new or different idea because of the psychological discomfort associated with change. Some common mental habits that inhibit creativity and innovation are:

1. Positive thinking.
2. Security hunting.
3. Stereotyping.
4. Probability thinking.

These habits tend to muddle creative thought processes and different thought processes must be used to enhance creative thinking.

1. ***Positive thinking:*** Because of the speed of change in the modern world, personal lives are filled with great deal of uncertainty and ambiguity. The creative person learns to accept a reasonable amount of ambiguity in his or her work and life. In fact, many exceptionally creative people thrive in an uncertain environment and find it exhilarating.
2. ***Security hunting:*** Many people try to make the right decision or

take the correct action every time. In doing so, they rely on averages, stereotypes and probability theory to maximize their risks. Although this strategy often is appropriate, at times, a creator or innovator must take some calculated risks. Sometimes these risks result in the innovator's being wrong and making mistakes. Yet by recognizing this as part of the innovative game, the creative person learns from his or her mistakes and moves on to create bigger and better things. We all know Thomas Edison failed numerous times when searching for the correct materials for the incandescent light bulb.

3. ***Stereotyping:*** The more descriptive the abstraction or stereotype, the less real it becomes. Predicting actions from stereotypes and averages can cause an individual to act on the basis of a distorted picture of reality. More important, relying on these abstractions can limit a person's perception of the real entities and possibilities in the world.
4. ***Probability thinking:*** In their struggle to achieve security, many people also tend to rely on probability theory to make decisions. An over-reliance on this decision-making method, however, can distort reality and discourage one from taking calculated risks that may lead to creative endeavours.

In the creative game, often an individual is looking at an opportunity or situation that may occur only once in a lifetime. In a single-event situation, intuition and educated guesses are just as useful, if not more useful, than logic and probability.

Creative Exercise of Tools

The following problem solving exercises are designed to help eliminate muddling mindsets.

1. Practise taking small risks in your personal life and at work, rely on your intuition and hunches. Keep a log of these risks and chart their accuracy and consequences. For example, try to draw to an inside straight in your next family poker game.
2. Go out of your way to talk to people who you think conform to a commonly accepted stereotype.
3. Take on a number of complex projects at work and at home that do not lead themselves to guaranteed and predictable results.

Allow yourself to live with a manageable amount of ambiguity. Notice how you react to this ambiguity.

4. When an idea is presented to you, first think of all the positive aspects of the idea, then of all the negative aspects and finally of all the interesting aspects of the idea.
5. When listening to people, suspend initial judgement of them, their ideas and their information and simply listen.

Creativity, Inventions and Innovation

Innovation, invention and creativity are often used interchangeably. Among scholars in the field of creativity, innovation is used to define the process by which a new product or idea is introduced. Innovation sometimes refers only to the first use of new thing or idea.

It is convenient to use innovation to refer to the process that generates an idea, develops it, and brings it into practice. In this sense of the word, creativity is then the first step in the invention process. As Edison said, "invention is 5% inspiration and 95% perspiration". Creativity is what Edison called 'inspiration, a generation of an original, useful idea, the critical first step in the process. Invention is the process of selection of the idea to be worked on and its detailed process by which the invention is first brought into use by an individual, company or agency.

Differentiating creativity, invention and innovation help us to see the differences among the required process elements more clearly. Creativity requires the ability to reach out to widely separated components, and to synthesize them. The creativity effort does best by generating as many useful, new ideas as possible from which to select one or two to develop. The rest of the overall invention process consists of selecting the idea(s) to develop, requires convergent thinking and the ability to discard irrelevant ideas, and it includes analysis as opposed to synthesis. The rest of the invention process consists of detailed development of the idea(s) into producible, workable form, a continuous (often tedious) effort which includes the solution of a myriad of design problems, each of which may entail repeating the selection process many times at a micro level. The invention process also includes rests or trails of all detailed parts as well as the whole, and repetitions of the effort.

Innovation and the Entrepreneur: Innovation is a key function in the entrepreneurial process. Most researchers and authors in the fields of entrepreneurship are, for the most part, in agreement with Drucker about the concept of innovation.

Innovation is a specific function of entrepreneurship. It is the means by which the entrepreneur either creates new wealth-producing resources or endows existing resources with enhanced potential for creating wealth.

Innovation is the process by which entrepreneurs convert opportunities into marketable ideas. It is the means by which they become catalysts for change. The innovation process is more than just a good idea. The origin of an idea is important and the role of creative thinking may be vital to that development. More important, a prospective entrepreneur must have the desire to bring a good idea through the development stages. Thus innovation is a combination of the vision to create a good idea and the perseverance and dedication to remain with the concept through implementation.

Entrepreneurs blend imaginative and creative thinking with systematic, logical process ability. This, combination is a key to success. In addition, potential entrepreneurs are always looking for unique opportunities to fill the needs or wants.

The Innovation Process: Most innovations result from a conscious, purposeful search for new opportunities. This process begins with the analysis of the source of new opportunities. Drucker has noted that because innovation is both conceptual and perceptual, would-be innovators must go out and look, ask and listen. Successful innovators use both the right and left sides of their brains. They look at figures. They look at people. They analytically work out and look at potential product users to study their expectations, values and needs.

Most successful innovations are simple and focused. They are directed towards a specific, clear, and carefully designed application. In the process they create new customers and new markets.

Types of Innovations: Four basic types of innovations exist. These extend from totally new to modifications of existing products or services. In order of originality these are the four types:

1. **Invention**: The creation of a new product, service or process often one that is novel or untried. Such concepts tend to be "revolutionary".
2. **Extension:** The expansion of a product, service or process already

in existence. Such concepts make a different application of a current idea.

3. **Duplication:** The replication of an already existing product, service or process. The duplication effort, however, is not simply copying but adding the entrepreneur's own creative touch to enhance or improve the concept to beat the competition.
4. **Synthesis**: The combination of existing concepts and factors into new formulation. This involves taking a number of ideas or items already invented and finding a way, so together they form a new application.

Sources of Innovation: Innovation is a tool by which entrepreneurs typically exploit change rather than create change. Although some inventions have created change, these are rare. It is more common to find innovations that take advantage of change. The internal and external areas that serve as innovation sources are presented next.

1. **Unexpected Occurrences:** These are successes or failures that occurs because they were unanticipated or unplanned, often end up proving to be major innovative surprise to the firm.
2. **Incongruities:** These occur whenever a gap or difference exists between expectations and reality.
3. **Process Needs:** These exist whenever a demand arises for the entrepreneur to innovate and answer a particular need. The creation of health foods and time saving devices are examples.
4. **Industry and Market Changes:** Industries and markets are always undergoing changes in structure, design or definition. The entrepreneur needs to be aware of and seize these emerging opportunities.
5. **Demographic Changes:** These arise from trend changes in population, age, education, occupation, geographic location and similar factors. Demographic shifts are important and often provide new entrepreneurial opportunities.
6. **Perceptual Changes:** These changes occur in people's interpretation of facts and concepts. They are intangible yet meaningful. Perception can cause major shifts in ideas to take place.
7. **Knowledge-based Concepts:** These are the basis for the creation or development of something brand new, trying into our earlier discussion of invention as a type of innovation. Inventions are

knowledge based; they are new products or new things, new methods and new knowledge. Such innovations often require the longest period between initiation and market implementation because of the need for testing and modification. For example, the spectra camera from Polaroid, which helped revolutionize instant photography, took almost five years to create, perfect, and bring to market.

Principles of Innovation: Potential entrepreneurs need to realize that innovation principles exist. These principles can be learnt and when combined with opportunity, can enable individuals to innovate. The major motivation principles follow:

1. Be action oriented. Innovators always must be active and searching for new ideas, opportunities or sources of innovation.
2. Make the product, process or service simple and understandable. People must readily understand how the innovation works.
3. Make the product, process or service customer savvy. Innovators always must keep the customer in mind. The more an innovator has the end user in mind, the greater the chance the concept will be accepted and used.
4. Start small. Innovators should not attempt a project or development on a grandiose scale. They should begin small and then build and develop, allowing for planned growth and proper expansion in the right manner and at the right time.
5. Aim high. Innovators should aim high for success by seeking a niche in the marketplace.
6. Try/test/revise. Innovators always should follow the rule of try, test and revise. This helps work out any flaws in the product, process or services.
7. Learn from failures. Innovators do not guarantee success. More important, failures often give rise to innovations.
8. Follow a milestone schedule. Every innovator should follow a schedule that indicates milestone accomplishments. Although the project may run ahead or behind schedule, it still is important to have the schedule in order to plan and evaluate the project.
9. Reward heroic activity. This principle applies more to those involved in seeking and motivating others to innovate. Innovative activity should be rewarded and given the proper amount of respect. This means tolerating and to a limited degree, accepting failures as a means of accomplishing innovations. Innovation

work must be seen as heroic activity that will reveal new horizons for the enterprise.

10. Work, work and work. This is a simple but accurate exhortation with which to conclude the innovation principles. It takes work, not genius or mystery to innovate successfully.

4.5.3 Self-Efficacy

Definition: Self-efficacy refers to an individual's belief that he or she is capable of performing a task. The higher your self-efficacy, the more confidence you have in your ability to succeed in a task. So in difficult situations, we find that people with low self-efficacy are more likely to lessen their effort or give up altogether, while those with self-efficacy will try harder to master the challenge. In addition, individuals high in self-efficacy seem to respond to negative feedback with increased effort and motivation, whereas those low in self-efficacy are likely to lessen their effort when given negative feedback.

Development of self-efficacy: Development of self-efficacy is necessary for the following reasons:

1. To make the individual believe that the participants can, will or should develop a motive because it is demanded by his career and life situation.
2. To experience achievement motivation as consistent with self-image, with prevailing culture, values and norms.

Tools used: The tools used for training of entrepreneur to develop self-efficacy is as follows:

1. Analyzing "who am I", individually and in small group, reinforcement in developing personal effectiveness through re-writing "who am I" and generating data in Achievement Orientation exercise.
2. Analysis of personal and social values to succeed in entrepreneurial career.

4.5.4 Risk Taking

Introduction: To be personally responsible for the risk involved in the establishment of an enterprise may be considered one of the important dimensions of entrepreneurial behaviour. Entrepreneurs have, however, certain characteristic attitudes towards risk. Generally, the choice of an occupation is governed by many other considerations.

Most people look for security in their occupation because of the 'fear of failure'. However, in the choice of an entrepreneur, the fear of failure forms the least important consideration. The entrepreneur bears the risk of launching a new business. Nonetheless, while opting for the risk, he does not like to be a gambler. The difference between a gambler and an entrepreneur needs to be clearly understood for a proper appreciation of entrepreneurial behaviour.

Objectives: Risk taking is an important aspect of entrepreneurial life. Entrepreneurs are calculated risk takers. They do not aim at goals that can be very easily accomplished. They like challenges. They also do not aim at tasks that are very difficult to accomplish, as they would enjoy a sense of success attained only after accomplishing a challenging goal. They are moderate risk takers. Moderate or calculated risk taking involves a number of processes as stated below:

1. Understanding the situation.
2. Gathering as much information as possible.
3. Assessing one's own resources.
4. Setting challenging goals for oneself, on the basis of the information and resources.
5. Testing one's own abilities.
6. Modifying the goals set on the basis of previous experiences (one's own and other's).

Exploring Risk Taking and Goal-setting Behaviour

Tools used: The following tools are used:

1. The ring toss game: The ring toss game provides an opportunity for an entrepreneur, potential entrepreneur or for any participant to examine his own risk taking orientations and associated behaviours.

This ring toss game was first used by Kurt Lewin in a study of the level of aspiration of Kindergarten children (McClelland, 1958). Mc Clelland used it later in a study of risk taking behaviour of children with high and low need for achievement. Later it was used on college students in a similar study by Atkinson and Litwin (1960). Its first use in training for developing achievement motivation was made in 1964 in an experiment conducted in India (McClelland and Winter, 1969). Since then this game is being used widely in achievement motivation and other training programmes.

It has the following objectives:

a) To enable the participant to examine his own risk taking behaviour i.e., whether he is a high risk taker, moderate, or low risk taker.

b) To enable the participant to examine the dynamics of achievement motivation (or affiliation and power motives) as they operate through his goal setting behaviour.

c) To enable the participant to study the extent to which he is sensitive to the information generated by himself, and use this information to modify his behaviour.

d) To help the participant examine his tendencies to take personal responsibility in accomplishing the tasks.

An early use of ring-toss game in the sequence design of the achievement motivation training is made to help the participants foresee the issues connected with taking risks. The game is usually played in three "rounds". The "first round" involves choosing a distance and throwing rings on a peg all by oneself. In the "second round", the participant goes through the same procedure as in the first round, but acts in the presence of his peers; and in the "third round" he acts under the additional influence of an incentive where he stands to earn more points by choosing longer distances.

2. Process Analysis: There are several techniques by which people can be helped to explore and understand the dynamics of their risk taking and goal-setting behavioral patterns. The entrepreneurs may be asked to recollect the various significant decisions they have made in their life, and detail out the process by which they have made those decisions. The process analysis may reveal some consistent patterns. The very decision of joining the programme by the candidate could be used for the process analysis as an illustration. The candidate can thus be helped to develop an insight into the process of his decision-making.

3. Problem solving: Simple paper-pencil exercises which help to develop insights into skill-utilization and goal-setting, could also be used. For example, a series of simple arithmetic problems could be given. He may be asked to indicate the number of problems he can solve, say, in a two-minute period. There may be one trail run in the beginning. But from the second run onwards the candidates would be required to indicate every time the number of problems he can do correctly in the next two minutes. The points to be scored in the end may be arranged according to some kind of a geometric progression, depending on the number of problems solved. If he solves 10 problems, he gets 50 points; 60 points for 11 solutions; 80 for 12; 110 for 13; and so on. In this exercise, he states in the beginning how many problems he could solve. If he cannot solve as many as he has stated in the beginning, he gets a zero score. Such instructions on "rules" to be observed provide a setting for examining one's own goal-setting behaviour.

After four or five trials, under a given set of rules, the instructor should help the participant to see his goal-setting behaviour by raising questions like: "How did your set your goal for the first trial? What was the possible clue or information that you used while setting the first goal? Did you think of generating information by asking the instructor on the general performance by others? What information was available to you in the subsequent trails? Did you use your own experience? How did you use others' experience? What was your goal (to win more points or to do better than others)? Were you trying to avoid failure? What was the impact of time on you? How did you feel when you succeeded or failed? What was the impact of each trial on subsequent trials? How did you change your goals for successive trials? What according to you, has contributed to your success or failure?"

Thus, several other performance exercises (line Darts and Dice) could be used to generate the dynamics related to goal-setting and risk taking behaviour.

4.5.5 Leadership

Meaning: Terry has defined leadership as "the ability to influence people to strive willingly for mutual objective". Livingstone regards it as, "the ability to awaken in others the desire to follow a common objective".

Thus, it is clear that leadership is the process of influencing the behaviour, activities and efforts of an individual or a group for achieving common goals.

Characteristics of leadership: A business manager is the leader of his subordinates as it possesses the basic characteristics of leadership as follows:

1. *Group of followers :* Without followers, leadership cannot be

imagined. It does not exist in vacuum. It is only on the followers or a group that a leader can assert his authority. A manager has a defined group of his subordinates as followers.

2. *Influencing Behaviour :* Leadership envisages the idea of influence. As McFarland observes: "The very essence of the leadership role in businesss is found in the context to which an executive can influence the behaviour of his fellow executives along the lines he himself desires". This influence is exercised for attainment of certain common goals.
3. *Reciprocal Relationship :* Leadership is not domination. It is a mutual relationship based on reciprocity of leaders and the lead. A leader does not only influence his group but, is at the same time influenced by it.
4. *Common goals :* Leadership is an activity of influencing people to make efforts for the attainment of certain common goals. It is the leader who defines the common goals, makes them understood to all and reconciles the common objectives with the individual ambitions and interest.

Importance of Leadership

The importance of leadership function in a modern organization can be very well understood reviewing the various functions which are generally performed by managers as a leader. The main functions of a leader manager are as follow:

1. He formulates objectives for his group.
2. He gives orders and instructions to do work.
3. He maintains discipline in the organization.
4. He maintains communication in the organization.
5. He listens to subordinates and responds to their needs.
6. He maintains unity and co-restiveness in the organization.
7. He inspires and motivates the various members of his group.
8. He represents the group to the outside world.

4.5.6 Communication

Effective communication is important to all of us but it is very important for the successful entrepreneurs. Effective communication is also necessary for smooth and productive working within the enterprise and outside the enterprise for good image of the business. Therefore, there is a need to have effective communication skill from the point of starting the process of setting up an enterprise.

What is Communication?

Communication is the medium through which we transfer our thoughts, needs, feelings, ideas and messages to others. It is said that "communication may not save us, but without communication we will not be saved".

Communication Skill

Whatever may be the channel or medium i.e., spoken or written words, television, radio, newspaper, public speeches, etc., the sender (one who communicates) and the receiver (one who receives the messages) are human beings. What happens when people talk together, when they write to one another, when they read? It sometimes happens that they are unsuccessful in exchanging their thoughts clearly and in a comprehensible manner. How is it that when one person speaks, the other person does not understand him/her properly? This happens because both are complex beings with different feeling, values, ideas, attitudes, needs and motives. And each person understands and accepts the communication which he/she sends or receives depending upon his/her capacity to interpret, based on his/her objectives, interests, needs, desires, and so on. And that is the reason why skills are required to communicate—to be direct, precise, honest and understandable.

Importance of Communication Skill for an Entrepreneur: In the process of business, the entrepreneur has to communicate (both oral and written) with various people or organizations. They are as follows:

1. *Banks or official institutions:* For the purpose of obtaining a loan for the project.
2. *Government or non-government agencies:* When the entrepreneurs need land, building, licences, no objection certificates, etc.
3. *Workers:* Effective communication is very important with workers to have cordial, complete and effective in order to ensure the greatest possible productivity and achievement of production target without any strikes or lockouts.

4. *Suppliers:* Communication may play an important role when the entrepreneur gets into terms and conditions with the suppliers. An entrepreneur influences and convinces the suppliers effectively with his communication skills.
5. *Customers:* It is ultimately that the entrepreneur has to sell his goods to the customers. He has to convince the prospective customers about the positive points of his product and influence them effectively. This is possible only if the entrepreneur has the effective communication skills.

Types of communication: can be as follows:

1. Verbal communication
2. Written communication
3. Non-verbal communication

Verbal Communication: It is unwritten messages. Message conveyed by word of mouth, face to face discussion, giving oral orders, telephone calls, lecturing, participate in debates, public address, conducting conferences, directly interviewing the persons, talking over intercom are the examples of verbal or oral communication.

Written Communication: If the message sent, is in black and white i.e., written, printed etc., it is written communication. Letters, notes, information circulars, brochures, reports, notices displayed on the board, written complaints, newspapers, magazines, etc., are various forms of written communication.

Non-verbal or Meta-verbal Communication: Communication is more than spoken or written words. It was discovered by the psychologists in the 90th century that non-verbal communication is also known as meta-verbal kinesics, body language or para language. One of the study says that words contribute only 7% to the total impact of the message, 38% is contributed by the tone of voice and the balance 55% by facial expression and body gestures.

Components of Meta-verbal Communication

Meta-verbal communication consists of four major components:

1. **Your appearance:** How you appear is the first signal by which others try to understand you. Your dress and grooming announce your profession, social and economic status, and attitude to tidiness and neatness.
2. **How you sound while talking:** Tone, pitch and rhythm of the

sound/voice supplement or contradict the verbal communication. Tone and pitch depends on whom you are talking to, whether you're subordinate, friend, colleague or boss. That also depends on the situation, for example, conversation in a small group, a speech or a presentation in a conference.

3. **How you use body language:** Body language has three aspects:
   i) Posture (standing or sitting)
   ii) Movement (working)
   iii) Gestures.

   When we speak, the whole body comes into action. Our face (eyes, ears, eyebrows, lips, nose and facial muscles) and neck are the most important zones of our body. Shoulders, hands and fingers are the next critical zone. Legs and feet form the third zone. All these parts signal a host of emotions, which convey more than words.

4. **How do you handle space:** The space that we maintain between others and us can be divided into four kinds. They are:
   a) *Intimate*: The intimate space is reserved for close relationships like those between husband and wife, parents and children, etc.
   b) *Personal*: Personal space is that shared with friends and colleagues.
   c) *Social space*: Social space is shared with your boss.
   d) *Public space*: Public is that of a gathering.

Communication Process

The figure shows us that when you send a message to another person or persons, it involves a channel. This channel or medium could be the spoken or written word, television, radio, newspaper, etc. The receiver (for whom it is intended) receives and interprets the message based on his/her perception and gives a feedback (an answer or understanding of the message).

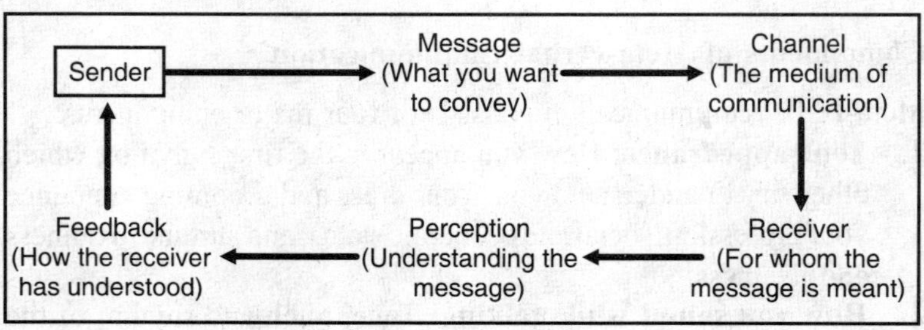

Stages in Communication

There are six stages in communication. They are as follows:

1. Conceiving the message.
2. Language of the message.
3. Selecting the medium for communication.
4. Decoding the message.
5. Interpreting the message.
6. Providing feedback.

1. **Conceiving the message:** At this stage a decision is made by the sender to communicate a message. The message may be the careful result of reasoning and thinking or responses to external factors. Some messages are made involuntary and some may be impulsive.
2. **Language of the message:** The sender has to put it (encode) into an appropriate language before a message is sent to the receiver. The languages of communication include the spoken word, the written word, the number, the picture, drawing and symbol and the non-verbal communication—expression, gestures and posture.
3. **Selecting the medium for communication:** Once the sender has chosen an appropriate language, he needs to select the right medium of communication. The medium could be the spoken or written words. The major factors influencing the choice of medium are:
   a) Effectiveness
   b) Need for tact
   c) Time
   d) Cost
   e) Complexities of message
   f) Simultaneous reception of information by receivers
   g) Need for instant feedback
   h) Need for speed.
4. **Decoding the message:** Messages can become ineffective if the receiver does not properly understand them. A message has to be understood before it can be absorbed or acted upon. The reasons for the failure to understand a message are:
   a) Lack of knowledge of language of sender.

b) Not knowing the sender's vocabulary (words or phrases) to the receiver.
c) When the receiver is a layman and the sender is a specialist.
d) Due to education, culture, outlook and attitude between the sender and the receiver.

5. **Interpreting the message:** After understanding the message (language) of the sender, the receiver also needs to be able to interpret it correctly. The underlying or actual message may be rather different from the words actually spoken because it may sometimes be sarcastic.
6. **Providing feedback:** Feedback is the response of the receiver to the message. A feedback is desirable because the sender can discover that the receiver has correctly interpreted the message. It is a check on how successfully the sender has been transmitting messages as originally intended and the receiver is ready for the next one.

Miscommunication

Sometimes miscommunication occurs due to the following reasons:

1. When the receiver makes his own judgement without understanding the meaning of the message and reply accordingly.
2. When both sender and the receiver give meaning to the message as per their own perceptions.
3. What the other party to the communication says is incorrect and irrelevant.
4. When parties are emotionally disturbed and miss the real message and give their own interpretation.

Developing Communication Skills/Tools Used

The following are the guidelines to develop communication skills for both sender and receiver:

1. **As a sender:**
   a) At the time of composing a message, you have to decide what sort of action or response you desire from the receiver.
   b) Choose a language most suited to your needs and the situation.
   c) At the time of encoding (forming) a message, take time to express your ideas logically. Give some thought to the language you intend to use.

d) Select the most appropriate medium, that is, whether to send a letter, a circular or make a telephone call, give a lecture or use radio or telephone facilities.
e) Make sure that you choose a language, which is understood by the receiver.
f) Be careful to see to it that your message is clear enough to avoid any misinterpretation by the receiver.
g) Make sure to get a feedback from the receiver.

2. **As a receiver:**

a) Give full attention to the message being communicated.
b) Check that the medium of communication used by the sender is meeting your needs.
c) Make sure that you understand the message fully.
d) Take care to interpret the message correctly.

Tool used: Role play can be used as a tool to develop communication skill.

Barriers to Communication

1. Obstinacy or unwillingness to discuss any problem or difference in opinion.
2. Prejudice fixed or rigid views or ignorance of the topic.
3. Lack of interest in the topic.
4. One way communication without caring for the others' opinion.
5. Anger, emotion, loud noise/tone or abnormal action.
6. Ego of personal nature or status consciousness.

4.5.7 Planning Action

Mere understanding of one's own personality and behaviour in the context of entrepreneurship is not sufficient for individual growth. To become an entrepreneur, one has to feel confident of overcoming one's shortcomings and to formulate step-by-step action plans to acquire the desired entrepreneurial characteristics to reach his goals.

There are instances where once the participants learn the system of analyzing the TAT stories, in the repeat process of rewriting other stories towards the end, they write carefully to score high. When they score high in contract with their previous scoring results, they start raising questions like, "Do you mean to say that instantly I have developed high achievement motivation which was not existing before?" Such questions are significant. In such situations, the trainer has to explain the theory of associative networks (McClelland and Winter, 1969) and try to help the participants understand that by writing highly achievement oriented stories and scripts. His motive level is not increased. What has increased is the capacity to use the achievement language. This in itself constitutes a step forward because unless he keeps practising the achievement language, he cannot expect his thinking to be achievement oriented. It is only with time and practice that his motive level is likely to go up. He should also explain that language is one of the dimensions of entrepreneurship. There are several associated behaviours which are characteristics of entrepreneurship. It is a means to move towards acquiring those behaviours that are associated with entrepreneurship.

Thus, the cognitive and motivational inputs provided so far to the entrepreneur must be reinforced through providing an opportunity to prepare a plan of actions step-by-step and to practise what he has learnt in the programme.

The concluding part of the programme is devoted to planning by individuals in concrete terms in the context of such learning for his immediate as well as long-term future. This will provide them opportunity to translate the conceptual learning into action through planning.

For the long-term plans, the entrepreneur has to set some broad goals covering next 5 years. Whereas, short term plans have to be set to attain more specific goals within a period of one year or so. Plans for six months following immediately however, have to be governed by goals stated in clear terms and are marked by greater details so as to make them more useful to attain higher level of entrepreneurial performance.

The detailed action plan covers specific areas like:

1. Activities that the participant proposes to ensure attainment of his goals.
2. Hurdles (personal as well as environmental) that are anticipated and the actions to be taken to overcome the same are proposed.
3. Helps that he proposes to take from different sources for specific purposes.

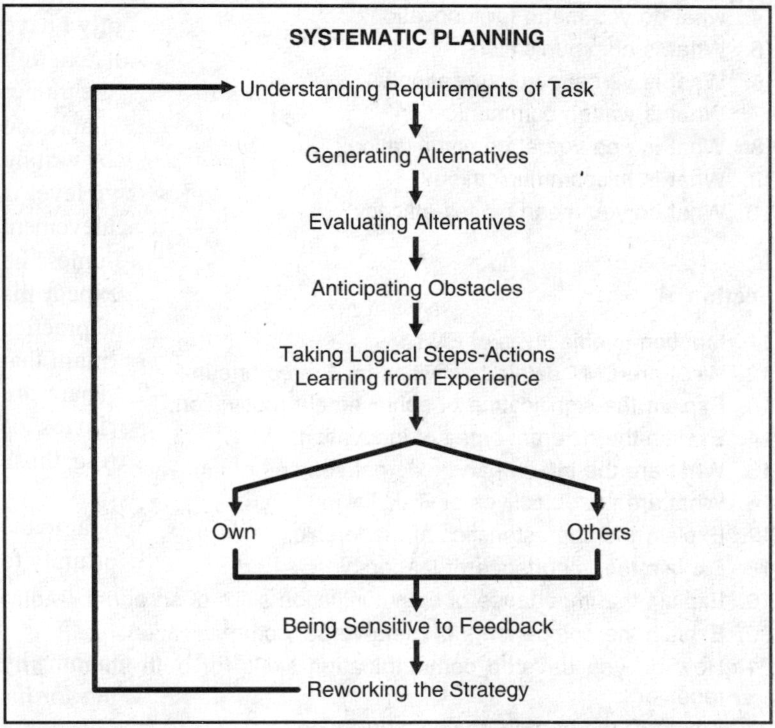

4. The way he would like to rate the probability of his achieving the set of goals.
5. The feeling that he is likely to experience either in eventualities of attainment or in non-attainment of the goals, etc.

Thus, the detailed plans of action covering those various dimensions not only help the entrepreneur internalize the cognitive inputs but also provide a definite direction to his forward movement in entrepreneurial performance.

EXERCISES

Section A

1. Mention any two objectives of EMT.
2. Define 'Achievement Motivation'.
3. Define 'Creativity'.

4. what do you mean for innovation?
5. What is communication?
6. What is verbal communication?
7. What is written communication?
8. What is non-verbal communication?
9. What is miscommunication?
10. What do you mean by self-efficacy?

Section B

11. Mention to objectives of EMT.
12. What are EMT delated activities for Entrepreneurs?
13. Explain the significance of achievement motivation.
14. Explain the different types of innovations.
15. What are the internal and external sources of innovation?
16. What are the objectives of Risk Taking?
17. Explain the characteristics of leadership.
18. Explain the importance of leadership.
19. Explain the importance of communication skills of an entrepreneur.
20. Explain the components of meta-verbal communication.
21. How do you develop communication skills for both sender and receiver?
22. What are the barriers to communication?

Section C

23. Discuss in brief the components of EMT to develop entrepreneurial competency.
24. Discuss the characteristics of persons with high need for achievement.
25. Discuss the different sources of development of n Ach and tools used to develop achievement motivation.
26. Discuss in brief the four phases of creative timing process.
27. Discuss in brief the different methods for developing creativity.
28. Explain the principles of Innovation.
29. Explain in brief the communication process.

SKILL DEVELOPMENT

1. Entrepreneurship Motivation Training (EMT) to develop entrepreneurial competency in the lab.
2. Visit EDI to learn more on training programmes.

PART B
SMALL BUSINESS

5

Small-Scale Industries

STRUCTURE

5.1 Introduction
5.2 Definition of Small-Scale Industries
5.3 Investment Limits for Small-Scale Industries
5.4 Objective of Promotion of Small-Scale Sector
5.5 Advantages of Promotion of Small-Scale Industries
5.6 Deficiencies in Small-Scale Industries
5.7 Importance and Role of SSI
5.8 Problems Faced by SSI
5.9 Steps to be taken to Solve the Problems
5.10 Strategies of Solve Problems of SSI
5.11 Government Policies to SSI
5.12 Government Assistance and Concessions for SSIs
5.13 Recent Govt. Actions
5.14 Organizational Forms or Ownership Pattern

5.1 INTRODUCTION

The small-scale industry has been recognized as one of the most appropriate means of developing the industrial economy of developing countries. Small-scale industries facilitate the tapping of resources which otherwise would remain unused. These resources included entrepreneurship, capital, labour and raw materials. They can mobilize rural savings which may otherwise remain idle or may be spent on luxuries or channelled into non-productive ventures.

They are fairly labour intensive, small-scale industries which create employment opportunities at a relatively low capital cost. In

India, there is a basic problem of absorbing the surplus manpower in non-agriculture jobs and providing additional employment opportunities for the growing population.

Such industries lead to the creation of employment opportunities as a dispersed basis not only in large cities and towns but also in smaller towns and far-flung regions. The establishment of small-scale industries would therefore made it possible to reserve the current trend of the migration of the people from rural to urban areas.

The development of small-scale sector has been of importance in India because, the Small-Scale Unit requires less capital outlay and at the same time, it provides more employment than the large-scale sector. A small-scale unit does not require highly sophisticated technology. It can therefore, be useful in backward areas where the people have yet to be trained to meet the challenge of sophisticated technology.

Small-sale industries contribute significantly to the strengthening of the industrial structure. Small-scale industries serve as seedbeds of entrepreneurship. They serve the developing economy not only by their output of goods but also by functioning as a nursery of entrepreneurial and managerial talent. This role of small-scale industries is of decisive importance in any economy.

Soon after independence our national leaders recognized the role of small-scale sector in the development of the economy of India and laid a solid foundation for its accelerated development through active policy support and creation of an institutional framework. The Industrial Policy Resolutions of the Government of India, from 1948 to 1991 visualized integrated growth of both the large and small-scale sectors and recognized the social and economic contribution of small-sector. These industrial policy resolutions states that the Government of India would stress the role of cottage and village and small-scale industries in the development of the national economy. The policy further envisaged that the decentralized sector should acquire sufficient vitality to be self-supporting and its development be integrated with that of the large-scale industry.

5.2 DEFINITION OF SMALL-SCALE INDUSTRIES

Most countries define small-scale industries, as an enterprise in terms of employment levels. Usually small-scale industries are taken to be those units which employ more than 5 less and than 50 or 100 workers. India is among the few countries that has used investment ceiling to define small-scale industries. Further, in India itself, different definitions are used for different purposes.

1. The Factories Act defines a factory as one, which employs ten workers or more if the unit uses power or twenty workers or more if it does not use power. All such units have to be registered under Factories Act and are subject to various labour laws including the provision of medical insurance and social security. Within this definition, those units which employ more than fifty workers (if using power) or more than hundred (if not using power) have to compulsorily register themselves (subject to amendments) with the state government in order to operate.
2. For the purposes of fiscal concessions, the criterion for determining a unit as SSI, depends upon the turnover of the unit in the previous year. Accordingly, if the turnover during the previous year is less than Rs. 400 lakhs (the limit was Rs. 300 lakhs upto 2004-05), then the unit is treated as a small-scale unit for the current year. But the amount of capital invested, manpower involved, the size of the factory etc. do not form the basis for treating the unit as a small-scale unit. Therefore, it is clear that the only criterion is turnover of the previous year.

But the most widely used definition of small-scale industry (SSI) in India is based on ceilings on investment in plant and machinery. Therefore,

Small-Scale Industrial Undertaking is defined as an "industrial undertaking in which the investment in fixed assets in plant and machinery, whether held on ownership terms or on lease or on hire purchase does not exceed rupees one crore."

[Provided that the investment ceiling in respect of the small-scale industrial undertaking manufacturing certain items shall not exceed rupees five crore.]

Ancillary Industrial Undertaking is an industrial undertaking which is engaged or is proposed to be engaged in the manufacturing or production of parts, components, subassemblies, tooling or intermediates, or the rendering of services, and undertaking supplies or proposes to supply or renders not more than fifty per cent of its production or services, as the case may be, to one or more other industrial undertakings and whose investment is fixed assets in plant and machinery, whether held on ownership terms or on lease, or on hire purchase, does not exceed rupees one crore.

[Provided that the investment ceiling in respect of the ancillary industrial undertaking manufacturing in certain items shall not exceed rupees five crore.]

Note 1 - No small-scale or ancillary industrial undertaking referred to above shall be subsidiary or owned or controlled by any other industrial undertaking.

Note 2 - a) In calculating the value of plant and machinery for the purposes the original price thereof, irrespective of whether the plant and machinery are new or second hand, shall be taken into account.

b) In calculating the value of plant and machinery, the following shall be excluded, namely,

i) The cost of equipment such as tools, jigs, dies, moulds and spare parts for maintenance and the cost of consumable stores.

ii) The cost of installation of plant and machinery.

iii) The cost of research and development equipment and pollution control equipment.

iv) The cost of generators sets and extra transformers installed by the undertaking as per the regulations of the State of Electricity Board.

v) The bank charges and service charges paid to the National Small Industries Corporation or the State Small Industries Corporation.

vi) The cost involved in procurement or installation of cables, wiring, bus bars, electrical control panels (not those mounted on individual machines), oil circuit breakers or miniature circuit breakers which are necessarily to be used for providing electrical power to the plant and machinery or for safety measures.

vii) The cost of gas producer plants.

viii) Transportation charges (excluding sales tax and excise) for indigenous machinery from the place of manufacturing to the site of the factory.

ix) Charges paid for technical know-how for erection of plant and machinery.

x) Cost of such storage tanks which store raw materials, finished products only and are not linked with the manufacturing process. and

xi) Cost of fire-fighting equipment.

c) In the case of imported machinery, the following shall be included in calculating the value of machinery, namely,

i) Import duty (excluding miscellaneous expenses as transportation from the port to the site of the factory, demurrage paid at the port).

ii) The shipping charges.

iii) Customers clearing charges.

iv) Sales Tax / VAT.

5.3 INVESTMENT LIMITS FOR SMALL-SCALE INDUSTRIES

Table 5.1 provides the history of evolution of investment limits for SSI since 1980. The attempt has been to keep revising the investment limits to keep up with inflation and hence to preserve the real value of investment limits. A curious development took place in 1999 when, for the first time, a reversal in investment limit was put into effect. The current definition is therefore more restrictive in real terms, relative to 1991. This definition is made under the Industrial Development and Regulation Act (IDR Act). The same Act also empowers the government to delineate industrial sectors for small-scale industry reservations. The current status of the investment ceiling for small-scale industries is provided in Table 5.2.

***Table 5.1** : Evolution of Investment Limits for Small-Scale Industries.*

Year	Investment Limits	Additional Condition
1950	Upto Rs. 0.5 million in fixed assets	Less than 50/100 persons with or without powers
1960	Upto Rs. 0.5 million in fixed assets	No condition
1966	Upto Rs. 0.75 million in plant and machinery	No condition
1975	Upto Rs. 1 million in plant and machinery	No condition
1980	Upto Rs. 2 million in plant and machinery	No condition
1985	Upto Rs. 3.5 million in plant and machinery	No condition
1991	Upto Rs. 6 million in plant and machinery	No condition
1997	Upto Rs. 30 million in plant and machinery	No condition
1999	Upto Rs. 10 million in plant and machinery	No condition

***Table 5.2:** Investment Ceilings for Small-Scale Industry (December 1999).*

Type of Small-Scale Industry	Investment Limit	Remarks
Small-Scale Industry	Rs.10 Million	Historical cost of plant and machinery
Ancillary	Rs.10 Million	At least 50 per cent of its output should go to other industrial undertakings
Export Oriented	Rs.10 Million	Obligation to export 30 per cent of production
Tiny Enterprise	Rs.2.5 Million	No location limits
Service and Business Enterprise	Rs.0.5 Million	No location limits
Women Enterprise	Rs.10 Million	51 per cent equity holding by women.

Note: A small-scale industry cannot be owned, controlled or be a subsidiary of another industrial undertaking. The policy framework for all segments is the same except for some incentives. The limits have been periodically revised upwards, but in December 1999, it has been revised downwards from Rs. 30 million fixed in December 1997.

A lower investment limit is prescribed for "tiny enterprises" which receive further concessions and services from the government.

Tiny Industries

Very small industries with an investment in plant and machinery of less than Rs. 25 lakhs are included in the definition of Tiny Industry. The number of persons employed in these units must be less than 50. The locational restrictions of setting up of tiny units have been removed by Small-Scale Industries Policy of 1992.

Cottage Industries

Cottage industries are called household industries which are organized by individuals with the help of members of the family and pursued as full-time or part-time occupation using local skills. Cottage industries include carpet weaving folk painting, toy making, carving of panels etc.

Village Industries

Village industries are defined as "artisans (irrespective of location) or small industrial activities vis., manufacturing, processing or preservation and servicing in village and small towns with a population not exceeding 50,000 (as per 1981 survey) and involving utilization of locally available natural resources and human skill, where individual credit requirements do not exceed Rs. 25,000.

Export-Oriented Unit [EOU]

An industrial undertaking in which the investment in fixed assets in plant and machinery, whether held on ownership terms, or on lease or by hire purchase, does not exceed Rs. 100 lakhs and has an obligation to export 30 per cent of production.

Medium Scale Industry

Medium Scale Industry are those units with investment in plant and machinery must be above the small scale industry limit and upto Rs. 10 crores.

5.4 OBJECTIVES OF PROMOTION OF SMALL-SCALE SECTOR

The following are the main objectives of promotion of small-scale industries:

1. To provide immediate large-scale employment opportunities as capital per unit of labour is less (for unemployed and especially for the educated youngmen and displaced person).
2. To avoid concentration of production from the viewpoint of ownership and location and method of ensuring more equitable distribution of income.
3. To provide opportunities for generation of new entrepreneurs.
4. To mobilize small capital resources. The overall quantum of capital resource is large when seen in a national framework but is not adequate for establishment of large industrial units.
5. To restrict the unplanned growth of urban centres which is inevitable if the unemployed start migrating to cities in the absence of employment openings in the present place of living.

6. To maintain and provide an orientation to industrial manufacturing, so that the local raw materials get utilized to the maximum extent
7. To promote local self-sufficiency at least in consumer goods (and incidentally reducing pressure on transport) and elimination of trader intermediaries, and
8. To help build decentralized pattern of growth.

5.5 ADVANTAGES OF PROMOTION OF SMALL-SCALE INDUSTRIES

The following are advantages of promotion of SSI or the major characteristics of SSI.

1. Employment Generation

The small-scale industry sector creates the largest employment opportunities for the Indian population, next only to agriculture. It has been estimated that an investment of Rs. one lakh in fixed assets in the small-scale industries sector generates employment for four persons. The small-scale industries sector has made significant contribution to employment generation and also to rural industrialization, because of its low capital intensity and high labour absorption nature. Thus, the employment growth rate for small-scale industries sector in the recent period is higher than that of the large-scale sector.

2. Growth Potential

The small-scale industries sector contributes 40 per cent of gross manufacturing. It has been estimated that an investment of Rs. one lakh in fixed asset in the small-scale industry sector produces 4.62 lakhs worth of goods or services, with an approximate value addition of 10 percentage points. In addition, the growth rate of small-scale industries sector during the various plan periods have been very impressive. It has been shown that throughout the nineties (barring the exception of 1995-96), small-scale industries sector grew at a higher rate as compared to the non small-scale industry sector.

3. Opportunities

The small-scale industry sector is ideally suited to build on the strengths of our traditional skills and knowledge by infusion of the technologies, capital and innovative marketing practices. The opportunities for the small-scale industries sector are enormous due to various reasons: (a) extensive promotion and support by the government (b) reservation for exclusive manufacture by small-scale industries sector, (c) low-level technical and managerial skills, (d) reservation for exclusive purchase by government, (e) growth in demand in the domestic market size to overall economic growth, etc.

4. Export Contribution

The number of small-scale industrial units undertaking exports is more than 5000. Overall small-scale industry exports contribute around 45-50 per cent of the total Indian export market, while direct exports account for nearly 35 per cent of total exports. The direct export channel includes merchant exporters, trading and export houses, export orders from large units or the production of parts and components for use in finished exportable goods, etc. Non-traditional products accounts for more than 95 percent of small-scale industry exports. The major small-scale industry items consists of low-skilled labour-intensive goods like garments (readymade garments, woollen garments and knitwear), leather products, gems and jewellery products, sports goods, plastic products, processed food, etc.

5. More Equitable Distribution of Income

The small-scale industry sectors are instrumental in resulting in a more equitable distribution of income owing to two reasons. First, it ensures income parity among the workers of small-scale industry sectors. Second, it is observed that entrepreneurial income is more equally distributed in case of small-scale industry sector.

6. Flexibility

Small firms are better able to adapt to changing and sometimes disruptive economic circumstances. Due to its flexibility, the sector is in an advantageous position to face challenges and changes. It is ideally poised to attract both technology and funds to generate rapid growth and sustained process of technology upgradation and quality improvement.

7. Contribution to Decentralization

The smaller firms prevent the concentration of power in a few hands. In addition, they also help in ensuring equitable distribution of wealth. A significant number of SSIs are located in the rural belt, while major industrialists are interested in locating their industries only near urban centres. Therefore, the absence of decentralization would cause accumulation of wealth only in certain areas.

5.6 DEFICIENCIES IN SMALL-SCALE INDUSTIRES SECTOR

The following are the deficiencies faced by small-scale industries:

1. Inherent deficiencies

a) SSIs generally employ old technologies, which do not allow them to compete with technically superior importable. Instead of encouraging their inefficiency through prolonged protection, provision of technical assistance and exposure to competition would boost their competitiveness and export intensity.
b) The lower plant sizes of SSIs generally do not allow them to enjoy the benefits of economies of scale. If large firms are allowed to carry out production in diverse areas, operation up to the economically viable point would render competitiveness to the firms.
c) A shortage of managerial ability and inadequate linkages among entrepreneurs results in high cost of production in SSIs.

2. Synthetic Export

The standard argument in favour of the policy of protection for SSI on account of their large contribution to exports is ill-founded. The large contribution originates not from their inherent advantages of producing these goods, but mainly from reservation of certain export goods production by SSIs. De-reservation of those sectors would enable large-scale industries to produce these goods more efficiently.

3. Subsidies

The interventions in markets for SSI services make sense only when their market-development effects outweigh their market-distortion effects. While deciding when and how to intervene, governments and donors need to begin with a good understanding of the structure and performance of existing markets. If the willingness to pay for support services is thought to be too low, is this because SMEs don't understand their true value, or because of the poor quality or inappropriate design of existing services? Are there few providers of services in the market because of a lack of knowledge of appropriate products, or because subsidized public institutions are crowding out private providers? Subsidies that are not targeted to the specific market failures constraining market development are likely to be more distortion than developmental, and since they do not solve the underlying problem, they may be more difficult to remove.

4. Reconsideration of the Reservation Policy

Following are some of the arguments against SSIs:

a) The SSIs producing reserved items are not allowed to cross the investment limits. This artificial cap on growth acts as a negative factor against the long-term interest of the sector. In order to comply with the norm on paper, SSIs often merely clone themselves and set up parallel units.

b) Since the policy environment prevents the successful units from growing, it acts as a dampener on entrepreneurship.

c) In line with the WTO obligation, the import policy and tariff reforms are undergoing reforms, and the SSIs are to face competition from imported goods. So, the reservation policy would eventually, lose its meaning. On the contrary, removal of reservations would enable the large-scale sector to enter and the resulting outsourcing and subcontracting arrangements would be instrumental in the growth of existing SSI units.

d) Since the technology and market characteristics for individual products differ, they do not have a single breakeven point. If reservation policy is to continue, the investment limits for individual products should vary, reflecting the minimum economic scale of production.

e) The policy of reservation has benefited only a few sectors. Out of the total of 200 products leading in value of output produced by the SSI sector, it was found that reserved products accounted for only 21 per cent.

f) De-reservation would as a whole promote technology upgradation, enhancement of productivity quality consciousness, product diversification, innovative marketing strategies and maximizing employment opportunities.

5. Increasing Concentration

It was expected that the SSI sector would be instrumental in lowering monopoly power of the firms. However, there is reason to believe that the concentration ratio is on the rise even within the SSI sector. The Abid Hussain Committee quoted from the NCAER study to note that in the garments sector, 14 units (17 per cent) accounted for not less than 82 per cent of production in the units. In electrical components, the share of two units was 36 per cent, and in detergents four units accounted for 37 per cent of production. These led the Committee to conclude that, ".. the market structure within the SSI sector has been showing clear indications of monopolistic competition, with an excessive number of tiny units crowding in to share in the rent created through policy of protection and subsidization, while success is achieved by a mere handful."

5.7 IMPORTANCE AND ROLE OF SMALL-SCALE INDUSTRIES

Entrepreneurship plays an important role in the formation of smaller enterprises. The small business sector is very important in most nations of the world. As many other things, small business offer the major economic advantages.

Therefore, entrepreneurship is needed to encourage small business for the following reasons.

1. They are labour intensive and provide more jobs.
2. They are the sources of many new goods and services.

3. They are suitable for the Indian economy which is capital-short and labour-intensive.
4. They contribute approximately 35 to 40 per cent of direct exports.
5. They have a higher per unit output of capital investment and per unit of energy used.
6. They are more flexible and innovative than large firms.
7. They may reduce economic and regional disparities and thus faster social stability and help in dispersal of economic power.
8. They may better serve small local markets in solving problems of unemployment and underemployment.
9. They may help in increasing the national productivity.
10. They may be less damaging to the environment.
11. They are cultivating the local natural resources and human resources effectively.
12. They can successfully compete with large firms.
13. They convert the persons from unemployment to self-employment which reduces the number of the unemployed and the burden on social assistance by coverage tax users to taxpayers.
14. The small-scale industries allow for creativity and flexibility, resulting in the ability to recognize and quickly seize business opportunities to suit changing local economic situations.
15. The sense of pride of small enterprises ownership often produces greater economic and political stability with increased productivity.
16. Small-scale industries are in tune with the local environment and culture, and are often able to make best use of the local resources and thus develop several local opportunities.
17. Often, small businesses are on the frontiers of new innovative technologies.
18. Small-scale sector can also reduce social frustrations of pressures, economic income disparities and political power disparities.
19. Small-scale sector gives self-empowerment to have increased status, improved lifestyle and the ability to control their own destiny. This concept is often applicable to: Disabled persons, retired personnel, civil servants, women's, ex-convicts, youth, unemployed, undereducated, middle-aged, professionals, technicians, etc.

5.8 PROBLEMS FACED BY SMALL-SCALE INDUSTRIES

The problems of small-scale industries can be broadly divided into internal or personal and external problems:

I. **Internal Problems:** Following are the internal or personal problem faced by an SSI which can be controlled:

1. Poor business philosophy.
2. Defect in the choice of an business idea.
3. Poor organisation structure.
4. Poor project implementation.
5. Lack of planning: Many social problems arises due to lack of proper planning include poor business locations, overextended capital requirements unrealistic sales projections, etc.
6. Lack of coordination or cooperation
7. Lack of proper control: It includes poor inventory control, poor financial control and over-investment in fixed assets, etc.
8. Lack of technical knowledge or know how.
9. Obsolete method of production and inferior techniques.
10. Poor quality of products of service.
11. Inadequate finance.
12. Low capacity utilization.
13. Inadequate training and skills.
14. Labour problems.
15. Funds diversion.
16. Inexperience in business: It means lack of technical skills and management skills.
17. Overambitious projects. This may lead to disaster.
18. Partner's dispute.
19. Mismanagement.
20. Wastage and pilferage.
21. Negligence to the problems.
22. Arrogance of entrepreneurs.

II. External Problems: The following are the external problems faced by SSIs:

1. Change in economic conditions.

2. Lack of infrastructure.
3. Lack of finance.
4. Recoveries.
5. Fluctuating interest rates on loans.
6. Unstable financial markets.
7. Change in industrial and financial regulations.
8. Problems due to taxation.
9. Lack of availability of raw materials.
10. Marketing related problems.
11. Problem of change in technology.
12. Change in labour market trends.
13. Competition from large-scale industries.
14. Problem to obtain licence: The problem is to obtain the permission and licence from the department of the state.
15. Problem of change in Government policies.
16. Competitive environment.
17. Inflation.

IMPORTANT PROBLEMS OF SSI

The various problems that are faced by the SSI sector hover around a few basic problems of finance, managerial capability, infrastructure and government policies. Following are the important problems faced by the SSI sector is discussed in details.

1. **Poor Business Philosophy :** Unfortunately, the business failures is due to not having a sound business philosophy or practices.
2. **Lack of Planning:** Many serious problems arise due to lack of proper planning. These include:
   a) Poor business location.
   b) Overextended capital requirements.
   c) Unrealistic sales projections, etc.,
3. **Management:** The failure of small business could be because of wrong decisions (management) in the following circumstances.
   1) Over investment in fixed assets.
   2) Poor inventory control.
   3) Poor financial control.
4. **Maintenance of quality:** Consistency in quality of product and services is most important for the successes of business.

Sometimes small businesses fail to maintain the quality of product and service.

5. **Neglect of customer's needs**: A more serious reason of business failure is a neglect of customer's needs and references.
6. **Inexperience**: Normally, entrepreneurs start their enterprise without having sufficient experience to succeed due to lack of technical and management skills.
7. **Arrogance:** Many small business entrepreneurs, particular inventors and innovative entrepreneurs with new products become deeply involved in their ventures. They become consumed with their own brilliance, convinced beyond reason (without market research) that their bright idea will change the world. Their arrogance will not allow them to take advice from others. All these may lead to failure.
8. **Lack of Finance :** Finance is the life and blood of SSIs. But there is lack of working capital for the business operations, long-term funds for the purchase of assets.
9. **Recoveries:** One of the most difficult problem of the small enterprises today is recovery from sales. That is delayed payment by customer.
10. **Lack of Entrepreneurial Enthusiasm:** Most of the SMI setups are result of the enthusiasm of a technocrat-entrepreneur. The setting up of the SMI against the odds shows the spirit of risk taking, hard work, tolerance for ambiguity and ability to cope with a complex bureaucratic structure. However, generally the technocrat-entrepreneur has no formal business education. This affects crucial decisions that need to be made in a business. Most of the critical decisions are intuitively made.

An NCAER study conducted on about 650 units over the country provides following related findings.

a) Most of the SSEs (93%) depends on their family and friends for important decisions.
b) Majority of the units (75%) chose the product line because they had some experience in that line or were aware that the demand prospects were better. Some of these are ex-employees of some large company and have borrowed ideas from their workplace. An objective analysis and proper prospecting was not usually done.

c) 90% of the entrepreneurs had not undergone any training prior to setting up the business.

d) About 90% of the enterprises did not have any quality for their products, and more importantly most of them felt that they did not require it.

The issues as regards finance and marketing are generally not handled professionally. There are many professionals that are now enterprising actively. And these entrepreneurs are conscious about the benefits of information based decision-making.

11. Change in economic conditions: Every business is affected by externalities live economic business cycles, fluctuating interest rates, interrupted supplies, labour market trends, inflation, change in government regulations and unsuitable financial markets, change in tax provisions etc.

Any rise in price due to the above external factors will lead to fall in sales or any change in prices of raw materials and increase in rate interest on loan lead to increase in cost, Therefore, a small change in economic conditions results in huge change in profits. Hence, small businesses are more susceptible to changes in the external environment.

12. Stagnation in growth : Stagnation in growth is a common feature. One of the reasons for this are complacency in the existing status, and the protective government policies that discourage shifting from the status of SME. The protective policies of the government have failed to increase the competitive capabilities of the sector. Again, the external changes in the environment are faster than the changes in the internal capabilities to keep up with the change.

13. The SSIs are their own service providers: In India there are no agencies that specifically cater to the needs of the SMI for marketing, equipment supply, training, skill acquisition, design and testing facilities. The SSIs, therefore, serve themselves for these needs.

14. Marketing Problems : Marketing has been a major problem for the SSEs. The NCAER study shows that the marketing of goods has been cited as the second most important reason for the closure of SSIs.

The marketing problems start right from the product selection stage. For any product to be successful, it is necessary to determine its marketability. As mentioned earlier, the technocrat-entrepreneur who ventures into a small business often lacks the skills to evaluate the market feasibility of the product. This is aggravated by the fact that there are no agencies that provide proper guidance and information in this respect to the SSI.

There are strategic deficiencies in the various aspects of marketing adopted by the SSIs. The pricing and targeting of the product is conventional in nature, shift to a niche market is also an option that the SSIs hardly think of. Lack of professional education and other guidance is one reason why the SSIs do not come up with innovative marketing strategies.

The perceived problem of finance, usually in the form of liquidity crisis, may go to some extent be related to marketing as a primary cause. Such problem may arise due to delayed payments from customers, provision of inadequate bank credit coming in the way of timely execution of supply orders or rejection of good supplied, etc.

15. Production bottlenecks : Most SSIs suffer severe production bottlenecks that do not allow them to work efficiently, produce quality goods and generate reasonable supplies. Important impediments to efficient production are:

1. Inadequate working capital and delayed payments.
2. Short supply of certain raw materials.
3. Limited space.
4. Bad working conditions.
5. Outdated machinery and equipment.
6. Lack of sufficient testing facilities.
7. Undependable power supply.
8. Frequent fluctuations in voltage.
9. Poor effluent disposal facilities.
10. Deficiencies in production management.
11. Low capacity utilisation

16. Technology obsolescence: Because of inadequacy of term loans the SSEs are not able to upgrade their technology. Term loan applications are often rejected on grounds of insufficient collateral/ security.

The NCAER study gives the following related findings.

a) More than 50% of the units were manually operated, about 40% used semi-automatic processes and less than 5% used automatic processes.

b) There is a close link between the size of the unit and the degree of automation. About 80% of the enterprises employing less than Rs. 2 lakhs capital are manually operated.

c) Better technology does not mean better machines only. It has to be coupled with higher and better operating skills. Further, better machines also need good quality of inputs else the machine itself can get damaged. Only about 44% of the units had installed testing facilities.

d) Many units are reluctant to change because of lack of relevant information and paucity of funds. They are not even aware of the changes in technologies that have been taking place over the years.

17. Risk Capital : The activities of the new SSI venture are risky. This keeps the banks from giving them credit. Thus, we see that a significant proportion of the units is completely self-financed.

18. Credit to the sector : The government directives pre-empt the bank funds for subscribing to government securities, and direct the made to the priority sector (40% of the total lending should be made to the priority). These affected the credit policies of the banks, making the lending activity directed towards meeting set targets of lending. The banks lend on collateral but the best possible use of the funds is not ensured. The basic conflict between the canons of sound banking, and the policy oriented objectives of social banking, has led to the current situation of high NPA ratio in Indian banking.

19. Lack of integration : The reservation of goods for manufacture by the SSI is based on the myth that the SME and the LSE (large-scale enterprises) are competitors. The policy fails to integrate the two sectors. The reservation creates production systems where in the LSE cannot exploit the economies of scale, and the complementarily between the sectors does not happen.

20. Lack of Infrastructure: Infrastructure includes no proper location, proper power supply, water supply and other facilities like communication, post office, etc.,

5.9 STEPS TO BE TAKEN TO SOLVE THE PROBLEMS

The following are some of the measures and strategies to be taken by SSI before and during the business operations.

1. Define the purpose and major objectives of business venture before commencement of business.
2. Plan the market with attention to a well-defined market segment.
3. Forecast sales and translate sales data into resources segments.
4. Document financial requirements and resources.
5. Plan to maintain positive cash flow.
6. Conduct a feasibility study of the project.
7. Formulate a marketing plan for the product.
8. Position the product or service in the appropriate growth market.
9. Establish on inventory management plan.
10. Plan the growth in accordance with availability of resources and limitations.
11. Plan properly to control the events and to prevent unintended consequences.

5.10 STRATEGIES TO SOLVE PROBLEMS

Strategies can be divided into :

1. Basic Strategy and
2. Advanced Strategy

5.10.1 Basic Strategy

It is essential for an ailing unit to sustain its existence in the immediate short turn. In the short run, it is a fire-fighting situation for the SSIs.

Some basic strategies that can enhance short term sustenance capability are given below. A major thrust in the short-term is to save costs and improve quality. The SSIs should follow the process explained below as basic strategy to solve problems.

1. Rational Evaluation

Do a rational evaluation of the possibility of survival. Are you in a dying industry? If yes, then close down.

2. Improve the Organisational Structure

Improve the organizational structure of the firm. Delegate but with a commensurate responsibility.

3. Take Suppliers into Confidence

Take the supplier in confidence of the recognisation efforts. Delay payments to get working capital.

4. Take Employees into Confidence

Take employees into confidence about the reorganization efforts. The employees form the most important resource of any organization. The employees of a SSIs are not always well educated to understand complex strategic decisions, and how do those decisions affect their work and output. Therefore, it is important that every strategic decision and its implications are explained to those implementing it in very simplified terms. The effect of the strategy should be linked to the changes in the bottom line.

5. Develop Internal Skills

The SSIs needs to upgrade its in-house skill development capabilities. It is observed that those workers who know particular operations tend to refrain from teaching them to others in the organization so as to maintain their exclusivity. Knowledge management practices that help the organization learn with time and past experience would reduce the indispensability of any person in the firm.

6. Get the basics right

The basic systems of any business organization consist of procedures and policies about the standard operations like buying, collecting from debtors, inventory management, time management, etc., because of the lack of formal business education technocrat-entrepreneur makes these decisions heuristically. Thus, the much-required discipline of analysis is lacking. Some specific suggestions about the basic systems are given below:

a) Working Capital

The working capital mismanagement is one of the main causes of strained conditions in SSI unit. This is aggravated by the unplanned expansion of the business that is not supported by the required WC. Therefore, the SSI unit has to ensure that the operating surplus has to be first employed towards meeting the WC needs. The capability to repay the debt comes in the long run from sustaining the sales.

b) Quality

Quality of the products is no longer a USP for any business. It is minimum requirement for a successful product. The SSI unit should upgrade its quality maintenance processes.

c) Production Planning

Production planning is essential to achieve lower costs. There are various aspects of the production process that need to be aligned to get good quality products at low costs.

d) Careful with Credit

Evaluating the customer before giving them credit can save bad debtors accumulating on the balance sheet. Some kind of market intelligence system should be put in place. Basic information like the business of the customer, the growth of the industry the customer is into, other information from the market in case of dealers, etc., can help determining the creditworthiness of the customer.

e) Distribution Costs

Distribution of the goods is amongst a non-value adding cost that every manufacturer has to incur. In the quest to reduce cost, every cost component has come under micro review of the business researchers. Transportation cost is one of them. The SSI unit must rationalize its distribution process by making use of basic tools like vehicle routing, transportation optimization, etc.

f) Servicing the Customer

Customer service and support can enhance the image of the SSI unit as a good supplier. The SSI is also in a better position to directly deal with the customer because there are few hierarchies and few key clients. Therefore, the marketing can directly look after the customer relationship function. The only one aspect where the marketing manager of the case-study company found the company one up the market leader was customer relations. "They get too professional", said the marketing manager about the marketing leader.

g) Information System

Information system is a key for the success of any business. There is a big lap in the way the information is managed in the SSI unit. There is no integrated use of the information generated in the various departments of the unit. There is a need to integrate the marketing with the production and that with the financial situation. This would enhance the coherence in the process employed in the business.

5.10.2 Advanced Strategies

The basic strategies talk about the short-term sustenance. But, in the long run, the company must get a strategic view of the direction it is moving into.

The advanced strategies are strategies for turning around the sector. The following are the methods to solve the problems :

1. Define your business or know your business : Most business in the SME sector are start-ups by technocrat-entrepreneur. However, as the size of the business grows the need for a coherent strategy aimed at a certain goal is needed. The SME should, to start with, define their business both currently and in the future. This definition should be based on a comprehensive evaluation of the strengths and the weaknesses of the firm internally and the opportunity that are available outside. There is the need to define the strategic intent of the company.

2. Enter into new fields or exploring new business : A total of 52% of the SME manufacturers in Japan in 1985, have had previous experience with entry into a new field. The mode of entry has been.

- 46% Diversification
- 41% Added grade or value to their products.
- 14% Changed business lines.

Following that model, the SME in India should be looking for greener pastures. This would require flexibility and being open to new possibilities. Some initiatives can be taken in the growing industries of the day like the software industry.

3. Selecting the right project : At times the project undertaken may be technologically sound, but their financial viability is under doubt. Therefore, it is important to ensure that to start with at least, the venture is viable and profitable. Besides, the SME has to both find and sustain barriers to entry by:

a) Continuous innovation of product or project.

b) Low profile invisibility to keep competitors away.

c) Focusing on difficult-to-please customers.

d) Technological gaps.

4. Product rationalization and process resequencing, The SSI unit generally has a small list of customers as compared to its large increase its sales, the SSI unit might end up producing whatever variety the customer demand and in any quantity. This leads to sub-optimal production decisions and product mixes. While it is essential to maintain the customer relationship, stretching it beyond a point can get dangerous for the very existence of the enterprise. A sub-optimal product mix can have adverse effect on product handling, inventory costs, advertising effectiveness, distribution costs, quality, etc.

The SSI unit must, therefore, rationalize its product mix. An ABC analysis of the sales levels of the various products, coupled with other market information should be used for deciding upon the product mix. Here, aiming a niche market is an option that should be actively considered.

Process resequencing is another cost reduction tool to be applied over the long-term. The production processes can be suitably modified coupled with technology change to reap cost benefits. Saving in production lead-time is another advantage that can be achieved with the use of process resequencing.

5. Matching asset expansion with sales growth : As the sales of the SSI unit begins to grow, the existing production capacity is stretched to meet the requirements. This is a very crucial decision point where the unit has to decide on whether it should expand its capacity. The following options should be kept in mind to decide on asset expansion:

a) Seasonal or temporary leasing of facilities wherever available.
b) Duplication of existing facilities.
c) Incremental addition to facilities as each bottleneck surfaces.
d) Acquisition of a new, next generation package of processing facilities for a higher capacity.

The choice of the option will depend upon the degree of commitment that the unit has to the product line, the seasonality of the increase in sales and the financial strength. The basic concern should be balancing the risk of over-expansion with the loss of opportunity. Compatibility of new machines with the old ones, standardization of product produced on different machines, etc, are other concerns.

6. Systematically expanding sales or planning sales growth : Often the SSI unit gets too focused on the existing customer and market area. Phansalkar suggests intensification and geographical expansion as sales expansion strategies, Under intensification, the sales push is increased on the existing market by increasing availability on the existing market advertising etc.

Geographical expansion implies looking for newer markets. The unit should look for greener pastures in another city, state or country.

However, sales expansion should happen in a planned manner instead of by default. The unit should take the following issuers in consideration while planning its sales growth:

a) The product changes required in new regions and the capability of the unit to meet such variety.
b) The trade-offs involved in the marginal profits and the cost of distribution to the new markets that would include transportation costs, margins to the dealer, etc.

The point to be stressed is that the unit must have complete knowledge of the markets, the distribution channel. Information can give a competitive edge. Extensive study of the market is essential to gain this information advantage.

5.11 GOVERNMENT POLICIES TO SSI

5.11.1 Industrial Policies of Govt. of India

The main objectives of the programmers for the development of the small-scale industries in various plans have been to promote large-scale employment on a decentralized basis, to improve the existing levels of skills and quality of products, and to raise production both for domestic consumption and export.

Assumption

The measures undertaken and programmes evolved to support the sector, have been determined by the nature of the perception of the policy-makers with regards to the operational problems and handicaps of the small-scale sector. The understanding of the policy-makers has been:

1. Since most of the small-scale units are organized on proprietary or partnership basis they to not have easy access to institutional sources of finance.
2. Due to capital scarcity the units end up in buying cheap and sub-quality machines which are difficult to maintain due to non-standardization.
3. As the units are small in size their requirements of raw materials are of limited quantities. Consequently, the raw materials cost work out to be high and the quality of a doubtful nature.
4. These units cannot take up advertisements or organize sales directly to the consumers. This makes it obligatory on them to depend on intermediaries and traders.
5. As many of the small-scale entrepreneurs are young and new to the manufacturing line they would not have adequate market know-how or the necessary knowledge of the various kinds of state supports available to them.
6. With limited resources small-scale units cannot afford to install quality testing equipment or afford to pay high rents for land and building in urban centres. This was particularly so for the new entrepreneurs.
7. The traditional techniques of production need regular upgradation. But this cannot be easily done by entrepreneurs with limited means; and

8. The large-scale manufacturing units can indulge in a variety of unhealthy and predatory practices to check the growth of the small-scale units.

The small enterprise is more susceptible to these factors than a large firm. Thus, small change in economic conditions results in huge changes in profits. Small business operation a relatively more intense, price-sensitive environment.

1. **Industrial policy statement – 1948.** The first policy statement 6th April 1948, emphasized the role of the SSI in the national economy is offering hope for individual village or co-operative enterprises and scope for the rehabilitation of displaced persons. The industries conference recommended that the small-scale industries were particularly suited for the better utilization of local resources.
2. **Industrial policy statement, 1956:** Eight years had passed, since the duration and the industrial policy in 1948, following thus, the constitution of India was enacted guaranteeing certain fundamental rights and an associating the preventive principles & state policy. The first 5 year plan was also then over. The parliament had accepted the socialistic patron of society as the objective and social and economic policy. Industrial policy on other policies were to be governed by these principles and directions.

   The industrial policy, 1956. Stressed the role of SSI in the development and the national economy. SSIs provide immediate large- scale employment. They offer a method of ensuring a more suitable distribution of the national income and they facilitate all effective mobilization of resources of capital and skill which might otherwise remain unutilized.
3. **Industrial policy 1977.** The Industrial policy statement 1977. drew up the list of industries to be started by large business houses so that, the competitive effort of small industries is not affected. The large industries were permitted to start in rural and backward areas.
4. **Small Enterprise/Industrial Policy 1991:** The small-scale sector emerged on a dynamic and vibrant sector of the economy during the eighties. The primary objective of the small-scale industry policy in nineties was to comfort more vitality and

growth competition to the sector to enable it to contribute to its full to the economy particularly in terms of growth of output, employment and exports. For the first time the Government came out with a separate small-scale industries policy. The government decided that the artificial divisions between small and large-scale industry which were conflicting should be cleared by the economic federations by a policy of integrated industrial development.

5. **Industrial Policy, August 2000:** The policy was out with strategic decision in the investment pattern. Classified the investment in small-scale and along with ancillary units. The without ceiling in respect of the small-scale industrial undertaking manufacturing items mentioned in the order dt. 9.10.2000 shall not exceed rupees 500 lacs.

5.11.2 Small-scale Reservation Policy

The policy of small-scale reservations was initiated in 1967 as a promotional and productive measure for the small-scale sector and the large-scale sector. Under this policy selected products were identified for exclusive production in the small-scale sector. The overwhelming consideration for reservations whether it is technically feasible to produce those in the small-scale sector, the manufacturing process of which is of a simple nature. That is essentially labour intensive and whether the small-scale units can meet the requirements of consumer, both in terms of quantity and quality. The rationale for reservation was based on the advantages of the small-scale sector like labour intensity and adaptability to a semi-urban and rural environment. Another objective was to make SSI products competitive with those of the large sector by offsetting the disadvantages of mass scale production, economics of scale, wider marketing network, better credit availability and publicity through mass and advertisements.

The basic features of the reservation policy :

1. The policy is applicable only to the manufacturing sector. It does not take into account the service sector including repairs of products.
2. No new unit in the medium or large-scale sector is allowed to be set up after the date of reservation nor is any further capacity expansion creation is reserved for the small-scale sector only.

3. Existing large-scale units which were manufacturing these reserved items at the time of reservation, were allowed to continue their activities indefinitely but their capacity was frozen at the existing levels that is they were prohibited from expanding further.
4. Creation of new capacity in the reserved areas is permitted among medium/large-scale units if they undertake to export a minimum of 75 per cent of their production (50 per cent in case of ready-made garments).
5. There is no restriction on the marketing by large units or big companies of products reserved for manufacture in the SSI sector.
6. A statutory Advisory Committee on reservation was established to undertake the review of items from time to time for:
   - De-reservation of items which are already reserved.
   - Reservation of new additional items.
   - Change of the nomenclature of the items.

A curious feature of this reservation policy introduced in 1967 was that it had no legal backing until 1984. It is remarkable such as this was not legally challenged. It was only in 1984 that the government plugged this legal inadequacy and put this policy on a statutory footing in the IDR Act. Initially, only 47 items were reserved in 1967. But the number has grown considerably. Since then at present the list contains more than 837 items.

5.12 GOVERNMENT ASSISTANCE AND CONCESSIONS FOR SSIs

The Government Assistance and programmes for SMEs are designed and coordinated by the Ministry of Small-Scale Industries (SSI). The ministry operates through three organizations attached to it.

1. The office of the Development Commissioner, also known as the Small Industries Development Organization (SIDO), which helps the Ministry to implement policies and programmes for promoting small-scale industries through a network of 30 industries Service Institutes (SISI), 28 Branch Institutes, 2 Extension Centre, 4 Regional Testing Centres, one Production Centre, 7 Field Testing Stations and several Tool Rooms, Process-cum-Product Development Centres and Technology and Training Support Institutes.

2. Small-Scale Industries Board (SSI Board), which is a 91-member body constituted by the government for advising the government on SSI policy and related issues.
3. National Small-Scale Industries Corporation Limited (NSIC), which is a public sector organization created for providing a variety of services to small-scale units, such as purchase of machines, marketing both within and outside the country, supplies to the government and public sector organization, procurement of raw materials and supplies training in industrial trades, etc.

Assistance and Concessions

Following are the assistance and concessions provided by the govt to SSIs.

1. Assistance for SME Exports

Following all the assistance to SMI exports:

a) SMEs are helped in participating in trade exhibitions. The government would meet their expenses in this regard on space rent, handling and clearing charges, insurance and shipment charges, etc.
b) SMIs are given triple weightage for being recognized as Export Houses, Trading Houses, Star Trading Houses, and Super Star Trading Houses.
c) Capital Goods Zero Duty Scheme is extended to SMEs without any conditions.
d) Export obligation fulfilment period for SMEs is extended to 8 years.
e) SMEs are given training in packaging for making their products attractive for exports.
f) Marketing Development Assistance (MDA) is given to SMEs to facilitate market research, publicity, etc.

2. Penalties for delayed payments to SSI Units

SSI units are vulnerable to delays in payments by customers. The latter would often be very large companies against whom the small-scale units can hardly take any action. The government has therefore enacted the Interest on Delayed Payments Act, which prescribes that the customers of SSI units should make the payments within 120 days of accepting the goods. Delays beyond this would attract interest at one and a half times the prime lending rate of the State Bank of India. Disputes on the matter should be settled fast, for which the state governments are asked to constitute industries Facilitation Councils.

3. Prime Minister's Rozgar Yojana (PMRY)

PMRY was launched on 2nd October 1993, with the ambitious target of creating one million jobs in five years by giving loans for the creation of tiny and micro enterprises. As the scheme was quite successful, it was extended beyond the five-year period and is still active.

4. Programmes on Pollution Control and Waste Minimization

Since 1998, SIDO has been conducting programmes for SMEs on Pollution Control and Minimization of Waste with a special focus on energy conservation. During the period of four energy conservation. During the period of four years up to 2002, SIDO has conducted more than 100 such programmes whereby more than 3000 SSI units were benefited.

5. Facilitating ISO-9000 Certification

Under the Quality Upgradation programme, SIDO would reimburse to SMEs 75% of the cost of ISO-9000 certification subject to a maximum of Rs 75,000/ case. The scheme started in 1984, and during the 7 years of its operation until 2001, SIDI reimbursed an amount of Rs 8.45 crores to 1384 SSI/ancillary units on the scheme.

6. Integrated Infrastructural Development (IID) Scheme

Under this scheme, the central government (by way of term loan) would contribute Rs. 5 crore in the ratio of 2:3 for the development of industrial infrastructure in rural and backward areas. The remaining expenses will have to be met by the concerned state government. The objective of the scheme is to promote the location of SMEs in rural and backward areas and facilitate linkage between agriculture and industry. In seven years (1994-2001), 57 such centres were established, which are at different stages of implementation.

7. WTO Cell

The World Trade Organization (WTO) Cell was set up in 1999 in the office of the Development Commissioner (SSI) in order to disseminate information and conduct workshops on WTO for the benefits of SSI units.

8. Subcontracting Exchanges

SIDO has set up Subcontracting Exchange and Vendor Development Programmes-cum-Exhibitions for helping SMEs to become suppliers and subcontractors for large companies. 34 Subcontracting Exchanges are currently functioning in select or branch institutes.

9. Marketing Development Assistance (MDA) Scheme

MDA is a new scheme launched in August 2001. Under this scheme SSI units/entrepreneurs can get the following five types of assistance.

1. Assistance to individuals for participating in overseas trade fairs and exhibitions,
2. Assistance to individuals to go on overseas study tours or as a member of a trade delegation going abroad.
3. Assistance for production of publicity material for overseas publicity.
4. Assistance to small industry associations to conduct sector-specific market studies aborad, and
5. Assistance to SSI Associations to initiate/contest anti-dumping cases.

10. SENET Project

Small Enterprise Information and Resource Centre Network (SENET) was a website created in 1998 to promote networking among seekers and providers of information on the SME sector. The purpose is to link all agencies involved in promoting SSI such as Central and State government agencies, NGOs, industry associations, training institutions, etc. The SENET project also helps in office automation.

11. Testing Centres

SIDO operates four Regional Testing Centres (RTCs) in Delhi, Mumbai, Chennai and Kolkata. These centres are equipped to test raw materials, semi-finished products and finished products in the fields of chemical, mechanical, metallurgical and electrical engineering. In addition to testing. RTCs also conduct awareness programmes for SSI unit on quality issues including ISO-9000 certification.

As the reach of RTCs are limited, SIDO has also created Field Testing Stations (FTSs) in seven other places (Jaipur, Bhopal, Kolhapur, Hyderabad, Pondicherry, Changanacherry and Bangalore). FTSs have the capability to test a variety of products like chemicals, dyestuffs, lamps, rubber products, castings, forgings, paints, varnishes, domestic electrical appliances, and so on.

Neither the RTCs nor the FTSs can be considered a success in the commercial sense. They spend more than they earn. This is also a declining trend in their utilization. It is true that initiatives of this kind should not be evaluated in purely monetary terms of their promotional impact. However, a better model would have been to provide some assistance for the SME units in a place to create such facilities for themselves on a collective initiative. When the units have some stakes in these facilities, they would take care of their commercial viability too.

12. Scheme for International Cooperation, Modernization and Upgradation

This is a scheme for facilitating one-to-one interaction between Indian and foreign enterprises for sourcing technology and exporting products and technology. In addition, the scheme has provision for conducting market potential studies, holding seminars and exhibitions, and sending and receiving delegates (government officials and exhibitions, and sending and receiving delegates (government officials and representatives of SME associations) for preparatory work for such events. Common expenses and the travel expenses of two government and association representatives are met by the scheme. Individual units have to bear their own expenses. Though the scheme is intended primarily to promote one-to-one interaction between enterprises, the visits are so timed that the delegations would also be able to visit some trade fairs and exhibitions in the country of their visit.

13. Trade Related Entrepreneurship Assistance and Development (TREAD) for Women

TREAD is a scheme for giving trade-related assistance to women entrepreneurs in the form of loans, grants, trade-related training and information, counselling and extension services. Grants up to one-third of the project cost will be given to non-farm group projects of women prepared through the involvement of NGOs. Of the total grants given for the project, 70% should be used for the direct benefit of the women entrepreneurs and 30% can be used for NGOs' capacity building.

14. Facilitating Surveys and Policy Research

Periodic surveys and studies are commissioned by SIDO to academic, research and training institutions in order to generate data for developing policies, strategies and action plans in promoting SMEs in the country.

The number and variety of government programmes to facilitate the SME sector, as my be seen from the selective and brief outline given above, are quite impressive. In exports, three years of GEM research there has not been much fault-finding with government programmes. There have been several mentions of policy inadequacies and bureaucratic apathy and incompetence. Perhaps one could conclude that the programmes are good but are made ineffective by inconsistent policies and faculty implementation.

15. Fiscal Concessions

Small-scale units receive fiscal incentives in the form of complete or partial exemption from excise duties, for instance, small-scale units operating from excise duties, that is, small-scale units operating in industries like footwear (employing less than 50 workers) tooth- paste, metal containers, roller bearing, zip fasteners, playing cards, carbon black (whose value of production is not more than Rs. one lakh) and confectionery, starch, various kinds of yarn, paper, steel furniture, bolts and nuts, grinding wheels, insulation tapes, paints and varnishes, aerated water, khandsari, soap, safes and strong boxes and metal containers, and vegetable non-essential oils (if no power is used) get complete exemption from excise duties. Similarly, differential rates of excise duties apply to industries like wires, cables and paper mills in the small-scale sector.

16. Financial Assistance

As a policy, public sector financial institutions and banks provide finance to the small-scale sector at concessional terms. State Financial Corporations (SFCs) are authorized to provide both risk capital and long-medium-and short-term capital on liberal terms. A number of commercial banks have special schemes for the grant of loans on easy terms to the sector. The Industrial Development Bank of India (IDRI) has established a special wing which exclusively deals with small, village and collage industries. Assistance sanctioned to the small-scale sector by the IDBI in the form of refinance of industrial loans and rediscounting of bills amounted to a total of Rs. 23,400 millions at the end March 1982.

17. Preferential Government Purchases

It is made compulsory for various government departments and agencies to buy their requirements of a number of items from the constituents of the small-scale sector. At the end of 1981 there were 384 items for which purchases were to be made only from the small-scale sector. In addition to these there are 11 and 15 items in whose case the DGS&D has to make purchases to the extent of 75 and 50 per cent respectively of its requirements from small-scale units. Price preference to the extent of 15 per cent is allowed to small-scale units in the case of items purchased both from the small and large-scale sectors.

18. Infrastructural Facilities

Since the beginning of the Second Plan the Government has taken up the task of establishing industrial estates in the country. Industrial estates not only provide readymade industrial sheds to minimize preliminary expense to individual small entrepreneurs but also offer common services at subsidized rates. The Small Industries Development Organization (SIDO), through a network of Small Industries Service Institutes (SISI), provides management consultancy, industrial design, common tooling and testing facilities, information or technical know-how, market advice and information for export promotion, etc. The National Small Industries Corporation (NSIC) and State Small Industries Corporations supply machines on hire purchase basis and assist small-scale units in securing Government orders. State Directorates of Industries have been assigned the task of providing scarce raw materials to the units in this sector.

19. Exemption from Certain Statutory Provisions

In view of the small scale of operations and investments, these units have been exempted from the provisions of industrial licensing under, the IDRA, 1951. Additionally, the provisions of section 58A of the Companies Act. 1956 are also made inapplicable to them. Companies falling under the category of small-scale industrial units engaged in the manufacture of number of products have been exempted from the provisions of the Cost Accounting Records Rules, 1977.

20. Bank Finance

Small-scale industrial units form part of the 'priority sector' along with agriculture, small borrowers, weaker sections, etc. for purpose of availing assistance and credit from banks. Loans to priority sector attract lower interest rates and are generally exempted from accessional credit constraints imposed by the Reserve Bank of India. The commercial banks are also directed to increase their landings to the priority sector.

The sum total of the concessions-direct and indirect-subsidies, preferential treatment and exemptions from the operation of some of the important regulatory provisions accorded to the small-scale sector add up to a substantial support for the sector. The significance of these concessions, however, cannot be assessed in terms of the financial outlays or direct costs to the state as many of the costs are hidden and non-quantifiable. If would also not be correct to assume that the concessions are uniformly available to all constituents of the sector. Viewed from the individual manufacturing unit's angle, one category of units may find one type of concessions more important whereas another group of small-scale units may find it far more rewarding to avail of other provisions of state policy package. For instance, a unit which enjoys financial support of a large and established industrial house of the country is likely to depend more on the facility of exemptions from the regulatory provisions whereas a small man may be quite happy if he could obtain a shed in an industrial estate. Similarly, an assembly unit may find government policy for preferential purchases to be more helpful than the availability of cheap raw materials.

To avail the state assistance and the variety of direct and indirect economic advantages, a unit must get official recognition as a small-scale unit. In a country like India, having a high degree of illiteracy and absence of effective channels for dissemination of official information, a large percentage of small-scale units are not likely to be even aware of the precise content and extent of state support available to them. One should, therefore, expect that only a fraction of the total number of small-scale units would have official recognition as constituents of the sector. Secondly, even if there was awareness of support policies towards the small-scale sector one has to recognize that availability of concessions and support has to be through the governmental system which has its own style and mode of operation. The groups which are not intended to be provided state support can indeed be the ones to take advantages of them; and the ones sought to be assisted may never come to know of their eligibility for such assistance. It is, for instance, an irony that the variety and form of concessions and other advantages available to cottage and rural industries are more widely known and understood in urban centres.

5.13 RECENT GOVERNMENT ACTION

The government is moving forward with the agenda of reforming the SSIs. Several reform measures are being undertaken to enable the SSIs to counter the competition from importable in the face of withdrawal of quantitative restrictions. The major policies initiated over the last couple of years to help the sector includes:

Policy initiatives in SSI sector during 2004-05

- The National Commission on Enterprises in the Unorganized Informal Sector was set up in September 2004. The Commission will, inter-alia, recommend measures considered necessary for improvement in the productivity of these enterprises, generation of large scale employment opportunities on a sustainable basis, linkage of the sector to institutional framework in areas like credit, raw material supply, infrastructure, technology upgradation, marketing facilities and skill development.
- Eighty-five items reserved for exclusive manufacture in the SSI sector were dereserved in October 2004. The total number of reserved items now stands at 605.
- To facilitate technology upgradation and enhancing competitiveness the investment limit (in plant and machinery) has been raised in October 2004, from Rs. 1 crore to Rs. 5 crore, in respect of 7 items of sports goods, reserved for manufacturing in the small scale sector.
- The Small and Medium Enterprises (SME) Fund of Rs. 10,000 crore was operationalised by the SIDBI since April 2004. Eighty per cent of the lending from this fund will be for SSI units, at interest rate of 2 per cent below the prevailing PLR of the SIDBI.
- The Reserve Bank of India enhanced the composite loan limit for the SSI sector to Rs. 1 crore from Rs. 50 lakh.
- With a view to integrate small and medium enterprises, facilitating their growth and enhancing their competitiveness (including measure for freeing the sector from "inspector Raj"), a suitable legislation is being finalised.
- A new "Promotional Package (for small enterprises is being formulated. This would for include measures to provide adequate credit, incentives for technology upgradation, infrastructural and marketing facilities, etc.

Major Measures Undertaken During 2002-03

- Dereservation of 51 items.
- Extension of SSI excise exemption scheme for certain industries.
- To encourage lending to SSIs, a National Award is given to a commercial bank for best performance.
- Stress on technology, upgradation projects and extension of the

coverage of ISO 9000 reimbursement scheme to include ISO 14001 scheme.

Major Measures Undertaken During 2001-02

- Enhancement of investment limit for units in various key SSIs.
- Raising the corpus fund set up under the Credit Guarantee Fund Scheme.
- Dereservation of 14 items related to leather goods, shoes and toys.
- A new scheme named Market Development Assistance Scheme was launched exclusively for the SSIs.
- Under the Cluster Development Programme, 4 UNIDO assisted projects have been commissioned.

Major Measures Undertaken During 2000-01

- Initiation of Credit Guarantee Fund Scheme and Credit Linked Capital Subsidy for Technology Upgradation for SSIs, aimed at addressing to the problem of collaterals
- Faced by the SSI units and to encourage technology upgradation.
- Enhanced excise exemption limit for SSIs.
- For improving credit to SSIs, enhancement of Composite Loan Scheme Limit, modification in collateral security requirement for loans up to Rs. 5 lakhs, setting up of RBI committees.
- Dereservation of readymade garments.
- Enhancement of investment ceiling for Small-scale Service and Business (Industry related) Enterprises.
- Continuation of the ongoing scheme of granting Rs. 75,000 to each SSI for obtaining ISO 9000 certification till the end of the 10th plan.
- Increasing the coverage of ongoing Integrated Infrastructure Development (IID) scheme to progressively cover all area in the country with 50 per cent reservation for rural areas.

Major Measures Undertaken During 1999-2000

- Announcement of a new Credit Insurance Scheme for providing adequate security to banks and improving flow of investment credit to SSI units, particularly export oriented and tiny units.
- The turnover limit to determine the working capital limit was enhanced.
- Lending by banks to non-banking financial companies (NBFCs) or other financial intermediaries for purposes of on-lending to the tiny sector, was included within the definition of priority sector for bank lending.

- A National Programme for Rural Industrialisation was announced, with a mission to set up 100 rural cluster every year, to give a boost to rural industrialisation.
- Inclusion of cotton yarn in the general excise exemption Scheme of SSIs.

The government policy on the whole has adopted a two-pronged approach. On one hand, the reserved items for SSIs are being increasingly opened up. This allows the existing units to enhance their economic viability by setting up an efficient plant size. In addition, it provides them opportunities for strategic alliances with major players. On the other hand, the government policy has focused on enhancing the investment ceiling of existing SSIs, credit availability, improving the infrastructure and facilitating technological upgradation. The coming years will testify whether the adopted approach is sufficient for improving the condition of the SSIs.

5.14 ORGANIZATIONAL FORM OR OWNERSHIP PATTERN

Before starting the industry or business, decide on the form of the business organisation at the time of launching the enterprise. This depends upon a number of factors, namely :

1. Nature of business activity and size of business.
2. Extent of control desired.
3. Tax burden.
4. Extent of capital investment.
5. Degree of liability acceptable, etc.

During the earlier years when the policy for promotion of the small-scale sector was evolved it was believed that the sector would mainly consist of partnership and proprietary undertaking. But today it is not. Now many small-scale units all registered as private or public limited companies under Indian Companies Act, 1956. In numbers they may be few but their share in the assistance (subsidies, loans, etc.) appears to be much greater. For various reasons entrepreneurs are opting for corporate form of organization. There are economic advantages in the new form and the managements can have far more flexibility of operation with reduced risks. This is, therefore, a preferred form. In administrative processing of applications it is not uncommon to see a built-in bias in favour of the new form over the proprietary or partnership organizations. A corporate entity is different from the individuals who may own or control it. Under the situation it is necessary to ask if the small-scale sector should remain open to the organized corporate sector of the Indian industry or, should some alternative organizational form promoted. It is a question that needs proper debate.

Table 5.3 : *Ownership structure of SSIs.*

Ownership	First All India Census 1972-73	Second All India Census 1987-88	DC (SSI) Sample Survey 1992-93	Manf. Enterprise Survey 1994-95
Proprietorship	61.00	80.48	78.03	97.65
Partnership	35.00	16.84	16.03	1.86
Co-operative	0.70	0.29	0.38	0.00
Limited Company	3.00	2.11	3.78	0.00
Others	0.30	0.28	1.78	0.00
Not reported	0.00	0.00	0.00	0.49
Total	100.00	100.00	100.00	100.00

Source : SIDBI (2002)

FORMS OF ORGANISATIONS

The form of organization to be selected will have to be one of the following:

1. Proprietorship

Proprietary organization are individually operated and a great majority of small-scale industrial units fall under this category. The tiny sector units and small-scale units with low capital investment are run by single individuals. This is primitive type where there is no organizational structure. The proprietor himself carries on the business in his home with the assistance of his family members or close friends.

2. Partnership firm

The whole concept of partnership is to embark upon a joint venture and for the purpose to bring in as capital money or even property including immovable property. Once that is done whatever is brought in would cease to be the exclusive property of the person who brought it in.

Features of Partnership Firm

i) Agreement between partners

A partnership is essentially a contract between the partners and the right during the subsistence of the partnership is to get his share of profits from time to time as may be agreed upon among the partners and after the dissolution of the partnership or with his retirement from partnership of the value of his share is the net partnership assets as on date of dissolution or retirement after deducting liabilities and prior charges.

The partnership may be formed with two persons who are capable of entering into an agreement. A partnership cannot be created with minor. There is no maximum number of partners. However, no partnership consists of more than 20 persons.

3. Cooperative Society

Governed by the Cooperative Societies Act, 1919 or other State Acts, a cooperative society is an association of persons voluntarily joining together to run a business organization with a view to provide service to members and the society in general. Members contribute the capital required and share the risks and benefits. A society has a separate legal entity with the limited liability of its members. The membership is voluntary and the functioning is on democratic lines through a managing committee elected by the general body of members.

4. Hindu Undivided Family (HUF)

This Act suits the traditional family business carried on by a 'Karta'. It is recognized as a separate legal entity.

5. Companies

The small-scale industries may also be incorporated as companies complying with the provisions of the Companies Act, 1956. Incorporation is the act of conferring judicial personality on a group of associated persons.

A company can be private or public depending upon the following:

i) A private company should have a minimum of two and maximum of fifty members while a public company should have a minimum of two members and there is no limit on maximum.
ii) There is a restriction on transfer of shares for a private company but not for a public company.
iii) A private company is to use "Private Limited" while a public company only has "Limited" as part of its name.
iv) A private company cannot float shares / debentures for subscription.

a) Private Company

A private company is one which -

i) Restricts the rights of transfer of shares.
ii) Limit the number of members to 50 excluding the present and past employees who continue to be members of the company.
iii) Prohibits invitation to the public for subscription of shares or debenture of the company.

The company should have minimum paid up capital of one lakh rupees or such high paid up capital as may be prescribed by its articles. The company prohibits any invitation or acceptance of deposits from persons other than its members, directors or their relations.

b) Public Company

A public company means, a company which is not a private company (Amendment) Act 2000, subjecting to the following conditions also.

i) Has a minimum paid up capital of Rs. 5 lakh or scale higher paid up capital as my be prescribed.
ii) In a private company which is subsidiary of a company which is not a private company.

Every existing public company shall enhance the paid up capital within a period of two years from the date of commencement.

EXERCISES

Section A

1. Define small scale industry.
2. Define ancillary industrial undertaking.
3. Define village industry.
4. What do you mean by export oriented unit?
5. Define medium scale industry.
6. What do you mean by a proprietary concern?
7. What do you mean bya partnership firm?
8. Define a company.
9. Mention any two features of a private company.
10. Mention any two features of a public company.

Section B

1. What are the exclusions while calculating the value of plant and machinery to define SSI?
2. What are the main objectives of promotion of small scale sector?
3. What are the advantages of promotion of small scale industries.
4. Explain in brief the deficiencies in small scale sector?
5. What are the general measures to solve the problems of SSI?
6. What are the basic features of the reservation policy of SSI?
7. What are the assumptions of industrial policies of govt. of India?
8. Distinguish a private company and a public company.

Section C

1. Discuss the deficiencies in small scale sector.
2. Discuss in brief the different forms of organisations.
3. Discuss the importance of small scale industries.
4. Discuss in brief problems of SSI.
5. Discuss the strategies to solve the problems of SSI.
6. Discuss in brief the government policies to SSI.
7. Discuss in brief the government assistance and concessions to SSI.
8. Discuss in brief the different forms of organisations.

SKILL DEVELOPMENT

1. Visit a SSI unit problems faced by them.
2. Find out the latest Government Policies, Assistance and Concessions to SBI.

6

Enterprise Creation

STRUCTURE

6.1 Starting a Small Industry
6.2 Entrepreneurial Function or Process of Starting a New Venture Based on Personal Competencies
6.3 Requirements to Start a Business Venture
6.4 Business Incubators

6.1 STARTING A SMALL INDUSTRY

Entrepreneurship plays an important role in the formation of small enterprise. Small-scale sector is very important in a country like India. Many of the small enterprises are run by entrepreneurs who started them in various ways, they are:

1. **Starting a business afresh:** Commencing the business from scratch, based on own product/service or ideas.
2. **Buying an existing business:** Purchasing a business previously started and run by someone else.
3. **Buying a franchise:** Starting a business or product/service whose rights are owned by someone else.

Once it is decided by the entrepreneur to start the business venture, he should move towards future activities in setting up the unit. It is the stage of taking concrete actions to establish the unit.

This chapter has been classified into three parts as follows:

I. Entrepreneurial process for starting a new venture based on personal competencies.

II. Requirements or steps involved in starting a business venture. This includes:
   a) Location
   b) Clearances and permits required, licensing and registration.
   c) Feasibility of the project to understand market, technical, financial feasibility, etc.

III. Business incubators.

6.2. ENTREPRENEURIAL FUNCTION OR PROCESS OF STARTING A NEW VENTURE BASED ON PERSONAL COMPETENCIES

As an entrepreneur, a person performs a number of functions. Entrepreneurship is the spirit of an enterprise. The relationship of the entrepreneur and enterprise is that of a soul and body. The former provides direction and energy whereas the latter processes the input and output so, entrepreneurial function is the process of starting a new venture by an entrepreneur. An entrepreneur performs this function based on personal competencies. The following are the various entrepreneurial functions. Each process has been explained below:

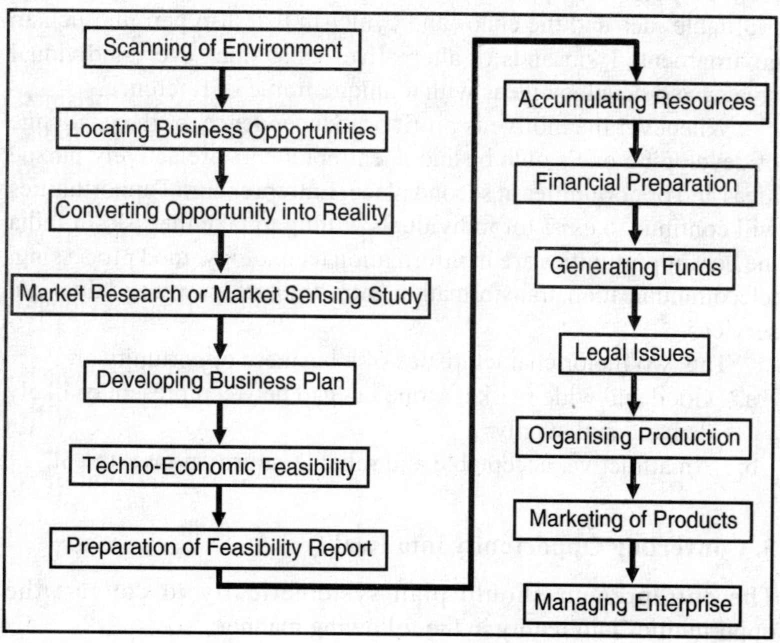

6.3. ENTREPRENEURIAL FUNCTION OR PROCESS

Entrepreneurial function is the process of starting a new venture by an entrepreneur. An entrepreneur performs this function. The following are the various entrepreneurial functions.

1. Scanning of Environment

Environmental scanning refers to the efforts an entrepreneur uses for examining the external and internal environment before making a decision on a new environment, governmental regulation and detailed evolution of industry to analyses industry characteristics, barriers to entry and competitive analysis.

2. Locating Business Opportunities

Free enterprise is the economic basis for all entrepreneurial activity. This means that any individual is free to transform an idea into business. The opportunities for potential entrepreneurs are unlimited. The constantly changing economic environment provides a continuous flow of potential opportunities if an individual can recognize a profitable idea and the chaos and cynicism that also permits such an environment. Thousands of alternatives exist since every individual creates and develops ideas with a unique frame of reference.

Whenever the motive is profit or independence, or the challenge of developing one's own business, entrepreneurs are actively pursue ideas and opportunities at second place. Entrepreneurial opportunities will continue to exist for individuals willing to take the risk. In India the best opportunities are in information technology, food processing, telecommunication, transformation, infrastructure, power and financial services.

The two major characteristics of a business opportunity are:

a. Good and wide market scope i.e. gap between present or likely demand and supply.
b. An attractive, acceptable and reliable return on investment.

3. Converting Opportunity into Reality

The entrepreneur should plan systematically to convert the opportunities into reality in the following manner:

1. Through creativity and innovative ideas, products and services.
2. By collecting necessary information about the perceived opportunity.
3. By acquiring technical and other required skill from organizations like small industries, service institute, the Khadi and Village Industries Commission, State Electronics Development Corporation, State Women's Development Corporation etc. or from private institutions.
4. By evaluating business opportunities through SWOT (Straights Weakness, Opportunities and Threats) analysis rigorously. This is a method, which compels entrepreneurs to think or reason out systematically and analyzing the important facts of strengths, weaknesses are always related to the individual or an organization interested in a business. Opportunities and threats are usually related to the outside environment.

4. Market Research or Market Sensing Study

Market research involves gathering of information about a particular market, followed by analysis of that information. Before the commencement of business, the entrepreneur should determine who will need your product or services, why they will be willing to buy them, characteristics of customers, who are your competitors, at what price the customers are willing to buy, feasibility to introduce the product in a particular location, etc.

5. Developing Business Plan

The entrepreneur has to prepare a written document that details the proposed venture is called business plan. It gives current status, expected needs and projected results of the new business. Every aspect of venture i.e. marketing research and development, manufacturing, management etc., A description of all of these facts of the proposed venture is necessary to demonstrate a clear picture of what venture is, where it is projected to go, and how the entrepreneur proposes to get there. The business plan is entrepreneur's road map for a successful enterprise.

6. Techno-Economic Feasibility

The success of an enterprise depends upon the entrepreneur doing the right thing at the right time. Starting a new enterprise is a very challenging and rewarding task. An entrepreneur has to take numerous decisions, right from the conception of a business idea, up to the start of production. Hence the identification of a project to be undertaken, requires an analysis of the project in depth. Therefore, an techno-economic feasibility of the project has to be conducted before preparing a feasibility report of the project for raising funds.

7. Preparation of Feasibility Report

Preparation of a feasibility report is a difficult task for an entrepreneur. The main purpose of the report is to provide information that is required for the project appraisal. This report would enable the financing agencies to purposefully evaluate the project before extending financial assistance. It contains background information about industry and enterprise, product characteristics, market position and trends, manufacturing process, cost of manufacturing, financial data etc.

8. Accumulating Resources

An entrepreneur operates in a competitive environment. In order to compete effectively, the entrepreneur must allocate resources efficiently. Three kinds of resources are available to the entrepreneur. They are human, material and financial.

9. Financial Preparation

In the process of arranging for resources financial planning is given importance. It focuses on:

a. Preparation of financial statements i.e. Balance sheet, income statement and cash flow statement.
b. Preparation of operating budgets.
c. Break-even analysis and ratio analysis as profit planning tool.

10. Generating Funds

Once the financial preparation, market research, estimated cost of production is ready in other words, business plan is complete, the entrepreneur has to obtain or arrange for required resources at right time and from the right place. Entrepreneur can obtain sources of funds from the following.

1. Personal source.
2. By issue of shares.
3. By raising loan (debt) from commercial banks or financial companies.
4. Venture capital from venture capitalists that are primarily investors.
5. Development of financial institutions like Industrial Development Bank (IDBI), Industrial Financial Corporation of India (IFCI) and Industrial Credit and Investment Corporation of India.

11. Legal Issues

Entrepreneur should have some knowledge about certain legal concepts that have implications for the business venture. Legal aspects that affect entrepreneurial venture may relate to:

1. Inception of venture.
2. Ongoing venture.
3. Growth and continuity of venture.

12. Organizing Production

Once the entrepreneur arranges the funds, he has to organize the production. Organizing production refers to making arrangements for purchase of machinery, appointment of workers, layout of plant, process planning etc.

13. Marketing of Products

Another important function of an entrepreneur is marketing of his product. Marketing includes of 4 P's i.e. Product, Price, Promotion and Place (distribution). Marketing is a comprehensive term and includes all set of activities necessary to direct and facilitate the flow of goods and services for the products to consume in the process of distribution. The entrepreneur should market the proper composition (4 P's). He has to decide the type of product, selling price, selection of promotion strategy i.e. personal selling, type of advertisement and media and distribution strategy i.e. channels of distribution and physical distribution system.

14. Managing Enterprise

The major role of an entrepreneur is to manage (all the above mentioned functions) money, material, production, labour, marketing, finance to ensure appropriate return on investment. Managing an enterprise is the most critical task for the future success of business enterprise. It is a great challenge to balance the activities of the organization and manage the growth. The survival and growth of a new venture require that the entrepreneur possesses both tactical skill and abilities.

After reaching the goal set by the entrepreneur, he should repeat the process to search for new opportunity for expansion and growth of the organization.

6.4. REQUIREMENTS TO START A BUSINESS VENTURE

Following are the basic requirements to start a venture:

1. Location
2. Licensing and registration
3. Feasibility of the project

6.4.1 Location

The location of a project is a very important factor. Normally, in small-scale projects the entrepreneurs are found to have a predetermined location. But there are several reasons because of which an entrepreneur may have to consider selection of location.

It is not enough to merely choose a location. It is necessary to select a site that suits the needs. Sometimes, the decisions are linked together. While selecting a location/site, it is necessary to give attention to criteria for selection and source of information.

6.4.2 Criteria for Location and Site Selection

For an entrepreneur, seeking to establish his own industry, the location of his unit is vital not only for the marketing or production considerations, but also for the commercial benefits available. Many entrepreneurs have thrived while others have failed because of the right/wrong choice of the location. Following are the factors to be considered for the selection of a location.

a) Basic Considerations

1. Location (city/town/village)
2. Population
3. Nearest large city (name and distance)
4. Connections to major cities (rail, road, air-distance, frequency)
5. Climate (minimum /maximum temperature, humidity, minimum/ maximum rainfall)
6. Distance from important geographical markets
7. Distance from major raw material sources and significance (or lack of it) of enterprise proximity to such sources
8. Distance and connection to relevant ports (in case of export/ import oriented enterprise)
9. Availability of manpower with required skills and prevailing wage rates
10. Overall industrial relations (strike/lockout/dispute) in the area
11. Law and order position in the area
12. Level of industrial development in the area and anticipated tempo
13. Composition of industrial development (in terms of types of industry and size/health of existing enterprises)
14. Proposed enterprise and govt. preference for types of industries at proposed location.
15. Whether readily built-up factory shed is available at the location and whether its size conforms to your need.

b) Physical Infrastructure Position

1. Land: availability and price
2. Existence of an organized industrial estate
3. Water supply : source (river, canal, tubewell), distance, quality (PH, hardness), rate, common storage facility, operating authority (Public Works Department, Estate-Corporation, Municipality)

4. Power supply: nearest substation, feeder type (industrial/rural) availability, quality of power, etc.
5. Effluent treatment and disposal (if relevant) : disposal point (land, sea, river), arrangement for treatment (individual, common), drainage arrangement for conveying the effluent (open, underground), treatment and conveyance charges
6. Approach road/internal roads
7. Street lighting
8. Responsibility for maintaining roads, drainage and street lighting (single or multiple agencies)
9. Annual maintenance charges

c) Commercial Infrastructure Position

1. Telecommunication (availability of new telephone connections, manual or automatic exchange, STD facility, telex facility, etc.)
2. Postal and telegram facility
3. Bank facility
4. Transport-operator facility
5. Weighbridge
6. Courier
7. Typing/photocopying
8. Warehousing
9. Proximity of offices of law-enforcing agencies (excise, sales tax, labour laws, factory inspection, pollution control, etc.)
10. Proximity of offices of industry-assisting agencies (State Financial Corporation, Industrial Infrastructure Corporation, raw material/marketing corporation, District Industries Centre which sanctions and disburses financial incentives)
11. Building/electrical/fabrication contractor facility
12. Shops for building material, spare parts and such other things.
13. Motor-rewinding, painting, gas-supply and such other industrial services
14. Technical, educational facility (e.g., industrial training institute, polytechnic)
15. Professional resource position (management/industrial consultants, financial/legal advisers, management/productivity associations).

d) Social Infrastructure Position

1. Housing: availability, quality, price (ownership and rent), public housing (actual and planned housing by State Housing Board, infrastructure corporation or such other agencies)
2. Education: primary, secondary and university education facility (quality, number of seats, ease of admission, medium of instruction)
3. Health: dispensary, hospitals, specialties
4. Recreational facility: cinema, restaurant, library, parks, etc.
5. Hotel accommodation
6. Service organization: Rotary Club, Lions Club, etc.

e) Financial Incentive Position

1. Investment subsidy (central govt./state govt.)
2. Income tax concession
3. Sales tax exemption/interest-free sales-tax loan
4. Promotor's contribution (margin) and interest-rate policy followed by State Financial Corporation
5. Octroi-exemption, electricity-duty exemption, local-tax exemption and such other incentives.

f) Site-specific Considerations

1. Vantage or otherwise location (e.g., on the highway), frontage, approach, etc.
2. Whether the proposed site is a part of an organized industrial estate
3. Direction of town-growth with reference to the site
4. Non-agricultural status of the site
5. Site-contours (levelled, hilly, pits, ravines, brick-kilns)
6. Site-shape (regular/irregular)
7. Immediate proximity to railway line, national highway, state highway*
8. Overhead telephones or power lines or underground water/ drainage/ gas line passing through the site*
9. Access to national/state highway or other roads provided by the state

10. Wind direction in relation to the site#
11. Soil-type+

Note:

* This may imply leaving out some portions of a plot for building purpose.

\# In India, normal wind-direction, except during winter, is north-south. If there is a dense population concentration in south, a factory involving gas/smell emission may cause a problem.

\+ Loose soil may increase construction cost.

Information Sources on Location

The information on locations or sites can be obtained from the following sources:

1. Industrial estate officials
2. Local authority officials
3. Revenue department officials
4. State Electricity Board
5. Public Works Department
6. Office-bearers of local industry associations
7. Knowledgeable personal businessmen residing at the location
8. Officials in banks/State Financial Corporation
9. Officials in District Industries Centres
10. Landowners, residents of nearby villages, towns, local Rotarians, etc.
11. Real estate agents.
12. Web Sites

Identify just two or three locations and then select a few possible sites at each of these locations. Next, compare these locations or sites according to the requirements.

Thus, the above mentioned considerations will help to judge how sound the location is or site decision and what are the strengths or weaknesses of the closer location or site.

6.4.3 Licensing and Registration—Government Procedures and Formalities

Licensing

A licence is a written permission issued by the government to an industrial undertaking stating such details, the geographical location of the industry, the article to be manufactured and other related particulars.

Objectives of Licensing

1. To limit industrial capacity.
2. To direct investment in industries according to plan priorities.
3. To regulate the location of industrial units so as to secure a balanced regional development.
4. To prevent both monopoly and concentration of wealth.
5. To protect small-scale industries against undue competition from large-scale industries.
6. To promote technology and economic improvements in industries by ensuring units of economic size and adopting modern processes.
7. To encourage new entrepreneur to start industrial units. Thus, widening the entrepreneurial base.

Licensing and Registration Procedure

Any entrepreneur who wants to start an industrial unit, no formal permission is needed from the government for this purpose. Industries employing less than 100 workers and having fixed assets less than Rs. 10 lakh need not obtain any licence under the industries development and regulation act.

However, small-scale industries have to confirm to the rules and regulations prescribed by the state or local authorities under the Factories Act.

Powerlooms do not come under the purview of the SSI.

Types of Registration

Registration are of two types, they are as follows:

1. Provisional registration
2. Permanent registration

Provisional Registration

Industries are issued a provisional SSI registration certificate for a period of one year.

Provisional registration is required to apply for the following:

1. A shed in an industrial estate or a developed land in an industrial area.
2. Corporation or municipalities for other licences
3. Power connection
4. Financial assistance from banks.

Permanent Registration

Certificate will be issued when an industry has commenced production process.

6.4.4 Procedure or Formalities for Obtaining Statutory Licence

In the post-liberalization period, the Government intends to reduce the nucleus of permissions or clearances required for the project, in a bid to attempt to free the industry from excessive bureaucratic controls.

The new industrial policy of 24 July 1991, industry licensing was abolished for all project except in 18 industries where strategic or environmental concerns are paramount or where industries produce goods with exceptionally high import content. With this nearly 80 per cent of the industry has been taken out of licensing framework.

However, to avail certain facilities, it is necessary to undertake necessary formalities. For setting up a small-scale unit, consider the sequence of formalities as listed below.

1. Small-scale Industry Registration

Small-scale industry registration is not compulsory. But as a practical compulsion, it is advisable to get the unit registered as small-scale unit with the District Industries Centre (DIC) of the district in which the project is proposed to be located. This registration is required by the Government for record purposes to plan for the future requirements of the industry and for getting loan from banks and financial institutions.

2. Sanction from the electricity company or board

Compulsorily get the sanction from the electricity boards for company. It is not required if the enterprise can be operated without power.

3. Industry-specific approval

These apply to selected industries like food, drug, etc.

4. Registration under Factories Act

This depends on the manpower size. The purpose is to ensure good general working conditions.

5. Shops and Establishment Act

This applies to almost all enterprises. Controls working time and employer-employee relationship.

6. Sales Tax registration

In the matter of levy and collection of taxes by the individual states in the Indian Union, a revolutionary step has been taken with the introduction of Value Added Tax (VAT) instead of the sales tax system with effect from 1-4-2005. Registration under sales tax or VAT is compulsory even for the small-scale industry.

7. Certificate of Boiler Inspectorate

This approval is required depending on the equipment used in the unit.

8. Pollution Control Clearance

The entrepreneur should also apply for obtaining a no-objection-certificate (NOC) from the State pollution control board depending on the type of industry he wishes to set up. If the industrial unit is likely to be a pollution hazard or may discharge effluents, the pollution control board issues NOC after stipulating certain conditions to install the facilities to control pollution.

9. Building Plan Approval

This is compulsory for the construction of an industrial unit from the local authority.

10. Acquisition of Infrastructure Facilities

If the entrepreneur plans to locate the unit (project) in one of the industrial estates promoted by the Government agency, he may apply for a ready built-up shed or plot of land. Once the shed is offered, he can start with production activities. In case of allotment of a plot, he can start building once the building plans have been approved. In either of these cases, after allotment, he has to apply to power to state electricity board as well as for water to the concerned authority.

11. Registration of Firm or Incorporation of Company

Simultaneously, the entrepreneur should also decide on the Constitution of the business, namely, whether it should be a proprietorship, a partnership or a private limited company. The decision would largely depend upon the size of the operations and the degree of risk involved. Having decided the constitution of the business, he may now undertake necessary formalities such as registration of partnership firm, incorporation of private limited company.

12. Import-Export Formalities

If you plan to import any item of capital goods or raw materials, you need to know the provisions of the current import policy of the Government of India. Similarly, if you propose to undertake the export of your products, you need to know the current export policy of the Government of India and accordingly, you are required to undertake certain formalities. The information on current policy of import and export can be had from the publication "Export-Import Policy" and the information on the procedural part is available from the "Handbook of Procedures on Exim Policy" published by the Ministry of Commerce, Government of India. Further, assistance in this matter can also be availed of from the regional offices of Director General of Foreign Trade situated in your state. In addition, concerned Export Promotion Councils also offer help in undertaking these formalities. There are certain states which have also established State Export Corporations in order to help the small-scale industries to undertake export of various items by way of preparing documents and administering export formalities. If such an organization exists in your state, you may avail of their assistance. For example, Gujarat has set up an Export Promotion Council at the state level to undertake export of their products to different countries of the world.

6.4.5 Important Labour Legislations

Anyone running an industry, shop or commercial establishment would do well to know the important features of the undermentioned acts and rules:

1. The Factories Act, 1948 and rules framed by the States flowing from the Act.
2. Shops and Establishment Acts.
3. Payment of Wages Act, 1936.
4. Minimum Wages Act, 1948 and State Government notifications.
5. Payment of Bonus Act, 1965.
6. Employees Provident Fund Act, 1952.
7. Employees State Insurance Act, 1948.
8. Employees Deposit Linked Insurance Scheme, 1976.
9. Payment of Gratuity Act, 1972.
10. Workmen Compensation Act, 1923.
11. Contract Labour (Regulation and Abolition) Act, 1970.
12. Industrial Employment (Standing Orders) Act, 1946.
13. Maternity Benefit Act.
14. Industrial Disputes Act, 1947.

6.5 FEASIBILITY OF THE PROJECT

After obtaining the above clearances, the entrepreneur should apply for term loan either to the state financial institutions or to a commercial bank, with a techno-economic feasibility report including market survey as well as documentary evidence justifying the claim. After the sanction is received, he may have to execute necessary legal documents mortgaging the assets.

The Entrepreneur now is required to prepare the feasibility report covering all activities listed below and the resources needed for the project. Chapter 7 deals in detail with the preparation of feasibility report or a 'Business Plan':

1. The background of entrepreneur and the constitution of business.
2. Market potential and market strategy
3. Selection of location.
4. Requirements of land and building.
5. Manufacturing process.
6. Requirements of plant and machinery
7. Requirements of utilities.
8. Requirements of raw materials
9. Estimated cost of the project
10. Proposed means of finance
11. Cost of production and profitability
12. Cash flow statement
13. Break-even point (BEP)
14. Internal Rate of Return (IRR)

6.6. BUSINESS INCUBATORS

In some places it is possible for a new venture to use an incubator approach in getting started. Business incubator is a facility with adoptable space that small businesses can lease on flexible terms and at reduced rents. Support services like financial, managerial, technical and administrative are available and shared, depending on the size and nature of tenants needed. Most incubators limit the amount of time, ranging from two or five years, a small business may occupy space in the facility.

The basic purpose of an incubator is to increase the chances of survival for new start-up business.

Types of Incubators

Four types of incubators exist and objectives of each type tend to vary.

1) Government sponsored

These incubators are organized by the Government organizations or departments.

2) Non-Profit sponsored

These incubators are organized and managed through associations, chambers of commerce, etc. Area development is the major objective of non-project sponsored incubator.

3) University or Academic Institutions

Most of them are considered science and technology incubators. The major goal of university related incubators is to transit the findings of fasten research and development into new products and technologies. Some of the academic institutions like IIMs are also acting as business incubators.

4) Privately Sponsored

These incubators are organized and managed by private firms or companies or cooperations. The major goal is to make profit.

Kinds of Services Offered

Most incubators provide the following kinds of services:

1. Project Report Preparation
2. Additional information and access to various types of financial and technical assistance.
3. Sharing equipment and services that would otherwise be unavailable or unaffordable. Such services are typically divided into three major categories:
   a) Offices and communication services such as typing, photocopying and phone answering.
   b) Business services such as business planning and financial management.
   c) Facilities and equipment services, including a reception area, conference rooms and computers.
4. Provision of an environment where small businesses are not alone, thereby reducing the anxiety of starting a new venture, etc.

Annexure–I

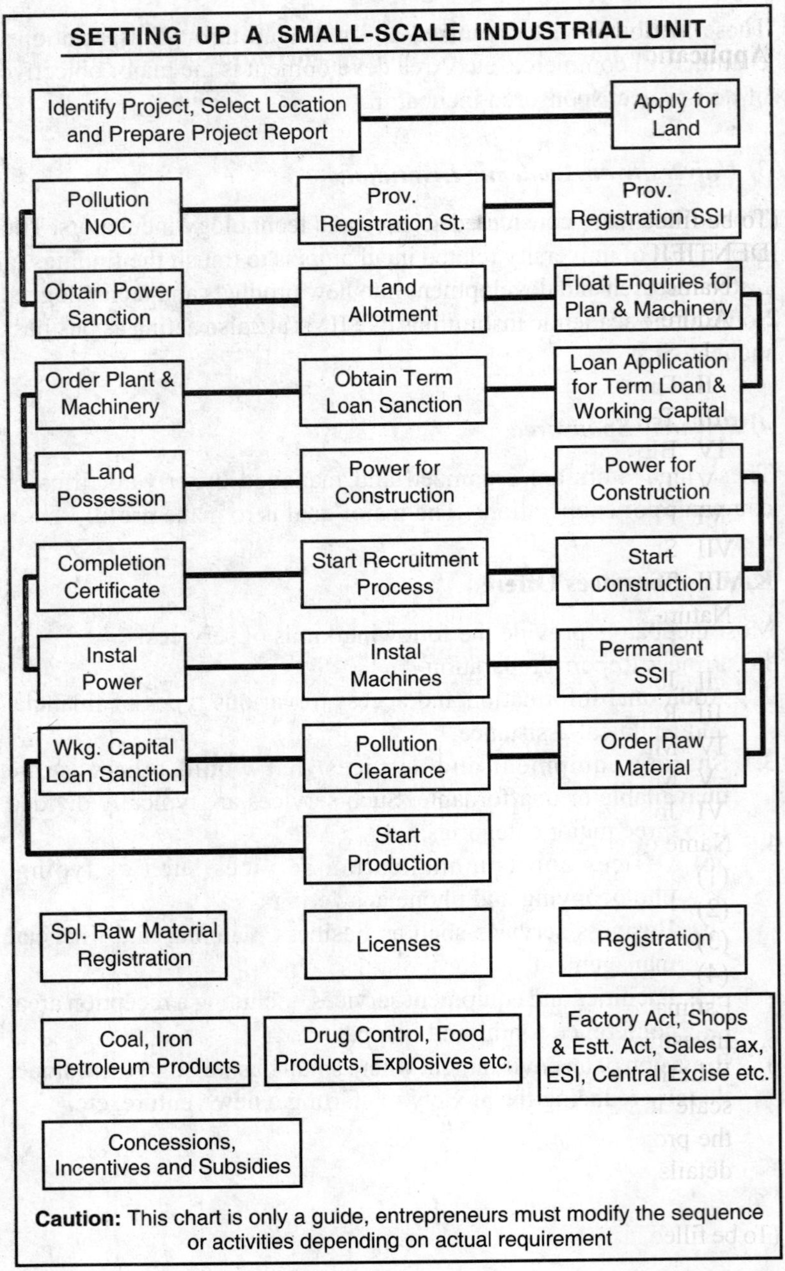
SETTING UP A SMALL-SCALE INDUSTRIAL UNIT
Identify Project, Select Location and Prepare Project Report
Apply for Land
Pollution NOC
Prov. Registration St.
Prov. Registration SSI
Obtain Power Sanction
Land Allotment
Float Enquiries for Plan & Machinery
Order Plant & Machinery
Obtain Term Loan Sanction
Loan Application for Term Loan & Working Capital
Land Possession
Power for Construction
Power for Construction
Completion Certificate
Start Recruitment Process
Start Construction
Instal Power
Instal Machines
Permanent SSI
Wkg. Capital Loan Sanction
Pollution Clearance
Order Raw Material
Start Production
Spl. Raw Material Registration
Licenses
Registration
Coal, Iron Petroleum Products
Drug Control, Food Products, Explosives etc.
Factory Act, Shops & Estt. Act, Sales Tax, ESI, Central Excise etc.
Concessions, Incentives and Subsidies
Caution: This chart is only a guide, entrepreneurs must modify the sequence or activities depending on actual requirement

Annexure–II

Application Form For Provisional Registration As Small-Scale Industry

PART-I

(To be filled in by all categories of Applicants)
IDENTIFICATION PARTICULARS

1. Name of the Unit:
2. Address:
   I. State ____________________
   II District ____________________
   III Tehsil/Taluka
   IV Block/Municipality
   V Town/Village
   VI PIN (Code)
   VII Street and Bldg. No.
   VIII Telephone No.
3. Nature of Industrial Activity:
   I Manufacturing (wholly)
   II Job Work (wholly)
   III Repairing/Servicing (wholly)
   IV Manufacturing and job work
   V Manufacturing and repairing/servicing
   VI Job work and repairing/servicing
4. Name of articles to be manufactured:
   (1) ____________________
   (2)
   (3)
   (4)
5. Estimated requirement of power (Annual)
6. Investment in machinery and equipment (proposed)
7. Whether any large/medium scale industry has interest in the proposed units, if so, give details.

KW

Rs H.P.

SIGNATURE........................

(To be filled in by applicants requiring indigenous scarce raw materials)

PART-II

1. Scare indigenous raw material required for production for one full year (approx).

	Item	Qty.	Value.
(1)			
(2)			
(3)			
(4)			

2. Details of machinery & equipment with value. Indigenous/ Imported

	Description	Qty	Value
(1)			
(2)			
(3)			
(4)			
(5)			

3. Proprietor/any or all of the partners/any or all of the Director own / having any interest in any trading firms dealing with materials same as those required in this scheme.

Date: SIGNATURE

(To be filled in by applicants requiring scarce and imported raw materials into Part-I and Part-II)

1. Imported raw materials required for production for one full year (approx).
2. Detailed scheme for the products to be manufactured in the enclosed proforma.
3. Specify the required plinth area for machine working, raw material and finished product stocking and the availability of the same.
4. Whether the product is for industrial purpose or consumer one.
5. Value added to the product (gross output value of raw materials and fuels).

6. Local availability of skills required to manufacture and in the State.
7. Competition in the line of manufacture locally and in the State.
8. Operation-wise flow chart for the products locally and in the State.
9. Demand prospect for the products state or country
10. Registered partnership deed/ memorandum of Articles of Association (to be produced).
11. Biodata of proprietor partners/directors and their permanent addresses.
12. Technical and/or managerial background of proprietor/partners/directors.
13. Their experience relevant to the line of manufacture.
14. Reputed suppliers of machinery and their address for the machinery required in the project.

Date: SIGNATURE

Declaration

We hereby declare that the following records will be maintained in the manner decided by the Import Trade Control Policy/Industries Commissioner or his nominee and kept at the premises for the manufacturing activity and will be made available for inspection by the officers of the industries department on any working day failing which the registration granted is liable for suspension for a period to be specified by Industries Commissioner.

1. Raw materials register
2. Finished products register.
3. Attendance register.
4. Sales-Tax registration and sales-tax payments
5. Register for yearly return.
6. Bill Books.

I/We also hereby declare that if this registration is given, the raw materials and components procured by this unit against import licence/

release order/State and Central quota will be utilized only for the manufacture of products specified in the registration certificate will be unstilted only for the manufacture of products specified in the registration certificate and no portion thereof will be sold or permitted to be used by any other party or diverted without the permission of the appropriate authority.

I/We hereby declare that information furnished in the above pro-forma are true and correct to the best of my/our knowledge. I/We fully understand that the registration granted to me/us on the basis of the information furnished is liable for cancellation in addition to any other penalty that the Industries Commissioner may impose or any other action that may be taken, having regard to the circumstances of the case, it is found that only of the statements of facts therein are incorrect of false.

I/We declare that the information given above is true to the best of my/our knowledge and belief.

I/We hereby inform that if according to rules, it becomes necessary for me/us to obtain the permission of Water Pollution Control Board, we shall obtain the same prior to getting permanent Small-Scale Industry Registration Number and shall submit the same to the General Manager, DIC

Signature of Applicant.

NAME AND ADDRESS

(To be filled in by the interviewer)

1. Type of legal organization
2. Social status of the entrepreneur. Educated Unemployed/Graduate Engineer/Technician/Artisan/Trader Ex-serviceman/Retired Civilian Scheduled Caste and Scheduled Tribe.
3. Past experience in the line, if any.

Signature of Interviewer

PRO FORMA REQUIRED FOR THE DETAILS OF THE SCHEME

I. INTRODUCTION

II. BRIEF DESCRIPTION OF PROCESS OF MANUFACTURE AND RAW MATERIALS

III. ASSUMPTIONS MADE IN CALCULATING THE COSTS.

(a) Number of working days per annum and number of hours per day.

(e.g., 25 days 8 hours)

(b) Approximate time required for completion of one unit of manufactured.

(e.g., 21/2 to 5 %)

© Approximate estimate of wastage in production.

(e.g., 21/2 to 5%)

IV. CAPITAL INVESTMENT:

(a) Factory and Office accommodation

(b) Machinery and Equipment

(i) Indigenous (item and cost)

(ii) Imported (item and cost)

© Working Capital:

(i) Raw materials

(ii) Wages

(iii) Miscellaneous, etc.

V. ESTIMATES FOR PRODUCTION PER ANNUM

(a) Raw materials :

(i) Indigenous (quantity and cost)

(ii) Imported (quantity and cost)

(b) Wages of Staff and labour

© Power requirement and cost

(d) Other items of expenditure (including interest) and depreciation.

VI. DEMAND AND SALES OUTLOOK

(Details in brief).

SIGNATURE.....................

Annexure–III

APPLICATION FORM FOR FINAL (PMT) REGISTRATION AS SMALL-SCALE INDUSTRY

PART-I

(To be filled in Duplicate)

(1) Name (Block letter)

(2) Registration No. (To be filled in by the applicant) (To be filled by D.I.C.)

Provisional Permanent

Number Provisional Permanent

Date Date

(Factory) (Office)

(3) District

(4) Tehsil

(5) Town

(6) Street/Bldg. No.

7. Fixed investment (a) Plant and machinery (b) Other Fixed assets

8. Employment Supervisory
Others

9. Nature of activity

Manufacturing/job work/Servicing/Repairing/Processing
(Strike out whichever not applicalbe)

10. Registration number
(Units Factories Act if any)

11. Reg. Number under
Shop & Establishment Act

12. Central Excise Number

13. Sales Tax Number

14. Year of Establishment | Main Source of Energy

15. Capacity

a) Manufacturing   b) Others

Sr No.	Item	Code	Annual Capacity Qty.	Value	Detail Job work Servicing Repairing Processing

16. Date of commencement of Production

17. Type of legal organisation*

18. Type of Entrepreneur (Code for social status)*

19. Whether Ancillary Unit? Yes/No

20. Whether Exporting Unit? Yes/No

21. Names of Proprietor/Partner or Board of Directors & their address (Document in Original to be produced) ____________

22. Name of the Chief Executive ____________

23. Other registration (if any) ____________

24. Employment

Supervisory	Skilled	Semi-skilled	Others	Total	Self-employment

*To be filled in by D.I.C.

25.	Fixed Investment (In case of rented Building, Building cost will be 150 times the monthly rent.)	Item	Capital Rs.
		Land & Building	
		Machinery & Equipment	
		Others	
		Total	
26.	Working Capital	Borrowing	(1) Long term Rs.
			(2) Short term Rs.

27. Electricity/Water/Coal etc. Required/Consumed.

Item	Unit	Required		Consumed	
		Qty.	Value (Rs.)	Qty.	Value (Rs.)

28. Particulars of important machinery and testing equipment having bearing on capacity

Sr. No.	Description of machinery installed	Specification	Approved Value Rs.

29. Raw Material

Sr.	Item	Estimated requirement for production of one full year Qty. Value (Rs.)	Actual consumption during the period Value (Rs.)
	(a) Imported		
	(b) Indigenous		

30. Exports (if applicable)

    (a) Are your products being exported? Yes/No.

    (b) Registration No. if registered exporter

    (c) item and value of exports as per yearly return enclosed (Fill in Appendix-II also if exporting)

31. Ancillary units (Fill in Appendix-I)

    (a) Whether registered/proposed to be registered as ancillary unit.

    (b) Registration No. (if any)

32. Type of organisation

    (1) individual proprietorship

    (2) Partnership-Joint family

(3) Partnership/others

(4) Public Ltd. Co.

(5) Private Ltd. co.

(6) Public Corporation/Special Act of Parliament/State legislature.

(7) Co-operative Society.

DECLARATION

In addition to the declaration given in the application for provisional registration, I/We hereby declare that I/We will continue to submit yearly reports (as per appendix-III) of the raw material received/ utilized, stock in hand/production and sales to the Industries Commissioner in triplicate regularly within three months after the end of the financial year. Failure to submit such returns within this prescribed period will constitute adequate ground for refusal to sponsor my/our application raw material etc.

Date Signature of the proprietor/partner

PART II

(to be filled in by D.I.C.)

1. Social status of the entrepreneur
2. Past experience in the line, if any, (particulars furnished by unit verified)

Permanent Registration Signature of the representative of the Director of Industries

Number PMT

Granted/refused for the following reasons.

General Manager

District Industries Centre,

_______________ District.

Appendix–I

(To be filled in by Ancillary Units only)

Investment ______________________________

Nature of activity ______________________________

Total annual turnover ______________________________

Quantum of Turnover as ancillary ______________________________

Name of parent unit	Value	Percentage of total turnover	Agreement of long term supply	As piecemeal sub-contract

Date

Signature

Appendix–II

(To be filled in by Exporting Unit only)

1. Name and Address of the Unit ______________________________
____
____

2. Date and No. of SSI Registration

Number				PMT				Date	

3. Name of items exported ______________________
4. Percentage of exports to total production ______________
5. Countries to which exported ______________________
6. Direct or indirect exports? If indirect give details ________
7. Testing facilities for items exported ______________
8. Whether a member of any export promotion council/exports inspection houses give details ________
9. If exporting for the first time attach copies of export enquiries received if any ______________

Date Signature

(This declaration is to be given by the unit who has not taken provisional registration) I/We hereby declare that the following records will be maintained in the manner decided by the Import Trade Control Policy/the Industries Commissioner or his nominee and kept at the premises for the manufacturing activity and will be made available for inspection by the officers of the Industries Department on any working day, failing which the registration granted is liable for suspension for a period to be specified by the Industries Commissioner.

1. Raw materials register.
2. Finished products register.
3. Attendance register.

4. Sales-tax registration and sales-tax payments.
5. Register for yearly return.
6. Bill Book.

I/We also hereby declare that if this registration is given, the raw materials and components procured by this unit against import licence/ release order/State or Central quota will be utilized only for the manufacture of products specified in the registration certificate and no portion thereof will be sold or permitted to be used by any other party or diverted without the appropriate authority.

I/We hereby declare that the information furnished in the above proforma are true and correct to the best of my/our knowledge. I/We fully understand that the registration granted to me/us on the basis of the information furnished is liable for cancellation in addition to any other penalty that the industries Commissioner may impose or any other action that may be taken, having regard to the circumstances of the case, if it is found that any of the statements of facts therein are incorrect or false.

I/We hereby undertake to submit yearly reports of the raw materials received/utilized stock on hand/production and sales to the Directorate of Industries in triplicate. Failure to submit this returns regularly by the end of the year will constitute adequate grounds for refusal to sponsor applications for import/allocations of raw materials etc.

I/We declare that the information given above is true to the best of my/our knowledge and belief.

Signature of the Applicant

Appendix–III

Proforma to be filled in by Unit to get Declared as small Ancillary Unit (Whose Investment on Machinery and Equipment Exceeds)

(To be submitted to the Director of Industries and copy to the SISI in the State)

---

1. (i) Name and address of the Unit :
   (ii) Date of establishment (for existing units :
2. Type of organisation (proprietary, partnership or private limited company and their names) :
3. SSI Registration number of the State Directorate of Industries :
4. Total investment in machinery and equipment :
   (i) Existing (purchase value)
   (ii) Proposed, if any
5. Details of machines and their capacity (Detailed list to be enclosed) :
6. Details of ancillary supplies during the year preceding registration if any :

Sr. No.	Name of the items	Actual production during the year	Detail of supplies	Supplied as percentage of total	Type of contract long/piece term meal
Parent Unit	Supplied	Qty. Value	Qty.	Value production	

7. Relationship, if any of the proprietors/partners to : Parent units

Signature of applicant with designation

(FOR USE IN DIRECTORATE OF INDUSTRIES OFFICE)

I: Certified that the capital investment on machinery and equipment of M/s ________________ is Rs. ________ (Rupees________________________ only).

For Director of Industries

(For Use in SISI Office)

II. Recommendation on technical competency/ production capacity :

Director, SISI

EXERCISES

Section a

1. Mention the different ways an entrepreneur can start his business.
2. What is a feasibility report?
3. What do you mean by Business Incubators?
4. What do you mean by 'Licensing'?
5. Mention the two types of Registration.
6. Mention the Purpose for which the Provisional Registration certificate is used.
7. What do you mean by permanent registration?

Section B

8. What are different types of incubators?
9. What are the different types of services provided by an incubator?
10. What are the objectives of licensing?

Section C

11. Explain in brief the various entrepreneurial functions.
12. Explain in brief the basic requirements to start a venture.
13. Explain in brief the formalities obtaining a starting licence.

SKILL DEVELOPMENT

1. Fill up the provisional registration form.
2. Fill up the final registration from.

7

Business Plan

STRUCTURE

7.1 Introduction
7.2 Meaning
7.3 Benefits of a Business Plan or a Project Report
7.4 When the Business Plan is to be Prepared?
7.5 How Long should the Business Plan be?
7.6 Composition of a Business Plan or Detailed Project Report
7.7 Guidelines or Steps for the Preparation of Business Plan
7.8 Common Pitfalls or Common Errors in the Preparation of Business Plan
7.9 Precautions

7.1 INTRODUCTION

Each year many fail and business owners see their dreams of success shattered. One important reason why such situations arise is that business owners do not plan carefully before they start to operate. They assume that they can learn as they go on with their business, but they find that problems get accumulated if not solved diligently. If these kinds of results are to be avoided, a business plan should be formulated.

7.2 MEANING

1. A business plan is "the road map for operating the resources to meet the goals and for operating the business and measuring progress a long way".

2. A business plan is "an outcome of an exercise meant to check the viability of an enterprise and analyse and firm up its essential parametres".
3. Business plan is "a document which provides answers to questions which are important for setting up an enterprise and then running it well".
4. A business plan is "a document which provides flesh and blood to a business idea". It focuses on the following:
   a) Steps or decisions an entrepreneur need to take prior to the business becoming operational. It gives indirectly and in brief things to be done in the initial period.
   b) Expected performance of the business.

There are various phrases used to refer to Business Plan document. They are:

i) Project Report
ii) Feasibility Report
iii) Techno-economic Feasibility Report
iv) Viability Report.

Business plan, therefore, is a summary of what an entrepreneur hopes to accomplish by being in business and how the entrepreneur intend to organize the resources to meet the goals.

The business plan may be prepared either by the entrepreneur or he can take the help of a consultant. But a well-perceived, well-made project report or business plan by the entrepreneur himself is helpful to him while running the industry. This is because, the process of preparing the project report/business plan enables him to interact with realities of the future when he actually implements the project. It is a "drill", a good training before jumping into a venture. Therefore, even he decides to take the help of a consultant, he must involve himself in the preparation of business plan or feasibility report.

7.3 BENEFITS OF A BUSINESS PLAN OR A PROJECT REPORT

The major benefits of a business plan are:

1. Helps in Reducing an Emotional Bias

The systematic approach for completing a business plan forces one to think thoroughly about the pros and cons of a business idea it helps in making decisions on whether to start the business or not.

2. Helps to Test One's Commitment

A business plan helps as a tool for measuring commitment of the people involved in it. It helps in measuring the commitment by oneself and by others who intend participating in the proposal before they actually join the proposal. Thus, commitment of an individual is vital for the success of any business venture.

3. Helps One to Develop a Consistent Strategy

A well prepared business plan in an impressive document, which tells the reviewers such as lenders, suppliers and prospective investors, both about the business and its profit potential. It serves to give them the required confidence that the proposer understands the business and the idea is viable.

4. Helps in Testing the Idea on Paper

By spending the time on the preparation of a business plan it helps to find out the major mistakes on the paper itself. It is a cheaper and easier way to correct before the implementation of the business plan.

5. Provides SWOT Analysis

A business plan provides a SWOT analysis, wherein the strengths, weaknesses, opportunities and threats involved in the plan are indicated.

6. Helps to Judge Viability and Profitability

It helps an entrepreneur to judge the viability and profitability of the prospective enterprise. If it reveals that proposal will be unviable, the entrepreneur will avoid a grave mistake of investing in an unprofitable venture.

7. Basis for Financial Assistance

A systematic approach in detailing a business plan enables the entrepreneur to convert the exciting ideas into a reality. The entrepreneur can justify the viability of the project and can receive support of others by providing good reasoning for the ideas and plans.

7.4 WHEN THE BUSINESS PLAN IS TO BE PREPARED?

For the preparation of business plan, a considerable amount of effort and expenditure is needed. Therefore, the entrepreneur should undertake only after fulfilling the following conditions.

1. He has already gathered preliminary information on the enterprise proposal.
2. He is confident of viability of the proposed enterprise.
3. He finds the proposal so exciting as to commit himself to a full-scale business plan investigation.

Once a potential entrepreneur has made a tentative decision of exploiting a specific opportunity, he has to prepare a detailed project report (DPR) or a business plan. A thoughtfully prepared project report or business plan is an important tool as it helps an entrepreneur in anticipating and solving problems. In the preparation of detailed project report or business plan, the entrepreneur has to consider several financial and implementation problems well in advance.

7.5 HOW LONG SHOULD THE BUSINESS PLAN BE?

There is no hard and fast rule as to the correct length of a business plan. The nature of the business operation may affect the amount of information to be included; whether it is a new business or an expanding one is another factor. The main objective of the business plan is to present the business or its future prospects as concisely as possible. At the same time, the plan has to cover all the important key issues.

7.6 COMPOSITION OF A BUSINESS PLAN OR DETAILED PROJECT REPORT

The business plan is a written document consisting of the following:

1. Assumptions or Estimates

The Business Plan consists of estimates of production, sales, raw material consumption, manpower needs, prices, etc.

2. Projections

It consists of the financial, production, sales, etc. projections for a certain period.

3. Information

It provides information on technology, competition, price, etc.

4. Calculation

It shows the calculation of costs, profitability, cash flow, etc.

5. Documents

Business plan or Detailed Project Report (DPR) also provides supporting documents for machinery and raw materials price, quotations, constitutional information such as partnership deed, documents for infrastructural needs like, land, building, land title, lease deeds, rent deeds, etc.

It is the basis on which a bank or any financial institution sanctions long-term financial assistance and working capital assistance.

6. Helps to Judge Risks

It educates the entrepreneur regarding device of risk underlying the enterprise proposal.

7. Helps to look at the Project Objectively

It enables the entrepreneur to look at the proposal objectively and encourages him to search for solutions with reference to pitfalls in his proposals.

8. It helps to identify the customers, market area, pricing strategy and competitive conditions under which entrepreneur must operate to succeed. This process often leads to the discovery of a competitive advantage or new opportunity, as well as deficiencies in the business plan.

9. First Impression is the Best Impression

A well-organized business plan makes it much easier for the lender or investor to assess the financing proposal and to assess the entrepreneur.

Thus, business plan is essentially future-mapping. It is difficult to anticipate what is likely to happen to an enterprise in distant future. Besides, a small entrepreneur is concerned mainly about near future. In view of this, eight years is the longest span of time for which projections are made under business plan for small enterprises.

7.7 GUIDELINES OR STEPS FOR THE PREPARATION OF A BUSINESS PLAN

While undertaking a detailed process of a business plan, it is necessary to take decision on various aspects of a business plan. They are as follows:

1. Decision on the basic project parametres.
2. Decision on Market Feasibility (Collection of Information and Analysis).
3. Decision on Technical Feasibility.
4. Decision on Financial Viability.
5. Economic Feasibility
6. Human Resources Aspect/Consideration
7. Social Aspects/Consideration
8. Implementation of schedule

7.7.1. Decision on the basic project parametres

Basic Parametres

While undertaking a detailed business plan or detailed project report, it is necessary to decide the following basic parametres of the project.

1. Project size or capacity of production.
2. Product-Range (Ex: TV, VCR, etc.)
3. Product mix (i.e., determining the relative importance of individual products in the expected product programme).
4. Product-Standard or Features. (Ex. Branded or unbranded and cheap or expensive product).
5. Target-market (i.e., type of customer in a particular geographical area).
6. Technology Choice (i.e., technology used in the production).
7. Positioning of an Enterprise: positioning the enterprise with a distinctive strength of the enterprise.

The above-mentioned basic project parametres are decided on the basis of the following considerations.

1. Overall Investment Limit.
2. Minimum Economic Viable Size.
3. Competition
4. Fiscal / Monetary Incentives.
5. Market Promotion Expenditure
6. Non-technical issues affecting production i.e. number of working days in a year and working hours per day.
7. Market prospects, technical capabilities and financial resources to determine product range.
8. The end product use and specifications, production capacity, financial resources, cost of manpower, equipment availability, technical competence of entrepreneur, raw material availability, etc. influence technology choice.

7.7.2 Decision on Market Feasibility (Collection of Information and Analysis)

After taking decision on basic parametres of the project, the attention should be given towards the market for the product. For this the information should be collected from the market through a market study and data should be analyzed.

I. Collection of Information

Market information is normally collected through a market study or market survey.

i) Market Study

Market study is usually focussed on gross market demand both for the present and the future. It highlights the gap between expected market demand and supply in respect of a given product. The gap may be positive or negative.

The market success is an outcome of favourable demand-supply gap as well as effective marketing programme.

Benefits of Market Study

Market study will help in the following ways:

a) It helps to evaluate the viability of an enterprise.
b) It will enable to cross-check the decision on production scale.
c) It provides preliminary information and insight to formulate marketing strategy and market related issues like product features, packaging, price, credit policy, discounts, method of selling, location, number of dealers, sales force size, expenditure of advertising, etc.

Stages of Market Study

Market study has three stages. They are:

a) Determining information needs.
b) Collecting information.
c) Analyzing collected information and arrive at conclusions.

a) Information Needs

The following information must be sought in the market study.

a) Product and segments.

b) Level of demand, its determinants, price and related matters.
c) Competition.
d) Distribution, trade practices and promotion.
e) Government policy.

b) Sources of Information

The information may be collected in terms of primary data and secondary data. Primary data is collected directly for some specific purpose from customers, dealers or salesmen, etc. through survey, observation, experimentation, etc.

Approaches for Collecting Information

There are two approaches to collect information:
They are,
i) Exploratory-cum-Desk Research (EDR).
ii) Detailed Market Research (DMR).

i) Exploratory-cum-Desk Research (EDR)

In this method, the entrepreneur has to meet various persons, read relevant information through news and features and try to arrive at answers to questions. Thus, the EDR means the following:

1) Locating published and unpublished material and reading it.
2) Interviewing customers, producers of machinery, raw material suppliers, middlemen and others.
3) Correspondence/phone calls.

ii) Detailed Market Research (DMR)

The following are the steps for the collection of information under the detailed market research.

1. Determination of market survey objectives.
2. Determination of information needs.
3. Collect information on target population.
4. Sampling.
5. Developing a questionnaire.
6. Questionnaire trail.

7. Selection of questionnaire administration method.
8. Ground work for physical survey i.e., recruitment of investigators, getting enough copies of questionnaire, etc.
9. Actual survey through personal interviews or mail.
10. Supervision to choose questionnaire administration work is called out properly.
11. Screening completed questionnaires.
12. Tabulating responses and analysis of data using statistical tool.

c) Analysis of Information

After collecting the above information it is necessary to analyse the information using the following tools. They are:

1. Simple Statistical Tools: like, percentages, weighted average, frequency distribution, etc.
2. Trend Analysis : The tool is used to analyse the rising or declining trend over a period of time.

7.7.3 Decision on Technical Feasibility

After taking the basic decisions like product-range, target market and product features, it is necessary to take decision on technical feasibility or arrangements i.e., financial matters associated with the following technical issues.

a) The Production

1. The manufacturing process of the product to be produced.
2. The sources of technical know-how.
3. Reliability of arrangement for technical know-how.
4. The requirement of plant and machinery or equipment.
5. The detailed specification of the plant and machinery or equipment.
6. Availability of plant and machinery.
7. Comparison and evaluation of suppliers of plant and machinery.
8. Selection of suppliers of machinery.
9. Plant and machinery procurement and erection schedule.

b) The Layout

10. Work out where exactly each facility like productions, raw material storage, individual machines, packaging, finished goods storage Adminstration and quality control departments will be located.
11. The space for each of the above mentioned departments.
12. The distance between one facility to another.
13. The flow of production process.
14. The space required for material handling and the manpower requirement.

c) Raw Materials

15. Identify all raw materials required for production of proposed product.
16. Ascertain the price of the raw materials.
17. Ascertain the credit-period with the suppliers, etc.

d) Packaging

18. Check the form and cost of packing.

e) Land Requirement

19. Requirement of land and built-up area.
20. Cost of land and building.
21. The special features of the built-up area or factory building.

f) Manpower

22. Number of employees required for the purpose of production (workers), supervision (technicians) and administration and sales etc. (staff), with their background, experience and their skill.
23. Sources of employees and their pay taking into consideration the minimum wages act, statuatory wage rate and market rate to calculate worker cost.

g) Location

24. Select the site that suits/ location the needs.
25. Compare these sites or location as per the requirements.
26. Ascertain the cost of site, etc.

7.7.4 Decision on Financial Viability

The main purpose of financial viability is as follows:

1. To find out how attractive or otherwise, the project is, from the financial angle.
2. To find out whether financial institutions are likely to accept the project by extending a term loan or working capital loan.
3. To find out how much money is required to set up the project and where it will come from.

Major Components of Financial Viability

1. Project cost.
2. Means of finance.
3. Capacity utilization and income estimate.
4. Expenditure estimate.
5. Profitability estimate.
6. Cash flow estimates
7. Risk analysis.

1. Project Cost

It should be noted that this exercise is a forecast or projection. The estimate of income, expenditure and profit for each is done separately. The number of years of projection size and the expectations of financial institutions prevailing in practice is a minimum of 5 years and a maximum of 8 years for small and medium-sized projects in India.

Project cost is the cost of establishing or investment required to set up an enterprise.

Elements or Components of Project Cost

1. Land and site or location development
2. Building and civil works
3. Plant and machinery
4. Other fixed assets
5. Technical know-how fee
6. Preliminary and pre-operative expenses
7. Working capital margin
8. Contingency and escalation

Individual elements of project cost have been given below:

a) Land and Site Development

- Cost of land.
- Land-related legal charges.
- Levelling and filling charges.
- Approach/ internal road construction charges.
- Fencing/compound wall charges
- Cost of gates.

b) Building and Civil Works

- Factory building.
- Office, godown and such other structures at project site.
- Well, tank, silos, garage at project site.
- Sewer, drainage.
- Architect's fee.

c) Plant and Machinery

- Price of machinery.
- Excise-taxes, freight, packing, transit insurance and octroi in respect of machinery.
- Stores/spares bought along with machinery.
- Foundation and installation cost.

d) Other Fixed Assets

- Furniture.
- Office equipment.
- Miscellaneous tools and equipment.
- Vehicles.
- Equipment, cabling for distribution of power.
- Laboratory equipment.
- Workshop equipment.
- Firefighting equipment.
- Effluent collection, treatment and disposal arrangement.
- Boiler.
- Diesel generating set.
- Other assets.

e) Technical Know-how Fees (Training Cost Included).

f) Preliminary and Pre-operative Expenses.

- Firm-floatation (Company registration, etc.)
- Feasibility report.
- Capital raising.
- Salary and administrative cost during implementation period.
- Rent, rates, taxes during implementation period.

- Travel cost during implementation period.
- Interest during implementation period.
- Insurance expenses in respect of loan.
- Trial production cost.
- BIS, Pollution Board and Explosive Licence, etc.
- Statutory deposits.
- Processing fees of FI.

g) Working Capital Margin.

h) Contingency and Escalation @10% of to IV)

The estimates are, in no of way, binding on the entrepreneur in terms of actual business decisions.

So, the entrepreneur has the liberty to change selling price, change method of depreciation, etc. from the business plan or project report.

2. Means of Finance

To meet the project cost an entrepreneur requires finance. Sources or means of finance can be from any of the following avenues :

a) Term Loan : Depending on the project cost, commercial banks or state financial corporation or state-level industrial development or national finance institutions can give the term loan.

b) Subsidy : An outright grant given by the State Government if an entrepreneur sets up a project in a backward area. A proportion of the cost of fixed assets is given. The proportion depends on the location and project scale (small and medium scale).

c) Equity Capital : It is the money which is raised from own sources (promoters) or from others i.e., general public. In a small enterprise, it is not likely that others contribute money.

d) Deposit or Private Loan or Quasi-Capital : This is not a common source for a small or new enterprise. The private loan is an unsecured loan from private lender (unless mortgage some personal assets or personal guarantee for its payments).

e) Deferred Payment Guarantee (DPG) : This is a means of financing the machinery. Initially an entrepreneur pay on portion of the machinery amount, then, the balance amount is paid in instalments over a period. DPG agency guarantees machinery supplier that it will pay the instalments when there is non-payment by the entrepreneur. Many foreign suppliers of machinery offers DPG facility through a Bank.

f) Special Assistance : Special Assistance can be received only if the entrepreneur is a woman or scheduled caste or scheduled tribe entrepreneur or an ex-serviceman intending to set up a business or setting up a very small project.

g) Venture Finance : Finance provided on the projects which are risky by certain agencies is known as venture finance. In example, Technology Development and Information Company of India (TDICI) an ICICI-sponsored company) Bangalore, Gujarat Venture Finance Corporation, Ahmedabad, etc. They do not follow the conventional definition of the project cost. They give money even for advertising and promotion for technology improvement, working capital, etc. if necessary even after implementation of the project. There recovery is linked to the performance of the project. They are almost partners both in case of profit and loss. But they stop monetary help after a few years.

Working Capital and Working Capital Margin

Working Capital : After establishing an enterprise, the money is required for raw materials, wages, electricity, etc., for the day-to-day operations is known as working capital. Portion of the total working capital requirement is given by banks and other financial institutions.

Working Capital Margin : The portion of the initial working capital requirement which will not be provided by the banks is called working capital margin. This way working capital margin is included in the project cost.

3. Capacity Utilisation and Income Estimates

The project cost, working capital and means of finance tell how much a project would cost and where the money comes from. But it is now necessary to assess how viable (profitable) the project is. For this purpose it is necessary to make further calculations or assumptions on capacity utilization, income and expenditure estimates.The enterprise in the initial years, in most cases does not work at 100% capacity level (installed capacity). This is due to the following reasons:

a) It takes time to win customer-confidence and build the volume of business.

b) Competition in the market.

c) Technical troubles i.e., not being able to produce as per the rated capacity.

d) Non-availability of raw materials.
e) Infrastructural bottlenecks. For example, power failure, manpower problem, etc.

Therefore, the projected production and income depends on installed capacity and actual capacity utilization of each year for a period of 8 years estimate of financial performance is calculated. Combine the production (capacity utilization) estimate and selling price assumption in order to arrive at the income estimate.

4. Expenditure Estimate

Expenditure estimate can be broadly classified in:
a) Cash expenses.
b) Non-cash expenses.

a) Cash Expenditure Estimate

The estimate of various cash expenditure is done using the relevant basis. They are as follows.

Cash Expenditure Estimate

Expenditure	Basics for Estimate
1. Raw materials.	1. In proportion to quantity of production.
2. Stores, consumables.	2. Actual production quantity.
3. Packing materials.	3. Proportionately related to production quantity.
4. Power, fuel and utilities.	4. Number of units produced.
5. Wages and salaries.	5. Partially related to production quantity.
6. Repairs and maintenance.	6. Higher expenditure on plant, building, etc.
7. Rent, taxes, insurance.	7. These are incurred irrespective of production quantity.
8. Administrative expenses.	8. These are incurred irrespective of production quantity.
9. Selling expenses.	9. Salaries of salesmen, advertising as fixed expense and dealer commission as variable as per sales quantity.
10. Interest on term loan.	10. Outstanding loan.
11. Working capital loan.	11. Depends on working capital on equipment.

b. Non-cash Expenditure Estimate

The following are the non-cash expenditure:

i) Depreciation.
ii) Amortization of preliminary expenses.
iii) Writing-off of technical know-how expenditure.

5. Profitability Estimates

To judge how profitable a small enterprise is, three ratios are recommended.

a) Capital Turnover Ratio: It shows annual income in relation to the project cost. It indicates the limits of profitability.

b) Profit Tax Ratio : It is the profit before tax to turnover ratio. This ratio indicates profitability of enterprise-operations.

c) Return on Investment Ratio : Investment here means project cost. The return on project cost is to be estimated.

6. Cash Flow Estimates

The enterprise must generate enough cash (Inflow of cash), so that the outflow of cash are met and is able to build up financial strength to undertake expansion or diversification. It is essential during implementation period as well as during the first eight years.

7. Risk Analysis

The profit estimates may go wrong as there is always an inherent risk in any business. So, it is necessary to judge the risk involved. There are two methods to judge risk. They are :

a) Break-even Analysis.
b) Sensitivity Analysis.

7.7.5 Economic Feasibility

Economic factors have to be taken into consideration while preparing a business plan or feasibility report. Economic considerations include:

1. The entrepreneur should identify the market potential in terms of current demand and projected future demand for the product.

2. The entrepreneur must consider the cost and project at different price levels.
3. The entrepreneur must analyse the strength, strategies, etc. of the competitors.
4. Data relating to general economic trends such as per capita income, level of consumption, expenditure, etc. have to be considered.
5. Data relating to price structure, discount patterns and sources of market information have to be collected.

7.7.5 Human Resource Aspect/Consideration/Feasibility

The entrepreneur has to analyse the managerial competence of the enterprise. It includes the key personnel i.e., management team, board of directors, executives, number of skilled workers, administrative staff required for the enterprise. For this purpose an appropriate organisation structure is to be decided.

7.7.6 Social Aspect/Consideration

Social aspect of a business plan means the source commitment of the enterprise towards the people and the community at large. It includes:

1. Maintenance of quality of the product.
2. Reasonable price or fair price of the product.
3. Ethical marketing approach.
4. Fair return on capital
5. Paying the tax obligations and following the rules and regulations of government.

7.7.7 Implementation of Schedule

It is almost end of the preparation of a business plan. Therefore, prepare a timetable for implementing the business plan to speed up the process of establishing the enterprise systematically.

Implementation of the timetable is not completely in the hands of entrepreneur. Because it depends on others for various things like loan, electricity, building plan approval, and so on. Therefore, provide for a margin while estimating time.

7.8 COMMON PITFALLS OR COMMON ERRORS IN THE PREPARATION OF A BUSINESS PLAN

After chalking out the business plan carefully, there is unlikely to make mistakes. But, there are so many entrepreneurs who make mistakes. It is important to keep these mistakes in mind and avoid committing in the preparation of a business plan. Some of the common errors committed in the preparation of a business plan are as follows:

1. Planning versus Plan

Business plan is made for various purposes. It is for understanding, term-loan sanction, working capital loan sanction, etc. There is a tendency to project the enterprise-performance in an optimistic manner and to hold back its negative features from the lending agencies. Some entrepreneurs get so preoccupied with producing a document acceptable to the lending agencies that they neglect the actual planning.

2. Capacity Utilization Estimates

Over optimistic and simplistic assumptions with reference to utilization of installed capacity is a pervasive feature of business plans made by beginners. There are so many entrepreneurs who assume 80% capacity utilization in the first year, 90% in the second year and 100% in the third year. The assumption is made in complete disregard of existing enterprise-performance, market conditions, competition-level and possible technical snags. The business plan, in such a case, is reduced to financial jugglery. It may be exciting to make such assumptions and derive satisfaction from financial performance projection. But then, the projection is based on a completely false premise.

3. Normally the actual project cost will be far more than the one estimated in the business plan. But, there are entrepreneurs who make very tight estimates. Particularly, working capital and preliminary or pre-operative expenses are underestimated. Obviously, profitability calculations go wrong.

4. Inadequate Working Capital Margin Money

As a result of an underestimated project cost or sanction of inadequate working capital loan or rise in working capital requirement (raw material prices may go up), the actual working capital margin requirement turns out to be far more. You have a first class enterprise ready, but not enough money to take it off the ground. It is frustrating. So, there must be adequate reserve (money) to meet the rise in the working capital requirement.

5. Means of Finance

There are entrepreneurs who rely excessively on others. They assume that loan-amount by SFC or bank will not reduce. They do not grasp the financing norms fully. They expect more assistance than what they actually receive. Then the problems begin. So, be conservative in the estimation of financial assistance from others.

6. Cash Flow during Implementation

Money is required at the time of implementation of the project. Normally, the cash flow is planned on a quarterly (3 months) basis. But if there is any delay in the disfusement of loan, the whole implementation plan is dissolved. Therefore, plan the cash flow on a weekly or fortnightly basis and organize the cash in such a way that a few weeks delay in cash receipt does not affect the progress of work.

7. Performance in the Initial Period

The entrepreneurs should have the patience as they are likely to face problems in the initial years. It is not enough to be prepared psychologically. Financial preparation is very essential. Normally, the business plan forecasts what would happen at the end of the year (profit or loss). But it is necessary to give attention in planning for the quarter or for six months.

8. Selling Price

Selling price for estimation in the business plan may be different from the actual selling price at the time of implementation of project.

9. Unconvinced Entrepreneur

Sometimes, even after the completion of viability exercise, the entrepreneur is not sure whether it is a sound business or not. Under such circumstances, the entrepreneur must decide to proceed cautiously and it is good to be aware of risks.

10. Business Plan

There are entrepreneurs who take the business plan completely at face value. They forget that it is a document primarily to help to judge whether to pursue a business idea or not. There may be some deviations. The entrepreneur must concentrate on making a plan work rather than worrying about deviations. So, switching over from business plan to business management is crucial.

11. Other Errors

11. Not providing sufficient contingency provisions.
12. Not providing cushion for fixtures, electrification, etc.
13. No getting all relevant and up-to-date information and supporting documents.
14. Over enthusiastic estimate for income and optimistic estimates about expenses.

7.9 PRECAUTIONS

Following are the precautions to be taken care of by an entrepreneur at the time of preparation of a business plan:

1. Always estimate the cost to be higher and income is less than anticipated.
2. Do not put any cost/price unless it is checked and verified this information personally.
3. Do not take any data directly from some other project report without updating them.
4. Do not consider full utilisation capacity in the first year itself.
5. Prepare the project report yourself.
6. Counter-check all calculations, like cost of project, etc.
7. Do not hesitate to take advice or opinion of other experts.
8. Consider the implementation time. The time when you prepare the report and the time when you implement the project would differ. Therefore, make necessary escalation provision for this purpose.

ANNEXURE–I

BUSINESS PLAN : THE KEY QUESTIONS

Following are the key questions to be assured before preparing Business Plans:

Product, Features, Capacity, Uses

1. What are you going to make?
2. What size/specifications-legal or commercial- will your product have?
3. On what scale will you make it? How many days in a year and how many hours per day will your enterprise operate?
4. What are the various uses of the product?

Market Prospects, Selling Price and the Cost of Selling

1. Who are the customers?
2. What is the present supply position?
3. What are the market prospects?
4. What kind of competition you are likely to face?
5. How much do you expect to sell during the first couple of years?
6. What price do you expect to realize in the initial years?
7. What arrangements should one make for selling the product?
8. How much will these cost?

Production Process and Technical Arrangement

1. Are there alternative production processes? Which one would you choose? What would be your source of technical know-how?
2. Do you expect any difficulty in terms of mastering production technology? If yes, how long will it take you to master it?

Plant Machinery, Suppliers and the Cost

1. What machinery/equipment would you need for production?
2. What support-equipment like boilers, electrical installations, quality-control equipment, effluent-treatment equipment would you require?

3. How much will each of these machine produce?
4. Will any machine remain idle or become a bottleneck in achieving the final output quantity?
5. Who are the suppliers of the machinery?
6. What would be the prices of the machinery?
7. How long will the suppliers take to deliver the machinery?

Location

1. Where will you locate the project?
2. What are the advantages / disadvantages of the chosen location?

Infrastructural Facilities

1. How much land would you need?
2. How much built-up area would you require?
3. Are there any special features of the factory-shed?
4. How much electricity, water, fuel, steam would you require?
5. What arrangements have you made to get these?
6. How much would the inputs mentioned in point No. 4 cost?

Raw Materials and Other Requirements

1. What is the requirement in terms of raw materials, stores, consumables and packing materials?
2. Are they easily available?
3. Who are the suppliers?
4. What is the price? How volatile is the price? Does it change according to the season?

Manpower

1. What is the manpower need (skills, number)?
2. How easy is it to get manpower?
3. What salary / wage would they be paid?

Working Capital

1. What is the amount of money required, once your enterprise is set up, to keep the business running?

2. What is the bank-policy regarding working capital assistance for such business?
3. How much working capital assistance from the bank do you expect?

Project Cost

1. What will be the total cost of establishing the enterprise?

Means of Finance

1. What are the various sources from which money will be raised to meet the project cost?
2. How much money will be raised from each source?

Capacity Utilization and Income Estimate

1. What will be, year-wise, expenditure on account of production, sale and administration over next 5 to 8 years?
2. What will be the non-cash and interest expenditure, year-wise, during such period?

Profit and Tax

1. What will be the profit before tax, year-wise, over next 5 to 8 years?
2. What will be the tax liability?
3. Is the expected profit enough to:
   - Repay the term loan?
   - Bring you an attractive return on your investment?

Risk Analysis

1. What are the risk factors of the enterprise?
2. How risky is the enterprise?

Other Questions

1. What are the government policies regarding this particular business?
2. What government clearances/approvals do you need?
3. How long will it take you to establish the enterprise?

ANNEXURE–II: CASE STUDY

A LIVE BUSINESS PLAN OR PROJECT REPORT OF SAFE ELECTRO CONTROLS

Table of Contents

1. Introduction

1. The industry
2. Utility to society
3. Employment generation
4. The product
5. Its usage

2. Administration and Management

3. Market Feasibility

1. Sales and Marketing

4. Technical Feasibility

1. The location and land and building
2. Scale of operation
3. Labour
4. Production
5. Raw materials
6. Machinery and equipment
7. Water and power
8. Transport and other infrastructural facilities
9. The production process

5. Financial Viability

1. Promoter's contribution
2. Interest and repayment of loan
3. Rent, salaries, purchases, labour, contingency,
4. Depreciation, bank interest, profit
5. Project cost
6. Revenue analysis for the first year
7. Cash flow for the first year

Conclusion

I. INTRODUCTION

India is also one of the countries where the voltage is not stable. This causes a lot of damage to electric equipment. Here, the need arises for a device which can protect these equipment.

i) The Industry

The voltage stabilizer manufacturing industry has now become a 700 crore industry and is also growing at a pace of 20-30% yearly. Due to the globalization, liberalization of the economy and the transformation of the middle class, the purchasing power of the consumer has increased tremendously. It is of use to almost everybody. Its demand is huge and is not affected by vagaries of season.

Till date, the manufacture of Electronic Voltage Stabilizers is by and large in the unorganized sector. Safe enterprises intends to create a very professional and organized manufacturing facility.

ii) Utility to Society

As mentioned earlier every household today requires the basic appliances like the television and the refrigerator. It has become a necessity at present in every home.

The unit has an immense advantage to the consumer. The society today are buying appliances for their homes as required and are hoping for these to last. What the consumer gets somehow does not match what he is looking for. Due to great voltage fluctuations their electrical goods get damaged.

A voltage stabilizer safeguards these appliances by adjusting the current to the requirements. Therefore, giving it a longer life.

iii) Employment Generation

For a long time in India, employment has become a major issue especially for those who cannot afford to get a degree. The unit is looking at providing employment to workers who are skilled.

iv) The Product

The product manufactured is a voltage stabilizer which stabilizes the electricity to fixed current. Electrical power that drives any equipment/ machine needs some regulation.

Specifications

- 150 VA
- Working range-Input 175 to 275V
- Output 200V to 250 V
- Voltage cutoff above V
- Mainly used for televisions

The Main Component of the Product

Transformer

Device that transfers electric energy from one alternating-current circuit to one or more other circuits, either increasing (stepping up) or reducing (stepping down) the voltage. **Transformers** are employed for widely varying purposes, e.g., to reduce the voltage of conventional power circuits to operate low-voltage, devices, such as doorbells and to raise the voltage from electric generators so that electric power can be transmitted over long distances.

Transformers charge voltage through electromagnetic induction e.g., as the magnetic lines for force (flux lines) build up and collapse with the changes in current passing through the primary coil, current is induced in another coil called the secondary. The secondary voltage is calculated by multiplying the primary voltage by the ratio of the number of turns in the secondary coil to the number of turns in the primary coil, a quantity called the turns ratio. Air-core transformers are designed to transfer radio-frequency currents.

v) Its Usage

Electronic voltage stabilizers are used for regulating voltage fluctuating.

Stabilizers, being highly affordable, are used by every household, commercial establishment, factory, etc. to protect their electronic appliances such as television, refrigerators, V.C.R, computers, etc., from erratic power supply. A good voltage stabilizer is designed to withstand the most unstable power supply fluctuations and surges of voltages, especially when power fails. Safeguarding those possessions that make our lives easier calls for a high quality of protection. The stabilizers produced by the unit are built to provide that protection for years, so that the purchase of the stabilizer is looked upon as a good investment.

2. ADMINISTRATION AND MANAGEMENT

Nature of the firm	:	Sole Proprietorship
Name	:	Amrita Kumar
Address (Resi.)	:	28, Aga Abbas Ali Road A-3 Swapnalok, Bangalore-560042
Qualification	:	Bachelor's Degree in Engineering (BE)
Name of unit	:	Safe Electro Controls
Address	:	345 2nd cross, 6th main Whitefield road Bangalore-560 056.

3. MARKET FEASIBILITY

Sales and Marketing

The market study was conducted and it has revealed that there is sufficient demand for the product, not much competition, the government policies are suitable to launch this product in the market.

Therefore, the company has no problems related to marketing.

4. TECHNICAL FEASIBILITY

i) The Location

The unit is proposed to be located in Bangalore. It is easily accessible by all means of transport. Hence, carriage of goods, both raw materials and finished products is very smooth and prompt. Further, being easily accessible, availability of workers and labourers poses no problem whatsoever.

Address of the office

345 2nd Cross 6th main
Whitefield road
Bangalore 560056.

Land and Building

The area in which the factory building is proposed to be housed is about 2400 sq.ft.

The building will be taken on rental basis, and the monthly rent is estimated to be Rs. 10000/-p.m.

ii) Scale of Operations

The scale of operations is on small scale. The investment totals to an amount of seven lakhs. Wherein the entrepreneur put in a quarter of the project cost, which amounted to Rs. 1,75,000 and the rest of the amount which amounted to be 5,25,000 is procured in the form of a loan from a bank.

iii) *Labour*

The unit is highly labour intensive. Every aspect of the business is done with the help of human labour. Right from unloading the raw-materials to the loading of finished goods, human force is involved.

No. of shifts per day : 1 shift per working day
No. of working days per month : 25 working days per month

The overall labour requirement of the unit is as under:
Excluding the proprietor the labour comprises :

Post	Number of employees	Salary paid
Supervisor	1	3000
Skilled workers	5-2000/each	10000
Clerical staff	1	2000

Since the location of the unit is very ideal, labour availability is abundant and no shortage or other problem is foreseen.

iv) Production

Production of units 2008

- No. of units to be produced per day = 40
- No. of units per month = 1000
- Therefore the No. of units to be produced annually = 12,000

Production of units 2009 (Projected)

No. of units to be produced per day = 50
No. of units per month = 1250
Therefore, the No. of units to be produced annually = 15,000

v) Raw Materials

The manufacturing process involved is assembling and fitting of stabilizers.

The various items required are as under:

- Transformers - Type 15
- Cabinets
- Relays
- Mains Cords
- Switch and Socket
- P.C.B.

Consumables

- Screws
- Nuts
- Bolts
- Copper wire, etc.

The above materials are available locally and no problem is foreseen in this area.

Apart from the basic raw materials as mentioned above, packing materials like boxes, covers, etc. are also locally procured.

vi) Machinery and Equipment

The unit is highly labour intensive and is characterized by the absence of technologically advanced plant and machinery. The only machines used in the factory are testing boards and motors.

vii) Water and Power

Water is not needed at any stage of production. Power is used for running the motors. No other machinery is run on power as the entire manufacturing process is labour intensive. Hence, water and power is primarily needed only of sanitation and lighting purposes. It is pertinent to note here that with the advent of summer, power and water is always in short supply and adversely affects the performance and survival of many industrial units. But in this case, as the unit is not dependent upon water and effect on the unit.

viii) Transportation and Other Infrastructural Facilities

The raw material is procured by the supplier and is assembled and produced in the unit. Therefore, the transportation of raw materials is taken care of by the supplier and the unit need not bear the cost.

The unit manufactures stabilizers for a bigger industry. The transportation of the finished goods is taken care of by the buyer and thus the unit has no cost for transportation.

As already discussed, the unit is located in the city of Bangalore, which is considered one of the prime industrial centre of India. As such, all the infrastructural facilities including transportation needed by the unit is easily available.

ix) The Production Process

Raw-materials procured
The raw materials required for the manufacture of voltage stabilized is firstly procured.

↓

Assembled & Fitted as per Specification
The raw materials are then assembled as per the specification. Each person is specialized in assembling one component of the stabilizer

↓

Tested
The stabilizer is then tested to check if it works

↓

Quality control check
The product is then put through tough high-quality tests for performance under different operational conditions.
The product is then checked for it's quality. This is done to make sure that the quality is a per the specification of the company it is being supplied

↓

Put in plastic roll-up cover
After the entire manufacturing process the product is then put into plastic covers

Packed

↓

After putting the product into plastic covers it is then packed into boxes which increase the aesthetic value of the product

↓

Dispatched
Finally the product is dispatched to the buyer

5. FINANCIAL VIABILITY

i) Promoter's Contribution and Bank Loan

The entrepreneur proposes to contribute a quarter of the project cost, which amounts to 1,75,000. The entrepreneur proposes to procure the rest of the cost from a bank in the form of a loan, which amounts to 5,25,000.

ii) Interest and Repayment of Loan

The entrepreneur has been able to repay the loan in two years. The entrepreneur began her repayment of loan on April 2006, starting with every month.

Income Tax

Income tax is calculated at latest rates announced on 28th February 2006 by the Finance Minister on Budget day.

Equipment

The entrepreneur invested a total amount of 40,000 on equipment which includes, testing boards, work tables, storing cabinets, etc.

Rent

The rent deposit

The rent deposit has been computed as ten months with one lakh being deposited for the year. Subsequently monthly payments amount to ten thousand.

Salaries

No. of shifts per day	:	1 shift per working day
No. of working days per month	:	25 working days per month

As mentioned earlier, salaries are paid to total of seven staff members, namely, one supervisor, five skilled workers and one clerical staff, which amounts to a total figure of thirteen thousand.

Sales

Purchases are made entirely on cash basis. Payment is made immediately to the suppliers. Creditors outstanding is 0 months.

Labour

Labour and administration expenses are paid on monthly basis.

Contingency

Contingency provision relates to such expenses which are not expressly provided in the statements. It is provided for @ 5% of the total project cost.

Depreciation

Depreciation is calculated as per the Income Tax Provisions using Reducing balance method.

Bank interest

Bank interest is assumed to be 14%. The entire amount of bank loan of Rs. 5,25,000 is assumed to be required in the first couple of months.

Profits

The net profit earned during the year is ploughed back into the company except for the amount drawn for personal use.

PROFITABILITY STATEMENT
2006 (1000 Units)

	Per Unit	Per Month	Per Year
I. COST OF PRODUCTION			
a) Raw materials & Consumables:			
Type 15 Transformers	60		
Relays	16		
Cabinets	18		
Mains Cords	11		
Switch & Sockets	06		
P.C.B (assembled)	12		
Sundry items	15		

b) Labour Charges	13		
c) Packing Materials	05		
Total Cost of Production	156	1,56,000	18,72,000
Sales during the year	220	2,20,000	26,40,000
Excess of sales revenue over cost of production	64	64,000	7,68,000

PROFITABILITY STATEMENT
2007 (1250 UNITS)

	Per Unit	Per Month	Per Year
II. COST OF PRODUCTION :			
a) Raw-materials & Consumables :			
Type 15 Transformers	60		
Relays	16		
Cabinets	18		
Mains Cords	11		
Switch & Sockets	06		
P.C.B (assembled)	12		
Sundry items	15		
b) Labour Charges	13		
c) Packing Materials	05		
Total Cost of Production	156	1,95,000	23,40,000
Sales during the year	220	1,75,000	33,00,000
Excess of sales revenue over cost of Production	64	80,000	9,60,000

CONCLUSION

The following information that has been presented is the projected plan of action of the entrepreneur, who wishes to start her own manufacturing of voltage stabilizers. The background information, and current market trends that the subject has researched shows clearly that the market for voltage stabilizers has good scope for business.

The financials that have been projected show that the business venture is a profitable venture. The entrepreneur has shown that she will pay back the loan procured in two years which shows that the venture is profitable as well as financially viable. The break even period has been achieved.

This report discusses the various aspects of the project and the profitability of the unit. The various calculations or ratios and projected cash flows are made on the basis of constructive assumptions and which are viable.

EXERCISES

Section A

1. What do you mean by Business Plan?
2. Mention any four benefits of a Business Plan.
3. Mention any four purposes of a Business Plan.

Section B

1. What are the necessary basic parametres of a detailed Business Plan?
2. What are the processes of taking decision on market feasibility?
3. What are the matters associated with technical issues of a Business Plan?
4. What are the major components of financial viability?
5. What are the main elements of project cost?
6. What are the economic factors to be considered while preparing a Business Plan?

Section C

1. Explain in brief the guidelines for the preparation of a Business Plan.

SKILL DEVELOPMENT

1. Visit an organisation and find out how a business plan was prepared by them.
2. Prepare a feasibility report (BP) by either collecting information from the organisation or with imaginary figures.

8

Implementation of the Project
– Assistance to SSI
– Sources of Finance
– Incentives and Concessions

STRUCTURE

8.1 Introduction
8.2 Under the Government System
8.3 Financial Assistance
8.4 Outside the Government System
8.5 Source of Finance
8.6 Financial Incentive for SSI & Tax Concessions
8.7 Assistance for Obtaining Raw Materials

8.1 INTRODUCTION

The basic approach towards the development of small-scale industries as outlined in various policy resolutions and national plans accepts the role of this sector as a major creator of employment opportunities with relatively low investment. The small-scale industry is also expected to facilitate mobilization of resources of capital and skill which may, otherwise, remain unutilized. By doing so, this sector of industry should help in raising levels of earnings and standards of living of a large number of artisans, craftsmen and entrepreneurs. This would be done by promoting entrepreneurship extensively with focus on villages and small towns. This sector is also expected to play a significant role in removing regional disparities through a deliberate policy and encourage the growth of non-farm occupations in villages and small towns. As such units can be promoted with far more smaller resources, the encouragement to the small-scale sector should also ensure prevention of concentration of economic wealth and power in the hands of few. Looking to the major expectations as narrated above from this sector, it is obvious that the Government of India has a special programme to assist this sector.

The Govt. of India initiated entrepreneurship development activities in the country within the first decade of Independence. The Industrial Policy Resolutions of 1956 itself had a small industry focus, and subsequently the Govt. took several initiatives to set up various institutions to support the small-scale sector by providing non-financial and Financial assistance.

Currently there are seven major types of service providers to entrepreneurs in the country. Some of the programmes are under the Govt. system and some of them are not under the Govt. system. (Figure 8.1) They are:

1. The Central Government.
2. State Government.
3. Financial Institutions
4. Non-financial Institutions
5. NGOs.
6. Academic and Training Institutions.
7. Industry Associations.

Thus, the categories discussed here are not to be treated as mutually exclusive but as part of a network for supporting the small sector. The classification of institutional assistance has been given in Fig. 8.1. An attempt has been made to discuss in brief, the major functions and linkages of the main institutions.

8.2. PART 1. PROGRAMMES UNDER THE GOVERNMENT SYSTEM

NON-FINANCIAL ASSISTANCE

The institution which come under the ministry of SSI at the national level under the 'Government system'and which are providing non-financial assistance to SSI, are discussed below in detail.

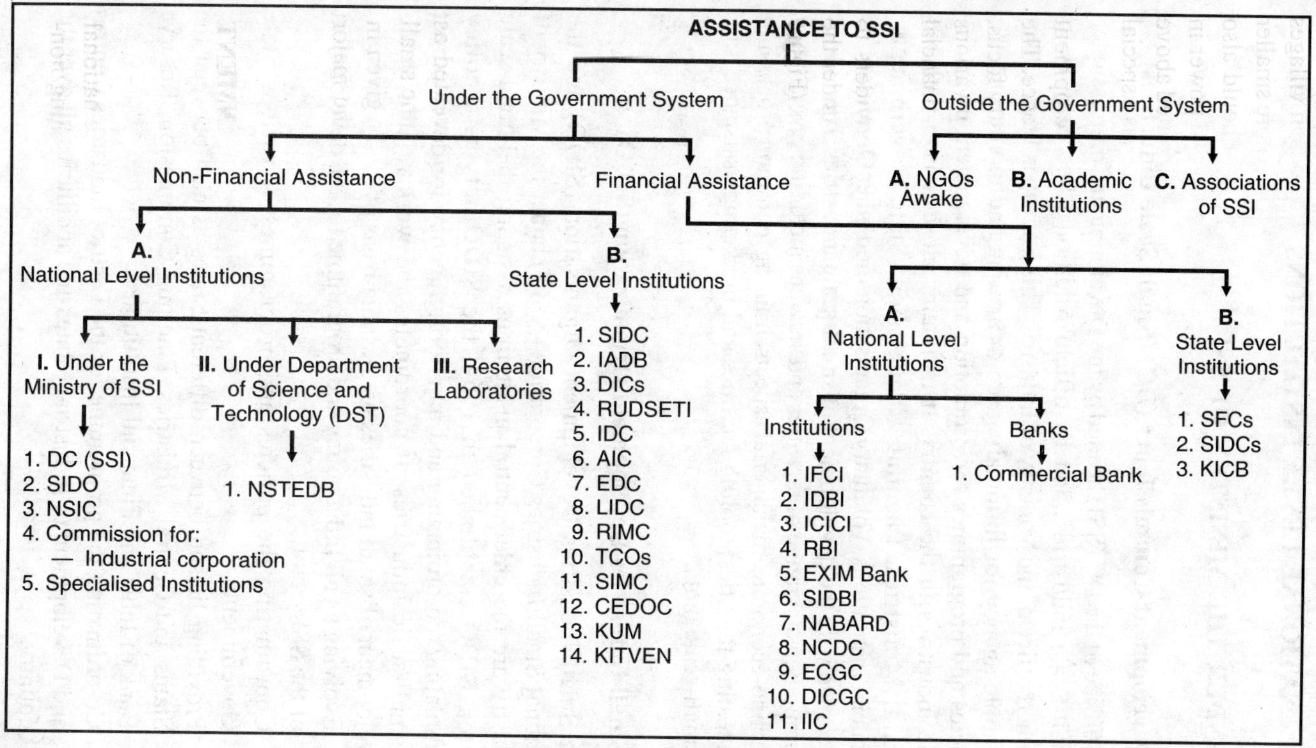

Fig. 8.1: Assistance to SSI

8.2.1 NATIONAL LEVEL INSTITUTIONS

I. UNDER THE MINISTRY OF SSI

1. Development Commissioner (DC) (Small-Scale Industries)

The Office of the DC (SSI) headed by the Development Commissioner (Small-Scale Industries) and Ex-officio Additional Secretary is an attached office of the Ministry of Industry. This is an apex body and is the noble agency for formulating, co-ordinating and monitoring the policies and programmes for promotion and development of small-scale industries in the country. It maintains close liaison with the Central Ministries, Planning Commission, State Governments. Financial Institutions, Voluntary Organisations and other Organisations concerned with the development of small-scale industries. It provides a comprehensive range of facilities and services including consultancy in techno-economic, managerial aspects, training, common processing and testing facilities, tooling facilities and marketing assistance, etc. to small-scale units.

2. Small Industries Development Organization (SIDO)

The Small Industries Development Organisation (SIDO) and the National Small Industries Corporation (NSIC) under the Ministry of Industry are the chief central institutions assisting the small-scale sector. SIDO established in 1954, the SIDO acts as a policy formulating, co-ordinating and monitoring agency for development of small-scale industries. It coordinates the work related to the development of small industries on all India basis by:

1. Evolving an all India policy and programme for the development of the SSI sector;
2. Coordinating the policies and programmes of various State Governments;
3. Providing liaison between different States as also between the States and Central Ministries, Planning Commission, Reserve Bank of India and Financial Institutions;
4. Co-ordinating the programme for the District Industries Centres and Development of Industrial estates and ancillaries all over the country.

Assistance is also provided by SIDO to the State Governments in formulating the schemes within the overall plan allocations and objectives. Central assistance to the States for development of small-scale industries is regulated by the Ministry of Industrial Development with the assistance of SIDO.

The important function of the SIDO is, however, to suggest a pattern of small-scale industries development for the country as a whole. This involves responsibilities for indicating the lines of manufacture which are suitable for the small sector and give to it all assistance in the form of promotion, procurement of raw materials and machinery and other technical advice from time to time. The SIDO provides a wide range of inspection services through its network of Small Industries Services Institutes, Branch Institutes, Extension Centres, Regional Testing Centres and other institutions at the field level.

The broad structure of Development Commissioner (SSI)/SIDO is given in the Fig. 8.2 below:

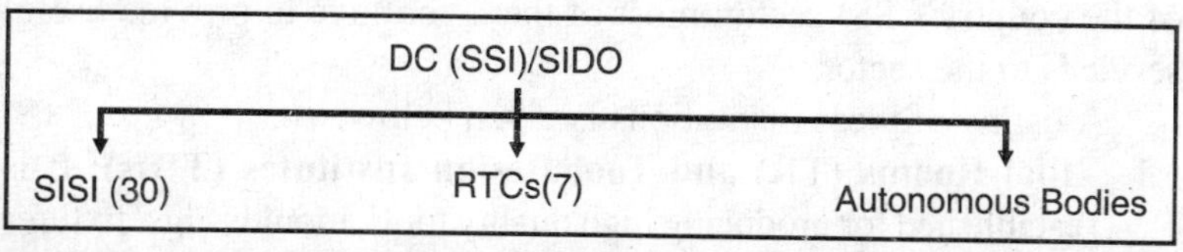

Fig. 8.2: *Organogram of the small industries development organisation (Note: Abbreviations used in the organogram are explained in the description that follow)*

a) SISIs and Branch of SISIs (for Training and Consultancy Services)

There are 300 Small Industries Services Institutes (SISIs) and 28 Branch SISIs. They provide a variety of services to existing and potential entrepreneurs/units, which include consultancy services, entrepreneurship development programmes, management development programmes, information services based on special surveys they periodically conduct, assistance in the areas of quality assurance, energy conservation, pollution control, export promotion, ancillary development, and so on. A special setup under the SISIs and Branch SISIs (some of them attached to industry associations), called Subcontract Exchanges for Ancillary Development (SCXs), has been created to facilitate the purchase of SSI products and services by medium and large enterprises as well as to facilitate exports from the SSI sector.

b) RTCs/FTCSs (for Testing Services)

Regional Testing Centres (RTCs) and their branches called Field Testing Stations (FTSs) and other specialized testing institutions provide various kinds of testing services to the SSI sector. These institutions also help the SSI units to improve their product and process quality.

c) Autonomous Bodies

This is a flexible part of SIDO's structure, which can accommodate any emerging needs of the SSI sector. For serving each of these needs, specialized autonomous institutions were created. While these institutions reflect the needs of a particular period in the development of the country's SSI sector, most of them continue to provide useful services to the sector.

A listing of these institutions is given below:

1. **Tool Rooms (TR) and Tool Design Institutes (TDIs):** It is established for producing high quality tools, moulds, jigs, fixtures and other components for the SSI sector and for providing training and consultancy assistance to tool makers. Some of these are with foreign (German & Danish) collaboration.
2. **Central Footwear Training Institutes (CFTIs):** It is established to enhance quality of footwear design and production and to train the manpower of this industry so as to facilitate increased sales in the local as well as the export markets.
3. **Product and Process Development Centres (PPDCs):** A series of institutions under the broad category of Product and Process Development Centres (PPDCs), which serve the traditional segments as well as the new and emerging segments of the industry. The latter include institutions like the Electronics Service and Training Centre (ESTC), Institute for Design of Electrical Measuring Instruments (IDEMI), Fragrance and Flavour Development Centre (FFDC), Centre for the Development of Glass Industry (CDGI), and so on.

4. **National Small Industries Corporation (NSIC):** The main job is to source and procure machinery for the SSI sector.
5. **Small Industries Development Bank of India (SIDBI):** It was set up primarily for refinancing the loans given to SSI units.
6. **Khadi and Village Industries Corporation (KVIC):** It focuses on the development of tiny and cottage industry units, particularly those manufacturing textiles and garments using the non-mechanized process, to provide long-term employment opportunities—KVIB will have tie-up with DRDA (District Rural Development Activity) to promote development programmes.
7. **Training Institutes:** There are five such national level institutes, whose names are given below:
   a) National Institute of Small Industry Extension Training (NISIET), Hyderabad.
   b) National Institute for Entrepreneurship and Small Business Development (NIESBUD), New Delhi.
   c) Indian Institute of Entrepreneurship (IIE), Guwahati, Assam.
   d) Integrated Training Centre for Industries, Nilokheri, Haryana.
   e) Small Entrepreneurs Promotion and Training Institute (SEPTI), Tiruvalla, Kerala.

3. National Small Industries Corporation (NSIC)

The National Small Industries Corporation was formed and registered at Delhi under the Companies Act in February 1955 as a Government Company for promotion and development of small-scale industries. It is engaged as the prime nodal agency for the development of small-scale industry in the areas of technology, finance, marketing, exports, technical training, consultancy and entrepreneurship development. The Corporation has set up its regional offices at Bombay, Calcutta, Delhi, Gauhati and Madras. In addition, branch offices have also been established in Allahabad, Bhopal, Bangalore, Chandigarh, Cuttack, Jaipur, Kanpur, Patna, Hyderabad, Pondicherry, Raipur, Trichur and Rajkot. Staff at field level has also been posted at Indore, Ahmedabad, Madurai, Salem, Trichur, Nadia, 24 Parganas, Hooghly, Ranchi, Cacher (Silchar) and Imphal.

The Corporation has been engaged mainly in the following activities:

1. Supply of both imported and indigenous machines to small-scale units on hire purchase basis;
2. Enlistment of small units for participation in the Stores Purchase Programmes of the Central and State Governments and other institutions;
3. Supply and distribution of certain types of raw materials, stores and components, including import of raw materials under its additional licences and IRMAC scheme;
4. Internal marketing of small industries products, mainly through consortia approach;
5. Export marketing of small industries products adopting a "single window" approach by providing a series of facilities to its export associates;
6. Co-operation with other developing countries in setting up small-scale projects on turn-key basis;
7. Development of prototypes of machines, equipment and tools, at its prototype development and training centres at New Delhi, Rajkot, Howrah and Madras;
8. Provision of basic and advanced training in various trades in the PDTCs;
9. Provision of common facilities at the PDTCs and initial production of certain machines as incidental to training.
10. Development and upgradation of technologies, particularly for projects based on wastes, etc. and
11. Implementation of Science and Technology Schemes entrusted to the Corporation by NCST.

4. Commissioner for Industrial Cooperatives

The main function is:

- Coordination of policies for industrial cooperatives.

5. Specialized Institutions

i) National Institute of Small Industry Extension Training (NISIET), Hyderabad.

Functions

a) Interdisciplinary approach in the areas of training, research and consultancy relating to the development and management of small and village industries (earlier known as Small Industry Extension Training Institute—SIET).

ii) National Institute for Entrepreneurship and Small Business Development (NIESBUD), New Delhi

Functions

a) coordinate research and training in entrepreneurship development and devices specific training programmes suited to various categories of entrepreneurs specially from the weaker sections of the society.

iii) Central Institute of Tool Design (CITD), Hyderabad

Functions

a) Training in the design and manufacture of tools, jigs, fixtures, dies and moulds.
b) Advisory and consultancy services including assistance in the design and development of tools.
c) Recommend measures to standardize tools, tooling elements, components, etc.

iv. Central Tool Room and Training Centres (at Ludhiana, Delhi, Calcutta and Bangalore)

Functions

a) Provision of tool room services and facilities in designs, manufacture and training. Tool rooms at Delhi and Bangalore are owned by the respective State Governments.

v. Central Institute of Hand Tools (CIHT), Jalandhar

Functions

a) Provision of improved technology, raw materials, designs and testing for hand tools industry.

vi) Institute for Design of Electrical Measuring instruments (IDEM), Bombay

Functions:

a) Provision of technical consultancy in the design and development of electrical and electronic instruments, calibration and testing, tool fabrication prototype fabrication and training.

vii) Central Machine Tool Institute, Bangalore. This provides technical competence in designing and making tools.

viii) Central Institute for Plastics Engineering and Tools, Madras (Ministry of Petroleum and Chemicals). Which provides technical building and research activities in the field of plastic and tools.

ix) National Institute of Foundry and Forge Technology, Ranchi. Provides technical assistance for foundry and forge plants.

x) Entrepreneurship Development Institute of India (EDI), Ahmedabad.

EDI established in 1983, is a non-profit making premier national Institute. It provides entrepreneurship education, training and research. It is an autonomous institute jointly sponsored by Industrial Development Bank of India (IDBI), Industrial Credit and Investment Corporation of India (ICICI), Industrial Finance Corporation of India (IFCI), State Bank of India (SBI) and with active support of Government of Gujarat. The EDI has been spearheading the concept of entrepreneurship throughout the country with a belief that entrepreneur need not necessarily be born, but can be developed through well conceived and well directed training activities. This in turn led to the emergence of several training programmes in the strategic thrust areas.

II. UNDER THE DEPARTMENT OF SCIENCE AND TECHNOLOGY (DST): (NATIONAL INSTITUTIONS PROVIDING NON-FINANCIAL ASSISTANCE)

The Ministry of Small-Scale Industries (SSI) is the government's main aim for entrepreneurship promotion and development, whereas the Department of Science and Technology (DST) designs and operates the special schemes for technology entrepreneurs. It was in 1982 that

DST set up the National Science and Technology Entrepreneurship Development Board (NSTEDB) for promoting hi-tech entrepreneurship in the country.

a. National Science and Technology Entrepreneurship Development Board (NSTEDB):

NSTEDB is the implementation agency of DST, just as SIDO is for the Ministry of SSI. The objectives of NSTEDB are as follows:

1. To create a 3-tier structure involving the district, state and central levels for promoting technology entrepreneurship.
2. To act as a technical consultancy organization for the government to provide information and advise on creating avenues for self-employment for technical personnel.
3. To create awareness about entrepreneurship by organizing camps in academic institutions.
4. To promote group self-employment.
5. To create national and regional institutions capable of providing entrepreneurship and management skills training to technical personnel.

The programmes and activities of NSTEDB are designed for achieving the above objectives. A list of such programmes are given below:

1. Entrepreneurship Awareness Camp (EAC).
2. Entrepreneurship Development Programme (EDP).
3. Entrepreneurship Development Cell (EDC).
4. Science & Technology Entrepreneurs Park (STEP).
5. Science & Technology Entrepreneurship Development Projects (STED).
6. Faculty Development Programme (FDP).
7. Skill Development through Science & Technology (STST).
8. Technology Business Incubator (TBI).
9. Technology Based EDP (TEDP).
10. Open Learning Programme in Entrepreneurship (OLPE)
11. Science-Tech Entrepreneur (Magazine).

Compared to the SIDO programmes, the NSTEDB programmes have more specific target groups and are operated through and with the help of a more enlightened group of institutions such as engineering colleges and science & technology centres. Hence, they are more visible and are perceived to be more effective in reaching the target groups. Achievements in this regard published by the NSTEDB are given in Table 8.1.

Table 8.1: Achievements of NSTEDB

Programme	Achievement (Nos)
Entrepreneurship Awareness Camp (EAC)	
Conducted	1018
Students Exposed	71260
Entrepreneurship Development Programme (EDP)	
Conducted	629
Persons Trained	14259
Units Set up	2684
Success	18.82%
Employment Generated	16,682
Entrepreneurship Development Cell (EDC)	
ED Cells Established	30
Science & Technology Entrepreneurs Park (STEP)	
STEPs	32
Units Set up	433
Jobs Generated	3279
Science & Technology Entrepreneurship Development Scheme (STEDS)	
No. of STEDS	13
Faculty Development Programme (FDP)	
Conducted	62
Faculty Trained	1575
Skill Development through Science & Technology (STST)	
No. of people trained	70,000

One of the major successes of NSTEDB is the Technology Business Incubator (TBI) programme, which is part of the STEP programme and hence not given separately in the table. All the TBIs are attached to engineering colleges and have been able to create a few successful enterprises, the number of which currently stands at 433 in about 30 STEPs, giving an average of 14per TBI. As the STEPs/ TBIs have started at different time-periods, the above numbers may not provide any indication of the TBI effectiveness. But the fact is that they are helping the process of new venture creation and employment.

III. RESEARCH LABORATORIES (NATIONAL LABORATORIES PROVIDING NON-FINANCIAL ASSISTANCE)

National laboratories coming under the purview of the Council of Scientific and Industrial Research (CSIR) and of other organisations and ministries of the Government is:

The National Research Development Corporation (NRDC), New Delhi releases the patents of new processes/products developed by national laboratories for commercial exploitation.

8.2.2 STATE LEVEL INSTITUTIONS (NON-FINANCIAL ASSISTANCE)

The State Level network of the institutions assisting the small-scale sector is headed/coordinated by the State Directorate of Industries and includes Small Industries Development Corporation, State Financial Corporation and institutions like District Industries Centres. The Directorate of Industries function as the executive agency for the village and small industries sector also. The Directorate acts under the overall guidance of the SIDO and the concerned central institutions associated with various programmes of assistance. The functions of the State Directorate include the activities which are regulatory as well as developmental. In the recent years, the emphasis is laid more towards the developmental function compared to the regulatory one. Certain programmes of assistance are implemented by the State Directorate directly, while it also implements other schemes, with the help of specialized agencies operating at the State Level for small and village industries. The following are the sixteen institutions operating at the state level.

1. Small Industries Development Corporation (SIDC)

The Small Industries Development Corporation functions to supply scarce raw materials to the units in the small-scale sector. It also provides machinery on hire-purchase. The Corporation extends assistance for marketing of the small industry products and provides them the facilities for display of the goods, etc. through trade centres.

The State Small-scale Industrial Development Corporation acts as an infrastructure agency and assists the small-scale sector by providing plots/sheds with ready infrastructure like water supply, drainage, communication network, etc. on easy payment terms. The financial corporations as well as banks provide long and medium term loans for acquisition of fixed assets through various schemes of financing for small-scale units. The State Level Financial Institutions are actively involved in attracting entrepreneurs to backward and rural areas and also promoting the entrepreneurship development especially amongst the technocrats, professionals and craftsmen.

The State Level Industrial Development Corporations play greater role in providing / promoting industrial development in the region. In Karnataka, a state level institution like KSSIDC is involved in promoting and formulating the industrial development by providing suitable structure for setting up of industry. The following are the important functions of KSSIDC.

1. Preparation of services report about the present and future development and industries in the area.
2. Creating industrial sheeds / plots
3. Providing suitable infrastructure facilities
4. Offering marketing assistance
5. Providing materials at concessional rates
6. Offering incentives to the SSI
7. Conducting rural industrialization programmes
8. Providing suitable consultancy services to the needy industrialist.

2. Industrial Area Development Board (IADB)

The State level Industrial Area Development Board plays greater role in providing/promoting rapid industrialization and to ensure decentralization of industries. The Board formulates and creates centre in the respective state by developing all infrastructural functions like power, water, telecommunication, banking, post-offices, residential housing, capitals, etc. Industrial estates are made available for small, medium and large industries in these growth centres.

The IADB has simplified procedure fixed tied up with the State Government for giving various clearances under single window arrangement to avoid various delays in implementation. The following are various committees (for allotment of industrial area) for setting up industries and clearance of projects:

a) **High level committees :** The high level committee headed by Hon'ble minister of small and medium industries clears the project investment beyond Rs. 50 crore.
b) **State level single window agency:** The state level single window agency headed by principal secretary to government for clearing projects involving upto 50 crore.
c) **District level single window agency:** The district-level single window agency is headed by District Commissioner.

3. District Industries Centres (DICs)

The concept of DIC came into existence in the year 1978, the main objective is to provide a foundation for the promotion of small, tiny, village and cottage industries and to provide services to support the industries under one roof. The main thrust and their programme is on the development of such industrial units in rural areas and small towns to create larger employment opportunities.

The following are the important functions of DICs:

1. Forming the industrial policy of the District.
2. Conducting survey of the District about the industries
3. Granting provisional Registration certificate (PRC) to start industries.
4. Issue permanent registration certificate (PMT)
5. Providing incentives/subsidy in backward areas.
6. Conducting EDP programmes in consultation with state level organization
7. Providing marketing assistance
8. Promoting modernisation programmes
9. Creating industrial estate and formulating survey report.

4. Rural Development and Self Employment Training Institute (RUDSETI)

The main objective of RUDSET is to encourage micro enterprises in rural and backward areas.

The following are the main objective of RUDSETs:

1. Establishing rural development centres
2. Collaborating with banks and financial institutions
3. Extending micro financing in rural areas.
4. Establishing specialized training centres in backward areas
5. Training self employed youth to start tiny and small industries.

5. Industrial Development Corporation (IDC)

Functions

Promotion of industrial units in the medium and large-scale sector including joint and public sector ventures.

6. Small Industries Marketing Corporation (SIMC)

Government of India and Government of Karnataka extending marketing assistance to small-scale sector in procurement of raw materials through purchase price preference. The state established Karnataka Small Industries Marketing Corporation (KSIMC) with the following objective:

1. To provide marketing assistance to the small-scale sector.
2. To provide opportunity to procure materials from Government department, public sector undertakings, stationary bodies and other institutions.
3. To provide purchase-price preference to SSI of the state.
4. To improve quality of the products.
5. To improve production i.e., manufacturing process
6. To reduce the prices
7. To augment exports.

7. Technical Consultancy Organizations (TCOs)

Technical consultancy service was set up in the 1970s and 1980s by IDBI, IFCI and ICICI in collaboration with state level financial institutions and commercial banks. At present there are 17 TCOs in the country.

Functions of TCOs

1. Preparing project profiles
2. Studying feasibility studies
3. Undertaking industrial potential surveys
4. Conducting entrepreneurs development programmes (EDPs)
5. Rendering technical and administrative assistance
6. Consultancy services for modernisation
7. Providing rehabilitation packages
8. Transfer and engineering services management
9. Export consultancy
10. Rural industrial programmes (RIP)
11. Turn-key assignment and audit
12. Consultancy services to respective state government
13. Retainer consultancy services.

8. Centre for Entrepreneurship Development of Karnataka (CEDOK)

As part of initiative to promote a strong entrepreneurial base, the CEDOK came into existence with the main objective to utilize the creative capabilities of local people particularly in less industrialised districts. CEDOK collaborates with national / international organization involved in entrepreneurship development. Partnership with private sector, CEDOK acts as centre of excellence and for the development entrepreneur in business management.

9. Electronic Development Corporation (EDC)

Function

Promotion of industries in the field of electronics including joint sector and public sector projects.

10. Leather Industry Development Corporation (LIDC) and Other Similar Commodity Corporations

Function

Development of specific types of village and tiny sector units relating to a particular trade.

11. Rural Industries Marketing Corporation (RIMC)

Function

Marketing of village industry products and provision of a variety of services needed by village and tiny units (Gujarat state has set up this corporation)

12. Karnataka Udyog Mitra (KUM)

Udyog Mitra set up specially to help NRI's MNC's to Indian entrepreneurs with information and guidance. KUM's packages of services ranging from identifying investment opportunities and site visits to obtaining clearance from Government agencies. KUM primarily acts as the Secretariat to the state single window agency to smoothen the way to investors/entrepreneurs intending to set up industries.

Features and functions

1. Informing industrial Expo's through mass media
2. Encouraging prospective investors and motivating them to establish units.
3. Providing information regarding opportunities for investment.
4. Locating / contacting prospective investors
5. Helps NRI's in promoting foreign investment
6. Organizing fairs, exhibitions and campaigns
7. Publishing literature in the form of papers, case studies, reports, periodicals, pamphlets, brouchers, digests journals, project, profiles, magazines and circulating or distributing them to the artisans and institutions.

7. Agro Industries Corporation (AIC)

Functions

a) Supply of agricultural machinery, machinery/equipment on hire
b) Development of agro-based industries
c) Sale of agro-inputs like fertilizers and pesticides.

13. KITVEN

Kitven is venture capital fund conceptualised and funded by Karnataka State Industries Investment and Development Corporation, Karnataka State Financial Corporation and Karnataka Small Industries Development Bank of India. Kitven fund is dedicated to companies in the information technology industry operating primarily in Karnataka.

Kitven fund's primary objective:

1. Develop competitive products and cutting edge technology
2. Manufacture and commercialize the product developed.
3. Move in value chain.
4. Expand and upgrade existing capacities to cater to a wider clients.

8.3 FINANCIAL ASSISTANCE

PROGRAMMES UNDER THE GOVERNMENT SYSTEM

Financial institutions are also called Development Financial Institution (DFIs) are owned and managed by Central Government or State Government with the adoption of economic planning, building up an appropriate structure of financial institutions has become a necessity. The first step towards building up a structure of financial institutions was taken with the establishment of the Industrial Finance Corporation of India in 1948, since then there is no going back, at regular intervals, either a new institution was set up or an existing unit in the private sector was taken over by the Government. As of now more than 70 DFI's in our country are catering to the different needs of industry.

8.3.1 National Level Institutions

Following are the national level financial institutions and banks under the Govt. system providing financial assistance.

I. FINANCIAL INSTITUTIONS

1. Industrial Finance Corporation of India (IFCI)

IFCI established in 1948 by an Act of parliament with the objective of providing medium and long term credit to eligible industrial concerns. The Industrial Finance Corporation of India (IFCI) has the distinction of being the first development bank of country. The advent of IFCI at this juncture had a special significance for the post-independence industrial scene of the country which was marked till then by a narrow industrial base.

Functions

1. Granting loans or subscribing to debentures payable with a period not exceeding 25 years.
2. Underwriting the issue of shares or debentures by industrial concerns subject to their disposal by the corporation.
3. Guaranteeing loans.
4. Deferred payment guarantees.
5. Guaranteeing foreign currency raised from or credit arrangement made with any banks or financial institution
6. Acting as agent for the Central Government or with its approval for the world bank in respect of loans granted or debentures subscribed.
7. Subscribing to the shares of any industrial concern
8. Acquiring, with the approval and IDBI an undertaking increasing the business assets and liabilities of any institution.

Assistance

1. Term loan assistance either singly or jointly
2. Setting up new industrial projects
3. Expansion of existing units or division into new lines.
4. Renovation and modernization of existing plans.

5. Term lending or bridge loans.
6. Personal guarantee of promoters / directors
7. Hypothecation of machinery and other movable property
8. Fixed assets loan
9. Rehabilitation of units / nourishment packages.

Financial Services

1. Equipment financing
2. Merchant banking and allied services
3. Equipment leasing
4. Equipment procurement scheme
5. Supplier's credit.
6. Finance to leasing and hire-purchase concerns.

Other Services

1. Promotional services
2. Consultancy services
3. Entrepreneurs Development Schemes
4. Assistance to backward areas.

2. Industrial Development Bank of India (IDBI)

Introduction

Commercial banks in India were on the model of European model of banking. They established mainly for extending working capital loans. Over the years it has realized the importance of credit investors and the concept of development banking as it existed in Germany. The first specialized institutions for term financing for industry viz., Industrial Finance Corporation of India (IFCI) came into being 1948, rapid pace of industrialisation under the 5 year plans underlined for a new institution with wider functions and much larger resource than the existing ones. Thus, the Industrial Development Bank of India (IDBI) was established in 1964 to meet the requirement.

The IDBI was originally constituted as a wholly-owned subsidiary of RBI. The new institution would benefit from the financial support, experience and authority of the Central Bank for effectively carrying out its tasks.

The following are the objectives and functions of the IDBI.

1. To serve as an apex institution for term loan finance for industry.
2. To co-ordinate the working of institutions engaged in financing, promoting or developing industries and assist in the development.
3. To extend financial, technical assistance.
4. To provide long-term credit
5. To develop industrial sector
6. To undertake market servey and economic studies
7. To establish better co-ordination among banks and DFIs (Development Financial Institutions)
8. To cater to the needs of term lending institutions for refinancing
9. Extending rehabilitation the sick SSIS
10. To promote entrepreneurship among the youth and also provide training by extending support to SIDO.

The IDBI grants financial assistance to industries which are in conformity with national priorities each project is appraised to its technically commercial viability financial strengths, managerial competency and total viability of the industrial sector. The following are the important parametres applied for grant of assistance to a project are:

1. Promoter's contribution to the project
2. Debt equity ratio (DER)
3. Break even analysis (BEA)
4. Internal rate of return (IRR)
5. Economic rate of return (ERR)
6. Discounted cash flow (DCF)
7. Debt service courage ratio (DSCR)
8. Foreign exchange net flow/flow (FENF)
9. Net present value (NPV)
10. Pay back period (PBP).

Due to complexity of increasing non-performing assets and in order to strengthen the on going process of financial restructuring, IDBI now converted as full fledged commercial bank as "IDBI Bank". Effective from Oct-2004, and at present, the IDBI is functioning as one of the scheduled commercial banks and conducting all the activities on par with any other scheduled commercial banks of the country.

In this regard IDBI functions are not restricted only to term lending but extended to collection of deposits, issuance of drafts, collection of drafts and other activities performed by any commercial/public sector banks.

Scheme of Assistance

1. Project related to modernisation
2. Textile modernisation scheme
3. Equity finance scheme
4. Project finance scheme
5. Technical development fund scheme
6. Venture capital fund.
7. Technology upgradation and modernization scheme
8. Energy conservation scheme
9. Loan underwriting schemes
10. Direct subscription and guarantee scheme
11. Refinance of industrial loan scheme
12. Bills re-discounting scheme
13. Seed capital scheme
14. Subscription to shares and bonds of financial institution

3. Industrial Credit and Investment Corporation of India (ICICI)

The ICICI was set up is 1955 under the Company's Act, 1956 to encourage and assist investment and industrial development financial assistance also to industry for setting up new units and also expansion and modernization purpose in particular.

Functions

1. Provide loans repayable over 15 years
2. Guarantees loans
3. Foreign currency loans to import capital investment
4. Provide finance through equity participation

5. Revolving credit facility
6. Promotional activities with a view of faster growth in the backward areas.
7. Underwriting new issues of shares and other securities
8. Managerial, technical services to industries.

Objectives

ICICI provides assistance for the creation, expansion and modernisation of industrial enterprises and in promoting capital participation in them. The assistance will be in the form and long and medium term loans, equity participation, sponsoring and underwriting issues of shares and debentures and guaranteeing respect and foreign currency loans from other sources.

ICICI has also undergone dramatic changes in the recent past now it is converted to ICICI bank functioning on par with other scheduled Commercial Bank.

4. Industrial Reconstruction Bank of India (IRBI)

IRBI set up in April 1971, originally it was Industrial Reconstruction Corporation of India, later it has been reconstituted as IRBI on March 20, 1985 to function as the principal reconstruction agency by providing assistance for reconstruction and rehabilitation of sick industrial units in consultation with development banks.

IRBI provides the following assistance:

a) Meeting essential capital expenditure for renovation, installation of balancing equipment diversification, expansion and modernisation.
b) Bridging the liquidity gap and providing margin for working capital.
c) Meeting liabilities considered necessary for the purpose of reconstruction

Further, IRBI also provides information on reconstruction works of sick industries. It undertakes the diagnostic studies aimed at the removal of shortcomings which had contributed to sickness. The IRBI takes steps to

1. Reconstruct the Management
2. Restructure the financial base,

3. Providing assistance and guidance in managerial, technical and marketing and allied fields suited to the needs of reconstruction work.

b) Arranging for financial assistance from other banks and financial institutions and government agencies.

5. Export-Import Bank of India (EXIM Bank)

The Export-Import Bank of India was set up on Jan 1, 1982 with a view to strengthen the institutional framework for encouraging the export of non-traditional products, i.e., engineering and capital goods and related services.

As leading public financial institution co-ordinating the working of institutions engaged in financing export and import. It is entrusted with the responsibility of financing, facilitating and promoting foreign trade. It can also provide financing export and consultancy and related services, assist Indian joint ventures in 3rd world countries, conduct export studies, finance export, oriented industries and provide international merchant banking services.

Financial assistance from EXIM Bank

a) Direct financial assistance to exporters of plant equipment, machinery and related services in the form of medium-term credit
b) Overseas investment finance to Indian promoters
c) Overseas buyer's credit for import of Indian capital goods.
d) Re-lending facility to overseas banks to enable them to provide term finance to importers for import of Indian capital goods.
e) Rediscounting of export bill
f) Refinance of export credit to eligible commercial banks in India against their medium to long-term credit.

In 1983, the EXIM bank introduced exim syndication facility under which it provides funds for export proposal and syndicate credit.

6. Small Industries Development Bank of India (SIDBI)

The SIDBI was set up as a wholly-owned subsidiary of IDBI by an Act of Parliament in 1989. SIDBI commenced its operation on 3rd April

1990, after taking over the outstanding portfolio under Small Industries Development Fund (SIDF) and national equity fund (NFF) of IDBI as of March 31, 1990. SIDBI has been assigned the role of the principal financial institution for promotion, financing and development of industry in the small-scale sector including tiny and cottage industries.

Functions of SIDBI

1. Refinancing term loan of SFCs (State Financial Corporations)/ Banks.
2. Discounting and rediscounting of bills arising out of sale of machineries and capital equipment.
3. Equity assistance is the form of NET (National Equity Fund)
4. Extending technical and other related support services
5. Promotion, development and growth of small-scale sector
6. Resource support to NSIC and SSIDCs
7. Supply of material, marketing of SSI products
8. Extension of hire-purchase and leasing facilities
9. Setting up of industrial estates and development of industrial areas and infrastructure.
10. Development of marketing infrastructure for creating new marketing channels for the products of the SSI.
11. Direct discounting of bills of SSI units, manufacturing capital goods.
12. Direct financial assistance in the form of long-term loans.

The various schemes of financial assistance for SSI units under the SIDBI scheme of assistance are as follows:

1. Refinance scheme for industrial loans for small and village industries.
2. Composite Loan Scheme.
3. Scheme for Scheduled Caste/Scheduled Tribe and physically Handicapped Entrepeneurs
4. National Equity Fund Scheme.
5. Special Scheme of Assistance to Ex-Servicemen
6. Seed Capital Scheme
7. Single Window Scheme (New project cost (excluding working

capital margin) is upto Rs. 10 lakh of the total working capital requirement at normal level of operation is upto Rs. 5 lakh.

8. Scheme for Women Entrepreneurs
9. Mahila Udyam Nidhi Scheme
10. Refinance Scheme for Quality Control
11. Schemes of Incentives for Exports
12. Equipment Refinance Scheme
13. Refinance Scheme for Rehabilitation of Small-scale Industries
14. Assistance to Small Road Transport Operator
15. Refinance Scheme for Refinance Scheme
16. Foreign Currency Refinance Scheme
17. Refinance Scheme under ADB Line of Credit
18. Refinance Scheme for setting up Industrial Estates
19. Bills Rediscounting Scheme.

7. National Bank for Agriculture and Rural Development (NABARD)

The National Bank for Agriculture and Rural Development refinances co-operatives and commercial banks and regional rural banks. Further it extends financial support to cottage and tiny units primarily in rural areas.

8. National Cooperative Development Corporation (NCDC)

Functions

1. Promotes and finances cooperative enterprises in processing, marketing, storage and export relating to agro-based industries.
2. Agro-service centres
3. Promotion of units for formulation of fertilizers, pesticides and insecticides
4. Workshop for fabrication of agricultural machinery/implements
5. Margin money for processing units
6. Technical training.

9. Export Credit Guarantee Corporation (ECGC)

Functions

Supports and strengthens export promotion drive:

1. by providing a range of risk insurance covers to exporters against loss in export of goods and services,
2. by offering guarantees to banks and financial institutions to enable exporters to obtain better facilities from them,
3. to give customer satisfaction service at low cost and with high efficiency.

10. Deposit Insurance and Credit Guarantee Corporation (DICGC)

Functions

Operates four guarantee schemes (a) small loans guarantee scheme, (b) small loans (small-scale industries) guarantee scheme, (c) small-loans (financial corporations) guarantee scheme, and (d) service cooperative society guarantee scheme.

11. Industrial Investment Corporation (IIC)

Functions

Finances medium and large units upto a certain investment ceiling with direct participation in share capital and underwrites new issues.

II. FINANCIAL ASSISTANCE FROM BANKS

Commercial Banks

Commercial banks usually provide short-term finance to meet the working capital needs. However, the commercial banks also provide term loans and they are eligible for the refinance from the IDBI. For this purpose for each district, one commercial bank is designated "Lead Bank". As lead bank, the nationalized banks play an important role by preparing credit plans for the concerned district for a specified period and set targets for various sub-sections of the priority sector and other sections to be attained by different banks. The implementation of the schemes is then periodically reviewed and suitable measures are advised to meet the specific requirement of industrial units of various locations.

8.3.2 State Level Institutions

State Financial Corporations (SFCs)

There are state financial corporations in our country, these institutions were set up following the Inactment of the State Financial Corporations Act 1951. The SFCs meet the financial requirement of small and medium enterprises. SFCs have been playing any effective role in the growth of small-scale and medium-scale units.

1. Granting financial assistance by way of term loans
2. Underwriting of shares, issues and guaranteeing loan
3. Project identification
4. Medium and long-term loans
5. Direct capacity participation
6. Equipment finance
7. Deferred equipment guarantee
8. Equipment leasing
9. Hospital/nursing home finance

Functions

1. Provides long and medium term loans for acquisition of fixed assets of small and medium industries.
2. Guarantees payment for purchases of machinery from suppliers within India.
3. Guarantees loans raised by industries from commercial banks, cooperative banks, etc.
4. Foreign exchange loans under World Bank line of credit.
5. Special capital assistance up to Rs. 200,000.

2. State Industrial Development Corporations (SIDCs)

These were set up in 1960 and in 1970 to act as a catalyst agent in the industrialization of state. The SIDCs are established on wholly-owned undertakings of state government.

Functions

The following are the important functions of SIDCs:

1. Granting financial assistance by areas of term loans.
2. Granting bridge loan agent investment subsidiary
3. Market intelligence services
4. Industrial promotional activities
5. Setting up industrial projects into medium and large sectors either in the joint sector i.e., in the partnership with private intrapreneurs.
6. Acting as agent of state and growth of subsidiaries incentive, etc.

Nine out of 26 SIDCs also function as SFEs to process finance to small-scale sector of the nine SFCs six are in the north-easterm region (Arunachal Pradesh, Manipur, Meghalaya, Mizoram, Nagaland, Tripura) and the remaining three are in Goa, Pondicherry and Sikkim.

3. The Karnataka Industrial Cooperative Bank (KICB)

The aim of KICB is to promote industrial development with extending short-term loans for acquiring man and machinery and also by providing need based working capital to the entrepreneurs.

Further the banks also extend facility like cash credit facility and trills discounting facility to the entrepreneurs. The banks also extend current account facility, so the entrepreneurs are able to operate the loan account and savings/business account as it makes the entrepreneur less dependant on scheduled banks.

8.4. PART 2. PROGRAMMES OUTSIDE GOVERNMENT SYSTEM

8.4.1 Non-Governmental Organisations (NGOs)

A second type of service-provider in this subcategory are the NGOs. Such organizations use entrepreneurship primarily as a means of creating self-employment among the poor and depressed sections of the society. Their major advantage is their thorough knowledge of their client groups and their ability to provide training and consultancy services to these 'clients' at substantially lower costs, often without charging any fees. The limiting factor for them is, as mentioned above, their limited vision of entrepreneurship primarily as a tool for self-employment. They may not see its larger role in promoting economic development, innovation and quality of life and generation of wealth for example:

a. AWAKE

Association of Women of Karnataka Entrepreneur: This is an NGO acting as one of the most important women entrepreneurship development organizations. Its main objective is to promote and strengthen the women entrepreneurship and offering skill and training in the special field in order to develop entrepreneurship skill. The following are the important objectives of AWAKE :

1. To promote women entrepreneur to establish small, tiny industries.
2. Provide suitable training and developing skill
3. Creating awareness among women abut skill and training to promote industry
4. Spreading entrepreneurship among rural women to take up cottage industries.
5. Promoting rural artisans and craftsmen.
6. Assisting in marketing the products by participating in trade fairs and exhibitions.

8.4.2 Programmes of Academic Institutions

It is naturally to be expected that academic institutions would have a larger perspective on entrepreneurship, and hence their programmes would include a greater variety of client groups and promote the larger objectives of entrepreneurship. It is on this argument that the involvement of academic institutions in entrepreneurship development is being recommended. In spite of the logical arguments supporting such involvement, it was shown by various studies (see our discussion on this above) that the results of such experiments are not very encouraging. The Indian academic community has not done any better. In fact, the level, intensity and variety of interaction between academia and entrepreneurs are far lower in India compared to the developed nations in the West.

Academic institutions in India, which are involved in entrepreneurship development activities, are of three kinds.

1. Training institutions started by the government as part of their overall strategy for entrepreneurship, that have subsequently become autonomous and have taken up a large number of activities on their own.

2. Specialized institutes set up by the government or private agencies in other areas and disciplines, such as Indian Institutes of Technology (IITs), Indian Institutes of Management (IIMs) and Indian Schools of Business (ISB), who have found synergies between their main programmes and entrepreneurship development activities and therefore have initiated separates centres and activities of entrepreneurship promotions.

The IITs and IIMs are not set up specially to cater to the country's need for developing entrepreneurs. These institutions have taken up entrepreneurship developments activities primarily because of their synergies with the core themes of their operations such as technology and management. Academic programmes in entrepreneurship are slowly developing from these institutes, and not from training institutions under the Government of India. Even the long-duration diploma programmes organized by the letter have a training focus, not by design but by the influence of their other programmes.

3. Universities and colleges, both public and private, that have taken up entrepreneurship development as part of their expansion.

4. NISIET and EDII: The two prominent institutions of this category are the National Institute of Small Industry Extension Training (NISIET), Hyderabad, and the Entrepreneurship Development Institute of India, (EDII), Ahmedabad. Both these institutions are very active in conducting training programmes for entrepreneurs and the two institutions together have more than 600,000 training man-days to their credit each year. The variety and reach of their programmes are quite large. They have different types of programmes addressed to different groups of clients. These are mainly the short duration training programmes, the long duration diploma programmes, seminars, workshops and conferences. The clients for such programmes are mostly from within the country. However, there are a few programmes for the international clients as well, especially for the trainers of entrepreneurs.

8.4.3 Associations of Small Industry Entrepreneurs

1. Federation of Associations of Small Industries of India (FASII)
2. Indian Council of Small Industries (ICSI)
3. National Alliance of Young Entrepreneurs (NAYE)
4. State small industry associations
5. District small industry associations

6. Associations at state and national levels for specific groups of industries
7. Chambers of commerce & industry and their federations.

Thus, though we can technically classify the entrepreneurship development activities of financial institutions academic institutions and NGOs as programmes outside the government system, none of them are completely delinked from the government. A large number of commercial banks and financial institutions, for example, are owned by the government and/or regulated by the government with reference to many of their policies including the ones on the SME sector. The same is the case with many academic institutions. It may be noted that in our discussion on the governmental schemes above, we mentioned some of these financial and academic institutions as part of the government system. While these institutions are directly under the government, most others are indirectly linked to the government. Even the NGOs often operate the governmental schemes or get funding support from the government. So the distinction between government and non-governmental programmes is not fully justified.

8.5 SOURCES OF FINANCE

In the initial stages of the enterprise, the entrepreneur may either invest his own money or take loans to augment it. A time may also come when the enterprise is not only established but it is growing. During this period, a considerable sum of money is required. So the entrepreneur has to consider various sources of finance. The major sources of finance are as follows:

1. Promoters
2. Public
3. Financial institutions
4. Commercial banks
5. Suppliers
6. Financing and leasing companies
7. Venture capital funding agencies.

1. Finance from Promoters

The required funds for the enterprise can be raised by the entrepreneur by himself or by the partners from their own source as capital or as loan. The big advantage is that the money is easily available without setting into hassles or procedures.

2. Finance from Public

This is another important source of finance through issue of shares or fixed deposit from public. Before going in for public issue, the entrepreneurs need to be cautious and knowledgeable about the procedure for the issue. Only if the company has reached a stage of growth (i.e., if the project or company is worth Rs. 1 to 2 crore) then this source would be suitable.

As regards public deposit, it all depends on the creditworthiness of the company and the rate of interest offered. Here too the Reserve Bank of India has prescribed certain guidelines.

3. Finance from Financial Institutions

The advantage of raising funds from financial institutions is that the repayment period for the loan is long. On the top of it there is a moratorium period for repayment in the beginning allows time to establish the firm and then start paying. This source still is the main and more acceptable funding source for all entrepreneurs.

4. Finance from Commercial Banks

Normally commercial banks provide money or finance for working capital and not for fixed assets like land, building, machinery, etc. But in some cases they do give long-term finance for fixed assets also. The repayment for the loan is shorter than that of the financial institutions and the rate of lending interest is higher. The moratorium period is also short. But the rules and regulations are a little more flexible than those of the financial institutions.

5. Finance from Suppliers and Distributors

This source is not yet popular in our country. This can be considered especially when the company is growing. This source can be availed when the money is required for a short period. In this case, the suppliers can give credit for machinery and equipment, raw materials even for technical know-how.

The advantage is that if the machinery supplied by the supplier is defective, the supplier has to correct the defect or replace it as the payment is spread over three or four years. Apart from this, since the machinery is purchased on the credit from suppliers, the depreciation can also be claimed. Sometimes, the profit margin on some machinery is so high that the suppliers may not even charge interest.

Another source similar to that of suppliers is distributors. When the product has good market and a established network, then the firm can even ask distributors to deposit a considerable amount of money to ensure stocks. Of course, this amount cannot meet all needs, but some extent of working capital requirements can be fulfilled.

6. Finance from Leasing Company

Lease finance can be availed for installing machinery and equipment, R&D facilities, computers and vehicles. In the recent years the number of leasing companies have grown by leaps and bounds. These companies are prepared to meet the needs for expansion of small and medium scale enterprises. If the growth requirement is for investment in machinery, then this is the best source of finance. Because, by investing only 15% to 20% of cost to firm can have required facilities with minimum procedure. The lease is generally for three to four years hypothecating the assets to the leasing company.

7. Finance from Venture Capital Funding Scheme

This source of getting funds is very popular abroad. But in India it is just emerging and not yet utilized widely.

The Small Industries Development Bank of India (SIDBI) has introduced a scheme of direct assistance under venture capital fund (VCF) scheme. The scheme is designed to provide VCF assistance to new or existing industries for : (objectives).

1. encouraging commercial application of indigenously developed technology
2. adopting imported technology to wider domestic applications, and
3. all matters connected with or incidental to the above.

The above-mentioned objectives limit the utilisation of the scheme as a funding resource. Besides, the size of investment under this scheme should range between Rs. 5 lakh and Rs. 250 lakh.

Factors for Selection of Source of Fund

1. Cost of raising funds
2. Cost of retaining funds
3. Time taken for raising funds
4. Tax implications
5. Terms and conditions for setting funds.

8.6. FINANCIAL INCENTIVES FOR SSI & TAX CONCESSIONS

In order to achieve the objective as set out in the industrial policy, the Govt. offers the following incentives and concessions for new investment made in the industrial sector. On or after 1 April 2001 for the purpose and various incentives, and concessions as detailed here under the status has been classified into four zones:

Developed Area	Zone—A
Developed Area	Zone—B
Backward Area	Zone—C
Growth centre/ Mini Growth Centre	Zone—D

Investment Subsidy

1. The Govt. will provide subsidy to all new tiny small sector industries. The details of investments subsidy available to tiny/small-scale industries in different zones is as follows:

Zone	Particulars	Industry	Interest/Subsidy
A.	Developed Area	NIL	NIL
B.	Developing Area	Tiny Inds.	10 percent value of fixed Assets. Max. 5 to
C.	Backward Area	Tiny Inds.	20 percent value of fired Assets subject 10 lakh.
D.	Growth Centres/ Mini Growth Centre		25% of value of FA Mx. 12.50 lakh

2. Investment subsidy would be available for industrial units making new/industrial investment under expansion, diversification and modernization and also investment subsidy would be available to all tiny and SSI undertaking expansion. Diversification or modernization without exceeding prescribed ceiling.
3. Additional subsidy to special category of entrepreneur: In addition to the subsidy, addition of subsidy to the extent of 5% of the value of fixed asset subject to ceiling of the 1 lakh shall be available for tiny/SSI except zone-D. In respect of entrepreneur belonging to scheduled caste, scheduled tribe and women entrepreneurs, special subsidy will be granted.

Entry tax exemption

Entry tax exemption will be extended to the industries including long and medium scale industries detailed below:

1. During the implementation of the project, machinery and equipment directly involved in production process, benefit will be available for a maximum period of 3 years from the date of project implementation.
2. On commencement of commercial production, raw materials, components, semifinished goods, consumables, diesel, furnace oil, and as consumables for the captive power generation units, tax exemption will be available as indicated below:

A.	Developed Area	NIL
B.	Developed Area	3 years
C.	Backward Area	5 years
D.	Growth Centres	8 years

Section 29 units: Industrial unit which are taken over by the corporation under section 29 of SFCs Act, SSI DC/KSFC are eligible for subsidy for exemption from payment of stamp duty and registration charges.

Special Concessions

100% Export oriented Units

These units are exempted from import licensing formalities. They are allowed to import capital assets, raw materials, components, consumables and spares under the Open General Licence (OGL) on the condition that their entire production will be exported.

Tax Concessions

Income Tax Concessions

The following concessions may be available to SSI subject to amendment made in the Act.

1. Tax holidays.
2. Investment allowance
3. Concessions to SSI in rural areas
4. Concessions to SSI in backward areas.
5. Depreciation, etc.

State Taxes/Value Added Tax (VAT)

Special schemes like exemption of tax for new industries or small-scale industries are not contemplated under VAT scheme.

Central Excise and Small-scale Industries

Central excise is a duty on manufacture or production of goods in India. Exemption from excise duty is given to manufacturers operating as small-scale industries, so as to encourage, their growth. From the past experience, the government of India has found that it is administratively inconvenient and costly to collect revenue from the numerous small units. Therefore, the Government has extended various concessions under the central excise law to small-scale industrial units by issuing notifications in this regard from time to time.

Packages and Incentives available to SSI Units:

1. SSI units having turnover upto 100 lakh in specified goods (goods eligible for SSI exemption) need not get registration under central excise and pay duty.
2. They can pay excise duty at 60% of tariff upto first 100 lakh turnover and avail the convert credit for the entire turnover below as well as above 100 lakh.

3. They have the option to avail the central credit after the turn-over has crowned the limit of 100 lakh.
4. SSI unit availing SSI concession need not submit monthly return. They can submit a quarterly return in form ER-3 return, by 20th of following month.
5. SSI units availing SSI exemption are required to pay duty on the 15th of month following end of the month, whereas others have to pay duty on 5th of the following month.
6. For the month of March duty has to be paid by SSI and other units by 31st March only.
7. Central excise inspector/preventive officers/audit officers can visit for inspections or verification with the prior specific approval of Assistant commissioner.
8. In the case of procedural irregularities except evasion of duty committed by SSIs lenient view is taken.
9. Audit of SSI unit once in two to five years.
10. While calculation SSI turnover of 100/400 lakh, some turnover of SSI unit as below cannot be considered:
    (a) Export sales are not considered. But export sales to Nepal and Bhutan are considered domestic sales.
    (b) Export under bond through merchant exporter to be excluded
    (c) Turnover of non-excise able goods should be excluded
    (d) Goods manufactured with others brand name to be excluded
    (e) Goods manufactured in rural area under others brand name to be included
    (f) Inputs brought by SSIs and cleared as such not to be included.
    (g) While calculations SSI limit of 100/400 lakh, the clearance of goods chargeable to NIL rate of duty or which are exempt from duty under any other notifications will not be considered.
    (xi) SSI units eligible for SSI concession under excise law need not be registered with the director of industries of any state.

8.7 ASSISTANCE FOR OBTAINING RAW MATERIAL

1. Promotion Councils

The Govt. has set up a number of promotional councils with a view to assist the promotion of export and import of goods/raw materials.

These councils are registered as non-profit making organisations for assisting industries. The following are the important councils:

1. The cashew export promotional council.
2. Cotton export promotion council.
3. Engineering export promotion council.
4. Gem and jeweller promotion council.
5. Handloom promotion council.
6. Leather promotion council.
7. Plastic & linoleum promotion council
8. Processed food promotion council.
9. Silk/Rayon promotion council.
10. Spices export promotion council.
11. Tobacco promotion council.
12. Wool and woolen promotion council.

The Govt. provides grants under specific heads for these councils and also appoints senior officials to act in the working committee and guide its operations.

2. The Karnataka Transparency in Public Procurement Act

Under the Karnataka Transparency in Public Procurement Act, 2000, special preference available to the small-scale industries sector. The Act is applicable to procurement of raw materials from Govt. Departments with price preference.

3. Assistance by Commercial Banks for Obtaining Raw Material

The nationalized banks and public sector banks provides working capital loans to entrepreneur for procuring raw materials. The financial facility depending upon the nature and activity and also size of the industry. Small industry requires frequent supply of raw material, hence the banks provides suitable working capital facility to the small- scale industry. Further, the financial facility will be in the form of revolving credit or cash credit. It can be used at a particular point of time and the facility can be revived frequently.

4. Assistance by Marketing Boards

The Govt. has set up marketing boards and corporations which procures raw materials and supply to the needy at concessional rate, in order to promote industrial growth and also to promote export with the sole intention of improving the quality of the product.

The state marketing board procure raw material and provide the same to needy at a rate fixed by the Government. However, the procumbent of raw material depends on the availability. The marketing Board like Karnataka Silk Marketing Board which procures cocoons from the farmers and distributes/offers the same to the needy at a cheaper rate when compare to the market rate.

EXERCISES

Section A

1. Mention any four non-financial institutions at the national level.
2. Mention any four non-financial institutions at the state level.
3. Mention any four financial institutions at the national level.
4. Mention any four financial institutions at the state level.
5. Mention any four autonomous bodies.
6. Mention any four special institutions at the national level providing non-financial assistance.
7. Mention any four parametres for grant of assistance to a project by IDBI.

Section B

1. What is IADB? Mention its functions.
2. What is DIC? Mention its functions.
3. What is KSIMC? Mention its objectives.
4. What is RUDSETI? Mention its objective.
5. What are the functions of Karnataka Udyog Mitra?
6. What is role of AWAKE in the promotion of entrepreneurship?
7. What are the functions of IFCI?
8. What are the functions of SIDBI?
9. What are the functions of NABARD?

Section C

1. What is NSIC? Discuss activities.
2. What is SIDO? Discuss its objectives and functions.
3. What is NSTEDB? Discuss its objectives and activities in brief.
4. What is SIDC? Discuss its functions.
5. What is TCO? Discuss its functions.
6. Discuss the functions and services provided by IFCI.
7. Discuss the role and functions and schemes of IDBI.
8. Discuss the role and functions of SIDBI.
9. Discuss the role and functions of (a) SFCs and (b) SIDCs
10. Discuss the role and functions of (a) NGOs (b) Academic institute (c) Associations of SSI.

Section D

1. Discuss the major sources of finance for an entrepreneur.
2. Discuss the incentives and tax concessions of SSI.
3. Discuss the assistance for obtaining raw materials for SSI.
4. Discuss the packages and incentives available to SSI units.
5. Discuss the non-financial assistance at the national level.
6. Discuss the non-financial assistance at the state level.
7. Discuss the institutions which are providing financial assistance at the national level.
8. Discuss the institutions which are providing financial assistance at the state level.

SKILL DEVELOPMENT

1. Vist any small-scale unit and find out the non-financial and financial assistance availed for institutions and prepare a report.
2. Visit tax authorities to collect tax concessions for small-scale units and prepare a report.

9

Industrial Estates

STRUCTURE

9.1 Introduction
9.2 Definitions
9.3 Objectives of Industrial Estates
9.4 Factors to be Considered while Establishing Industrial Estates in India
9.5 Types of Industrial Estates
9.6 Reasons for Failure of Industrial Estates

9.1 INTRODUCTION

The term 'Industrial Estate' is often used interchangeably with industrial district, industrial park, industrial zone, special economic zone, eco-zone etc.

An industrial estate is a "self-contained geographical area with high quality infrastructure facilities, which houses businesses of an industrial nature".

An industrial estate is administered or managed by a single authority that has a defined jurisdiction with respect to tenant companies. The authority makes provision for operation and management i.e., enforcing restrictions to tenants and planning with respect to plot sizes, access and utilities.

The industrial estates offer industrial, residential and commercial areas with developed plots or pre-built factories, power, telecom, water sanitation and other civic amenities such as hospital, security etc.

The main targets of industrial estate are high value adding small and medium scale industries, which do not have the capacity to invest in developing their basic infrastructure facilities, but have the capacity to pay for the services provided to them.

Hence, industrial estates are regions where infrastructure facilities are provided for and thus a conducive environment is created to attract small and medium scale industries.

9.2 DEFINITIONS

The United Nations has defined an industrial estate as "a planned clustering of enterprises, offering standard factory buildings, erected in advance of demand and variety of services and facilities to the occupants."

According to P.C. Alexander, an industrial estate is 'a group of factories, constructed on an economic scale in suitable sites with facilities of water and ward and first-aid and provided with special arrangements for technical guidance and common service facilities."

Almost all the states have taken initiatives in India to set up industrial estates to boost the economic activity. The state industrial development corporations (SIDC's) have developed the industrial estates as a catalyst for economic growth.

9.3 OBJECTIVES OF INDUSTRIAL ESTATES

The objectives of establishment of industrial estates in India are as follows:

1. To foster the development of industry as well as entrepreneurship by providing economics and incentives.
2. To encourage the growth of small scale industry.
3. To achieve decentralized development in small towns and large villages.
4. To encourage growth of ancillary industries in the townships, surrounding major industrial undertakings, both in public and private sector.
5. To shift small scale industries from generated areas to estate premises with a view to increasing their productivity.
6. To attract investments.
7. To generate employment.
8. To leverage on raw material sources, skilled manpower resources, proximity to end-use markets etc.

9. To add to and improve social infrastructure in terms of healthcare and educational facilities.

Thus, industrial estates can positively influence the socio-economic development and industrialization of the region.

9.4 FACTORS TO BE CONSIDERED WHILE ESTABLISHING INDUSTRIAL ESTATES IN INDIA

1. Industrial estates must be planned with a view to developing them into a healthier industrial growth in an area rather than as a cluster of merely inward looking group of production units.
2. While planning an industrial estate, due consideration is given to 'secondary growth' in order to regulate any haphazard growth around the estates.
3. While planning industrial estates in an area uniform pattern need not be followed. The organizational structure in a particular area or region may be adjusted taking into consideration factors such as, special requirements of an area, economic development, availability of skills, talents and enterprise level of development of the region etc.
4. Industrial estates have to be properly co-ordinate with the broader development programme. They have to be not only an integral part of the industrial development programme but also of the overall economic development programme of the area or region.
5. Homogeneity (rather than heterogeneity) is to be guiding criterion while selecting industrial units. This would lead to better planning and utilisation of common facilities, inter-firm co-operation and inter-linked development.
6. Location of the industrial estate is to be decide only on techno-economic considerations. A techno-economic feasibility study must always precede the setting up of an estate.
7. Instead of building sheds in advance, these may be built on the expressed demand as revealed at the time of conducting techno-economic or feasibility studies.
8. Elaborate and costlier construction has to be avoided and instead, functional types of sheds at cheaper rates may be provided.
9. To keep construction cost to the minimum, adequate attention

should be given to reduce the cost by improving design efficiency, increasing the size coverage and reducing to the minimum the area allotted for non-factory purposes.

10. The success of industrial estates has to be demonstrated by the government through prescribing minimum factory standards.
11. In backward and rural areas, greater efforts would have to be made to stimulate local entrepreneurship. The industrial estate in such areas have to play a promotional role and get as pace-settles in the process of industrial development besides guiding the entrepreneur in selecting the right lines of manufacture, it may also be necessary to offer additional incentives for locating industrial units. These incentives may be in the form of concessions credit, rebates in various taxes, professional allotment of scarce raw-materials etc., concessions could be given preferably as a "package deal".
12. The selection of products to be manufactured in the industrial estate should be in accordance with other development programme viz., mechanization of agriculture, utilization of agriculture produce, electrification etc.
13. While general purpose industrial estates are very useful for backward and rural areas and in urban areas, functional or special types of industrial estates may be preferred in view of the emphasize on modernisation ancillary development etc.

9.5 TYPES OF INDUSTRIAL ESTATES

Industrial estates can be developed as follows:

1. ***General Industrial Estate or Parks*** (***GIP***): This type of industrial estates caters to all types of industries. For example, Industrial Model Township at Manesar (Haryana) which has facilities to house different types of industries like auto and auto components, high precision industries, textiles, pharmaceuticals, software etc.

2. ***Special Industrial Parks*** (***SIP***): This type of industrial parks focuses on a specific industry like software technology park, at Whitefield in Bangalore etc.

3. ***Growth Centres*** *:* These centres may be 3-tier centres, namely, mega growth centres, mini growth centres and micro growth centres.

a) Mega Growth Centres: Mega growth centres provide modern and quality infrastructure facilities for rapid industrialization to attract investments.

b) *Mini Growth Centres:* Industry specific mini growth centres are set by the government at different locations in the state where specific industrial activity needs to be boosted. The location of the growth centres is done by keeping in mind the inherent locational advantages like availability of raw-material man-power connectivity and market.

The government provides two following facilities at such growth centres:

i) Highest slab of capital investment and interest subsidy.
ii) Highest slab of other relevant subsidies.
iii) Quality infrastructure support which includes good road connecting to the nearest highway.
iv) Priority in power allocation.

These growth centres could shift the focus growth of industries into rural areas, yet these growth centres are located near main highway and the district headquarters. This helps in generating employment for the local population. The examples of mini growth centres are electronics park, also based food processing park, chemical park, plastic park, silk park, software technology park (STP) biotech park etc.

c) *Micro Industries Park:* Micro industries park are set-up to give boost to village based industries at each block level. This park provides basic infrastructure facilities to rural entrepreneurs, artisans and craftmen. This will give a fillip to employment and rural growth.

*4. **Private Industrial Estates**:* The private sector can get itself involved in various capacities for developing industrial estates. **As a promoter**, the private sector company could play the role of a developer. **As an investor**, the private sector company may be involved actively or passively.

Implementation of an industrial estate project of the private sector company is usually through the formation of a special purpose vehicle (SPV) or development company or as the external agency responsible for mobilization of resources, marketing the estate to private investors and later for operation and maintenance etc.

The first example of such an arrangement in India is given in the Box below:

Box 1: Mahindra Industrial Park Ltd. (MIPL) – A case of private participation in India

The MIPL will be the first planned private sector industrial estate located in the Chengelpattu district of Tamil Nadu. MIPL is an SPV with a unique and pioneering institutional structure comprising of a partnership of three giants in the Indian industry. The institutional framework is as follows:

The Promoter : The Rs. 6000 crore Mahindra & Mahindra group is the promoter of the park from the private sector which also owns an equity stake in the project.

The Investor: Infrastructure Leasing and Financial Services, which focuses mainly on commercialization of infrastructure projects, is the Financial Institution investing in the project.

The Government Agency: Tamil Nadu Industrial Development Corporation is the Government agency involved in the project to reflect the commitment of the State Government in the completion of the project.

The Implementing Agency: MIPL has hired Jurong Town Corporation (JTC) International to do the master planning of the park. JTC is the private sector player, which has been hired to implement the project.

9.6 REASONS FOR FAILURE OF INDUSTRIAL ESTATES

While there have been numerous success stories, a few of the projects have also failed due the following reasons:

a) Some of the industrial estates failed as they were set up with sole motive of inducing industrial growth in backward regions. This motive led to improper selection of location, resulting in the inability to sustain industrial activity in these regions.
b) Lack of funds.
c) Inability to tailor the estate to the characteristics of the region.
d) Improper implementation and design leading to poor quality of infrastructure facilities.
e) Frequent changes in administrative heads and political interference.
f) A profit motive is missing the industrial estates.
g) Concessions to industries in the area in the form of fiscal and tax incentives to attract more units is missing.

ANNEXURE–I: CASE 1

Haryana State Industrial Developmental Corporation

The Haryana State Industrial Developmental Corporation (HSIDC), was established in 1967 by the Government of Haryana to act as a catalyst for promoting and accelerating the pace of industrialization in the State. The main objectives of HSIDC include identification and promotion of large and medium sector projects and facilitation of infrastructure development. HSIDC has till date promoted 33 Industrial Estates in the State. HSIDC, with a paid-up capital of Rs. 35.56 crores has been able to catalyse investment to the tune of Rs. 544.70 crore in these estates. HSIDC also recorded an all-time high income or Rs. 25.05 crore and a gross profit of Rs. 6.06 crore in 1999-2000. The success of HSIDC has been on account of the following reasons:

- It seeks co-promoters from the private sector aggressively.
- Has a locational advantage of being situated near cities like Delhi and Chandigarh, which are large markets.
- Its ability to adapt the design of industrial parks based on the local characteristics.
- Its ability to provide financial assistance to entrepreneurs and established industries. The financial services offered by HSIDC include equipment finance, bill discounting, merchant banking services, forex advisory services, etc.

CASE 2

Gujarat Industrial Development Corporation

The Gujarat Industrial Development Corporation (GIDC), was created by the Government of Gujarat to spur industrial development in the State. GIDC has till date, planned for 257 Industrial Estates of which 169 are functional. As part of the New Industrial Policy 2000, the Gujarat Government has decided to spur the growth of the Industrial Estates by formulating the 'Industrial Park Scheme 2000'.

The Industrial Park Scheme 2000 recognizes the need for private sector participation in setting up industrial parks and creating employment opportunities. In order to encourage private sector investment in this sector, the State Government has decided to implement an incentive scheme for setting up employment-oriented industrial parks, high-tech parks, investment-oriented parks and trade centres.

Details of the various incentives provided by the State Government are highlighted in Table VI.1 (overleaf)

ANNEXURE – II

Scheme for Promoting Industrial Parks

Type	Condition	Criteria for assistance
Employment Oriented Park	To develop facilities for setting up a minimum of 100 units or more or creating more than 2,500 employment opportunities in the Industrial Park	Subsidy at the rate of 10% of capital investment up to a maximum of Rs. 1 crore
	200 units or more than 5,000 employment opportunities	Subsidy at the rate of 10% of capital investment up to a maximum of Rs. 2 crores
Hi-tech park	—	Subsidy at the rate of 50% of capital investment, subject to a maximum of Rs. 250 lakh will be admissible
Investment park	—	Subsidy at the rate of 10% of capital investment subject to a maximum of Rs. 250 lakhs will be admissible
Trade Centre	Trade centre having a built-Up area of 5,000 sq.mtr or More for use	Subsidy at the rate of 10% of the eligible capital Investment—maximum cash subsidy of Rs. 50/- lakhs
	Trade-centre having a built-Up area of 10,000 sq.mtr or more for use	Subsidy at the rate of 10% of the eligible capital investment—maximum cash subsidy of Rs. 100 lakhs.

ANNEXURE–III

QUESTIONNAIRE TO BE SUBMITTED FOR NEW INDUSTRIAL ESTATES (IE)

A. GENERAL FEATURES

This information provides a profile of the estate to assist in identifying possible environmental issues.

• ***Industrial Estate***

Name : ....

Address : ....

....

Operations to start by Month-Year : ....

• ***Contact Person for Environmental Aspects***

Name : ....

Function : ....

Phone : ....

Fax : ....

E-mail : ....

• ***Ownership***

Public : ....

Private : ....

Public/Private partnership : ....

• ***Scale of the Project***

Total area of development (in hectares) : ....

Total number of units/companies proposed : ....

Total number of workers (approximate : ....

• ***Proposed Land Uses (Percentage of Total Area)***

Export Processing Zone : ....

General Industrial Zone : ....

Commercial Zone : ....

Residential Zone : ....

Landscaped Green Areas : ....

Undeveloped Areas : ....

Roads : ....

Others : ....

• ***Nature of the Industries Proposed in the IE***

Number of Units	***Likely No. of Workers***	***Production Volume***

Petrochemical Processing : ....

Iron and Steel Processing : ....

Non-ferrous Metal Industries : ....

Chemical manufacturing : ....

Energy Generation : ....

Construction Industry : ....

Transportation Sector : ....

Communication Technology : ....

Food Processing : ....

Drinks Manufacture : ....

Textile Manufacturing : ....

Leather Processing : ....

Electronic Manufacturing : ....

Pharmaceutical Production : ....

Plastics Formulation/Processing : ....

Paint Manufacture : ....

Ceramics/Glass Manufacture : ....

Pulp and Paper Production : ....

Packaging Manufacture : ....

Metal Plating : ....

Others : ....

• ***Service Industries Proposed in the IE***

Transport : ....

Warehousing : ....

Chemical Storage : ....

Recycling : ....

Waste Treatment/Disposal : ....

Laboratories : ....

Information Technology : ....

Banking, Finance and Insurance : ....

• ***Details of Environmental Features On Site Within 25km Radius***

Reserved Forests : ....

Vegetation / Tree Cover : ....

Wetlands, Swamps, Mangroves : ....

Lakes : ....

Rivers and Creeks : ....

Sea Coast : ....

Protected Areas : ....

Places of Tourist Interests : ....

• ***List of the Human Habitations Nearby***

Rural/Urban Area	Number of Inhabitants	Distance (km)
....	....	....

• ***Transport Links***

Bus : ....

Train : ....

Others : ....

INFRASTRUCTURE FACILITIES PROPOSED IN THE IE

This identifies a number of services and features that may be linked to environmental performance. *Who provides or is responsible for the following services, tools or actions?*

1. o-Industrial Estate Authority
2. o-Operation Units
3. o-Government Authority
4. o-Private Sector
5. o-Other (Please Specify)

• ***Energy (also State Requirement in K Cal)***	**1**	**2**	**3**	**4**	**5**
Centralized energy supply	?	?	?	?	?
Individual energy supply	?	?	?	?	?
Supply and recovery of waste heat (cogeneration)	?	?	?	?	?
District heating system	?	?	?	?	?
Energy from waste facility	?	?	?	?	?
Energy from renewable resources facility	?	?	?	?	?

• ***Water (also State Requirement in KL)***

Municipal Service	?	?	?	?	?
Tube Wells	?	?	?	?	?
Treatment Facilities	?	?	?	?	?
Waste Water Disposal	?	?	?	?	?
Liquid Waste Disposal	?	?	?	?	?
Waste Water Recycling	?	?	?	?	?
Rain Water harvesting	?	?	?	?	?
Sewage Disposal @	?	?	?	?	?

• ***Solid Waste (in Metric Tons)***

Solid Waste Disposal @	?	?	?	?	?
Composting of Biological Waste @	?	?	?	?	?
Industrial Liquid Waste Disposal @	?	?	?	?	?
Hazardous Waste Disposal	?	?	?	?	?
Waste Exchange Clearing House	?	?	?	?	?
Multi-material Resource Recovery	?	?	?	?	?
@ Including Collection, Storage & Treatment	?	?	?	?	?

• ***Transport (Attached Traffic Risk Assessment Report)***

Traffic and Transport management Plan	?	?	?	?	?

• ***Management***

Environmental Monitoring	?	?	?	?	?
Effluent Monitoring	?	?	?	?	?
Air Emission Monitoring	?	?	?	?	?
Environmental Auditing	?	?	?	?	?
EMP and Implementation of Risk Mitigation Measures	?	?	?	?	?
Environmental Technology Assessment	?	?	?	?	?
Environmental Training and Education	?	?	?	?	?
Emergency Preparedness and Response Capability	?	?	?	?	?
Self-Regulation and Operational Standards	?	?	?	?	?
Finance and Insurance Service	?	?	?	?	?

• ***Miscellaneous***

Restoring Natural Features of the Site ? ? ? ? ?
Landscaping and Gardening ? ? ? ? ?
Analytical and Laboratory Services ? ? ? ? ?
Protection and Security System ? ? ? ? ?

MAIN STAKEHOLDERS

List of units requiring individual environmental clearance (in future).
Details of issues raised in the environmental public hearing.

Finance Arrangements –

• ***Local Financial Institutions and Banks*** ? Yes ? No
If yes, what influence do they have ?
Owners ? Yes ? No
Conditionalities on Investments and Credits ? Yes ? No
Other (…………………..) ? Yes ? No

ENVIRONMENTAL IMPACT ASSESSMENT

To Cover

- **Baseline Conditions**
- **Impact assessment Including Carrying Capacity of the Area**
- **Social Impact Assessment Including Rehabilitation Action Plan (if any)**
- **Risk Assessment and Onsite and offsite Emergency Response Planning**
- **Environmental Management Plan**
- **Details of Environmental Parameters to be Monitored (Frequency and Implementation Agency)**

POTENTIAL ENVIRONMENTAL THREATS

This assessment is for the entire estate, not for individual units.

- ***Areas of Concern***

1. "Imminent threats' to human health and/or the environment ('imminent threats' means high-risk threats that require immediate action to reduce risk and liabilities)

Threat Actions proposed to be taken

....

....

....

....

2. Likely Environmental 'trouble spots'

Trouble spot	Actions proposed to be taken
....	....
....	....

3. Major sources & quantities of wastes (solid, air, liquid) likely to be generated in the IE

Sources	Inventory	Actions proposed to be taken
....	....	....
....	....	....

Habitat/wildlife issues of concern	Actions proposed to be taken
....	....
....	....

4. Potential sources of industrial accidents, explosions and fires, health and safety issues

Potential sources	Actions proposed to be taken
....	....
....	....

5. Sources of environmental threats in adjacent areas

Sources	Actions proposed to be taken
....	....
....	....

CHECKLIST OF ENCLOSURES

1. Land purchase agreement
2. Land use/Zoning particulars—relevant portions from the prevailing local Regulations
3. Cost estimates inclusive of land cost

4. Landscape plans with proposed tree plantation
5. Water balance statement
6. Rainwater harvesting plan
7. Storm water drainage
8. Material balance studies, if carried out
9. Common effluent treatment plant details with a write up
10. Statement on the machinery and manpower during construction
11. Fire protection measures and approvals obtained
12. Proceedings of Environmental Public Hearing also provide response to points raised in the public hearing
13. Approval of competent authorities in case of conversion of agricultural land, change of land use, DC rules
14. Construction schedule (CPM/PERT chart)
15. Approval from special bodies (State Industries Commissioner/ SIDC/financial institutions)
16. Approvals if applicable from ASI, Civil Aviation, ecologically sensitive areas, coastal development regulation, etc.
17. Solid waste collection, treatment, storage, transportation and disposal plan
18. Vehicle parking and management
19. Environment Impact Assessment Study (including executive summary)
20. Schedule-II Application Form for EC
21. Questionnaire for IE

May be addressed to:

Joint Secretary (CCI-II)
Ministry of Environment & Forests,
Paryavaran Bhawan, C.G.O. Complex,
Lodi Road, New Delhi-110003
Telefax: 24362551
E-mail: chandramohan@nic.in

Director, IA Division,
Ministry of Environment & Forests,
C.G.O. Complex
Lodi Road, New Delhi-110003
Telefax: 24360695
E-mail: biossk@menf.delhi.nic.in

EXERCISES

Section A

1. What do you mean by Industrial Estate?

Section B

2. What are the objectives of Industrial Estates?
3. What are the reasons for failure of Industrial Estate in India?

Section C

4. Discuss the factors to be considered while establishing industrial estates in India.
5. Discuss the different types of Industrial Estates.

SKILL DEVELOPMENT

1. Collect the Questionnaire to be submitted for new industrial estates.

10

Sickness in SSI

STRUCTURE

10.1 Introduction
10.2 Definitions
10.3 Symptoms of Industrial Sickness
10.4 Factors Affecting Sickness or Causes of Sickness
10.5 Consequences of Industrial Sickness
10.6 Supportive Measures from Government
10.7 Preventive and Remedial Measures of Sickness

10.1. INTRODUCTION

In common parlance, sickness means not being healthy, that is, any industrial undertaking ceases to generate incremental return to the expected level or when there is decrease in productivity which result in sickness. In other words, healthy unit is one which earns a reasonable return on capital employed and which builds up reserves after providing reasonable return on capital invested and creates reserve after providing for depreciation. The sickness in any industry irrespective of scale exists in different degrees in almost all the countries and is a part of economic development activity of the country. In any growing economy it is natural that inefficient and non-viable enterprises go out of existence and new units come into existence. But beyond reasonable limits sickness affects the generation of national wealth.

10.2 DEFINITION

1. **RBI (2001)** defines sickness as: An SSI unit should be considered sick if it is unable to pay its debt, i.e.,
   a) any of the borrowal accounts of the unit remains substandard for more than six months i.e., principal or interest, in respect of any of its borrowal accounts has remained overdue for a period exceeding one year. The requirement of overdue period exceeding one year will remain unchanged even if the present period for classification of an account as substandard, is reduced in due course; or
   b) There is erosion in the net worth due to accumulated cash losses to the extent of 50 per cent of its net worth during the previous accounting year; and
   c) The unit has been in commercial production for at least two years.

   The RBI has issued the above definition as a direction to the financial institutions so that sickness can be identified early and rehabilitation of the unit made possible. We refer to sickness as a state where it is unable to pay its debts, to put a time limit to sickness, especially in case of SSI, is not feasible.
2. **The Sick Industrial Companies Act (SICA) 1985** defines a sick industry as "An industrial company which has at the end of any financial year accumulated losses equal to or exceeding its entire net-worth and has also suffered cash losses in such financial year immediately preceding such financial year.
3. **According to the Development Commissioner (DC) SSI,** "A unit becomes sick if its:
   (a) capacity utilisation is less than 50 percent of the highest achievement during the preceding five years (incipient sickness).
   (b) net worth has been eroded by more than 50 percent or
   (c) the unit has remained closed for a period of more than six months.
4. **According to IDBI**, a unit may be considered sick if it has defaulted the payment of three instalments,
5. **According to State Bank of India**, "A sick unit is one which fails to generate an internal surplus on a continuous basis and depends for its survival upon frequent infusion of funds."

10.3 SYMPTOMS OF INDUSTRIAL SICKNESS

The existence of various signals over a long period of time becomes symptoms of industrial sickness. The symptoms are as follows:

1. Continuous shortage of cash
2. Deteriorating financial ratio.
3. Continuous decrease in the price of shares.
4. Frequent-request to banks and financial institutions for funds
5. Delay and default in payment of compulsory dues.
6. Delay in audit of annual accounts
7. Degradation in the employee's morale.
8. Disparities among the top and middle management level.

Sickness in Small-scale Sector

The small-scale sector has grown phenomenally over the years and has contributed to the Gross Domestic Product (GDP) along with growth, there has also been gradual increase in the incidence of sickness in this sector.

Performance of the SME sector is often measured in terms of the extent of sickness prevalent among them. The measure of sickness is considered to be appropriate for SMEs as this sector is particularly vulnerable to the vagaries of the external environment as well as the lack of experience or clout on the part of SME promoters. The Reserve Bank of India conducts periodic studies on industrial sickness. Data on sickness in the SSI sector for a seven-year period (1993-99) as reported in the Handbook of Industrial Policy and Statistics 2000 (p. 374) along with the computation of some relevant percentages are given in Table 10.1.

Table 10.1

As at the end of	No. of sick units	Total No. of SSI units	Sick units as %age of SSI units	Amount out-standing (Rs. crores)	No. of viable units	Viable units as %age of sick units	Amount out-standing (Rs. crores)
March 1993	2,38,176	23,90,000	9.96	3,442.97	21,649	9.09	798.79
March 1994	2,56,452	25,71,000	9.97	3,680.37	16,580	6.46	685.93

Table 10.1 contd.

Table 10.1 contd.

March 1995	2,68,815	26,58,000	10.11	3,547.16	15,539	5.78	597.93
March 1996	2,62,376	28,03,000	9.36	3,721.94	16,424	6.26	635.82
March 1997	2,35,032	29,44,000	7.98	3,609.20	16,220	6.90	479.31
March 1998	2,21,536	30,80,000	7.19	3,856.64	18,686	8.43	455.98
March 1999 (P)	3,06,221	32,12,000	9.53	4,313.48	18,692	6.10	376.96

Note: (P) Provisional: *These units include village industries as well.
Source: Completed from Handbook of Industrial Policy and Statistics, 2000, Office of the Economic Adviser, Ministry of Commerce & Industry. p. 374 & Economic Survey 2002-03, GOI, Ministry of Finance & Company Affairs p.15

The absolute figures in the original table showed an increasing trend in sickness (the number going up from 2.38 lakh to 3.06 lakh). But when the percentages of sick units out of the total SME units were computed, the figures showed that sickness in SMEs has been decreasing (from about 9% in 1993 to 6% in 1999). Even though the amount of money locked in these sick units (more than Rs. 4000 crores) is really a cause of concern, a 6-9 percent sickness rate cannot be considered to be unusually high. One could therefore dismiss the generally held belief that sickness is rampant in the SME sector. The sector has done reasonably well at least on the sickness criterion.

10.4 FACTORS AFFECTING SICKNESS OR CAUSES OF SICKNESS

India no doubt, has gained considerable experience to promote the entrepreneurship at grass roots level but it has been seen that majority of entrepreneurs give away in the first few years after they start their enterprises. An entrepreneur has to face many problems during life time of his business.

Following are the problems faced by an entrepreneur which leads to sickness:

1. Internal Problems (Factors)

1. Choice of an idea.
2. Feeble structure
3. Faulty planning
4. Poor project implementation
5. Poor Management
6. Poor production
7. Poor Quality of Project
8. Problem of market for the goods
9. Inadequate finance
10. Labour problem
11. Low capacity utilization
12. Lack of vertical and horizontal integration
13. Inadequate Training and skills
14. Loose organization
15. Lack of storage
16. Dispute among partner or director
17. Mismanagement of funds

2. External Problems (Factors)

1. Due to infrastructure
   - (a) Location
   - (b) Power
   - (c) Water
   - (d) Post office
   - (e) Bank
   - (f) Communication facilities
   - (g) Transportation
2. Financial problems
   - (a) Capitals
   - (b) Working capital
   - (c) Long-term funds
   - (d) Recovery
   - (e) Rate of Interest
3. Marketing problems
4. Taxation
5. Raw materials
6. Industrial and Financial regulations

7. Inspection problems
8. Technology problems
9. EXIM policy of the Govt.
10. Globalization.

IMPORTANT CAUSES OF SICKNESS

1. Managerial Capacity

The most important cause for the ailment of an Industrial undertaking in the small sector is attributed to lack of managerial competence or capacity. About 75% of SSI are proprietorship units. The corporate units are family concerns registered as Pvt. Ltd., companies having two or three family members, or close relatives or friends, without an organized structure, which are unable to attract high quality professionals and suffer from more number of employee's turnover. The entrepreneur should, therefore, induct professionals in the board to enable to function without difficulty.

2. Working Capital

Most of the SSI purely depends on the need based financial assistance in time. The proprietary concerns are unable to get the need based financial assistance from the banks and financial institutions, most of the time, the balance sheet did not show the encouraging trend to able to qualify to the required norms of banks and financial institutions. Hence, they suffer from lack of financial support from banks.

3. Cash Management

Cash is an important asset for the operation of the business, cash is the basic input, that keeps business run, any mismanagement of cash leads to bankruptcy. Good book keeping and frequent checks on cash transactions will provide greater scope and also provide suitable remedy to take appropriate remedial action. The person behind the project should ensure effective keeping of accounts and have check at regular intervals. More vigilance restricts the leakage of funds.

4. Marketing of the Product

Most of the industrial units failed to address the problem of marketing of their product. Once the product is produced, it should reach the market and to the end users without any hindrance. The marketing and network to push the product quickly is lacking.

5. Technical Knowledge/Know-how

Frequent changes in the technology affects the smooth functioning of the unit. Outdated technology will cost more to produce the goods when compared with the latest technology. Hence, technical know-how will improve the production substantially. In order to minimize the production cost, technical soundness is to be improved by acquiring better equipment.

6. Tax Policy of the Government

Frequent changes in the policy of the Government and also the tax structure, leads to sickness where the promoter is required to show his income. Hence, suitable policy of the Govt. will bring down the sickness of the industry.

10.5 CONSEQUENCES OF INDUSTRIAL SICKNESS

Following are the consequences of industrial sickness:

1. Substantial investment in sick units causes a great national loss in the form of wastage of scarce resources and decline in production.
2. Industrial sickness causes a great loss to entrepreneur and investors. Due to this, value of investors will decline, prospective investors and entrepreneurs and are discouraged and get frustrated. Industrial climate becomes non-conducive to industrial development.
3. Due to industrial unrest, industrial units often delay the pay to their staff. As a result strikes, lockouts and other forms of industrial unrest occur. This industrial unrest is a set back to production in the industry.
4. Closure of sick and non-viable industrial units causes widespread unemployment in the country. Loss of job causes tension and other social unrest.

5. Financial institutions suffer huge loss when the borrowing becomes sick.
6. Government gets sizeable proportions of the revenue by way of taxes and duties levied on industrial units. When large number of sick units are there, scope for tax revenue to the Government is substantially reduces. Ultimately this reduction affects various social and economic development in the country.

10.6 SUPPORTIVE MEASURES FROM GOVERNMENT

Considering the growing sickness in the industrial sector, the Government has shown a greater concern. The industrial policy statement, 1977 averted the growing sickness both in large and small-scale sectors. The policy observed about managing sick industrial unit by providing suitable nursing packages to overcome from the problems of the sickness. In many cases large amount of funds have been pumped through rehabilitation.

1. Sick Industrial Policy (1978)

The first policy statement on sick industries was announced in the parliament on 15.5.1978. The policy make it clear that where management are either unwilling or unable to perform their role, the financial intuitions and the Government should intervene to fulfil their larger social responsibilities of ensuring efficient use of national resources.

The policy statement 1978 guided the following:

a) Sick units in the small sector will be given special attention. Banks and financial institution are asked to devise rehabilitation scheme for revival of sick units.
b) The government and other purchaser of the products of SSI will be directed to settle dues of SSI on priority basis and commercial banks to ensure that credit given to large-scale units for working capital is applied first towards meeting dues of small-scale units.
c) In order to protect the investment, small scale units are forced to close down for reasons beyond the control of the entrepreneurs.

2. Sick Industrial Policy (1981 & 1985)

The Policy Statement of 1978 was revived in 1989 and 1985 in the light of experience gained since 1978 in its implementation. Revised guidelines have been laid down for Central Government/ State Government Financial Institution. The policy allowed to tackle the issue of sickness and to analyse the problems faced by the industrial units.

10.7 PREVENTIVE AND REMEDIAL MEASURES OF SICKNESS

Sickness in any industry does not come overnight, but it takes years. One can visualize the symptoms well in advance. 'Prevention is better than cure, but very few take preventive steps. Many promoters establish units with an intention of taking advantage of liberal concessions and subsidy being offered by the Central and State Governments, but fail to anticipate any problems.

1. Preventive Measure of Sickness

The following preventive measures can be taken by the entrepreneur:

1. Identification and detection of sickness at the incipient stage which is the first and foremost preventive measure to detect and reduce or avoid industrial sickness.
2. Identification of sickness needs appropriate yardsticks. Such yardsticks should be developed.
3. To avoid social disorder, solve labour problems, merger of large number of sick units will be a welcome proposition.
4. To prevent sickness, sick units must be permitted to close on negotiated settlement.
5. Proper steps should to taken to rehabilitate weak units to strengthen viability.
6. Rehabilitation of sick units are provided only in the form of funding but other problems like marketing etc, should be given equal weightage.
7. Early warning system (non-realisation of bills/lack of inventors)

2. Remedial Measures of Sickness

Following are the remedial measures to overcome sickness:

a) Rehabilitation of Sick Industries

The Sick Industrial Companies Special Provisions Act 1985 addresses itself to the rehabilitation of sick units which are engaged in all types of industrial activity except ship building.

b) Refinancing Schemes Under Rehabilitation

The Industrial Development Bank of India evolved a new scheme of RSR (Rehabilitation Scheme of Refinance). Under this scheme in which an industrial undertaking financed by the financial institution facing any financial constraint and encountering any problem, financial institution provides additional fund (i.e., inducement of fund) to recover from the problem faced by the unit. Extension of repayment period is also offered to those eligible units.

c) Re-scheduling/Rephasement of Loans/Advance

The financial institutions and banks are evolved a regular procedure of rephasing of loans of advances by taking into account of problem faced by the industrial unit. The rephasement/re-schedulment will be in accordance with the time limit and the extension of time should not be more than 15 to 20 years. The eligible units will have to qualify the basic. Criteria that the sickness should not be due to mismanagement.

d) Debt Reconstruction Scheme (DRS)

The scheme evolved to encourage the SSI units facing with huge losses. The capital loss should be more than 50% of the initial capital, and the unit should have suffered loss of more than 50% cash loss to become eligible to qualify for the availment of D.R.S. Scheme. Under this scheme additional fund is allowed the interest will be rephased.

e) Seed Margin Money Scheme

In order to assist the sick industrial units, the Central Government has evolved a margin money scheme for the revival of viable sick unit to supplement the various efforts of the State Government. The Reserve Bank of India, Commercial bank and Financial Institution offer seed margin money at 10% of the project with the reduced rate of interest to overcome any financial setbacks.

f) Bride Loan Scheme

Any units facing with shortage of working capital and facing certain problem in mobilizing funds due to non-realization of bills in time. Those industrial unit eligible for investment subsidy from the Government can approach, banks and financial institution to avail bridge loan, against to subsided component eligible from respective state.

g) Kapur Committee

Kapur Committee made the recommendation that to encourage banks to take up rehabilitation of potential viable sick small-scale industries. Some relaxations in income recognition and asset classification norms provided. Small Industries Development Bank of India and Industrial Development Bank of India evolved new schemes of rehabilitation packages to nourish the sick industrial unit.

h) BIFR

The Government of India and Reserve Bank of India should be requested to direct commercial banks and financial institutions to provide information on sickness to the boards like BIFR for implementing the rehabilitation programmes. The existing BIFR case are being monitored at present and there is temporary stop for further addition of cases to BIFR.

i) Negotiated Settlement Scheme

The banks and financial institutions are allowing the debt ridden account to get closed in the books of account by providing easy and honourable exit policy. In which to chronic accounts get closed where the banks/FI sacrifice a portion of principal or interest or both depending upon cases. The OTS or negotiated settlement policy which allows the bankers/FI to put an end to the default accounts.

EXERCISES

Section A

1. Define sickness.
2. Mention any four symptoms of industrial sickness.
3. Mention any four internal factors for sickness.
4. Mention any four external factors for sickness.

Section B

5. Explain the important symptoms of industrial sickness.
6. Explain the consequences of industrial sickness.
7. Discuss the preventive measures of sickness.

Section C

8. Explain the factors affecting industrial sickness.
9. Explain the re-financing schemes under rehabilitation of sick units.

SKILL DEVELOPMENT

Visit a sick unit and list out the reasons for sickness and what are the refinancing schemes under rehabilitation provided by to the sick unit.

11

Business Crisis: How to Overcome Them

STRUCTURE

11.1 Meaning
11.2 Types of Business Crisis

11.1 MEANING

The Institute for Crisis Management defines a business crisis as "a problem that : (1) disrupts the way on organisation conducts business and, (2) attracts significant new media coverage and/or public security." Typically these crises have the capacity to visit negative financial, legal, political or governmental repercussion on the company, especially if they are not dealt with in a prompt and effective manner.

Hundreds of potential threats exist for every organisation. Corporate crisis can take the form of plant fires, loss of competitive secrets, workplace violence, plant defects, embezzlement and extortion, industrial accidents, sabotage and natural disasters. The crisis could also be starting crisis, financial crisis, prosperity crisis, and management succession crisis.

Any of these events as well as numerous others, can cause an immediate and prolonged financial loss to the company. It desires an intensive communication effort to investors, employees, consumers and other entities and series of regulatory and competitive challenges.

11.2 TYPES OF BUSINESS CRISIS

Despite viable business ventures and adequate finance and large number of small and medium enterprises have been failing. These failures are mainly due to the unexpected events or due to the incompetency of entrepreneur, the promoter, the owner-manager. Therefore the business crisis may be classified into:

a) Sudden crisis or
b) Smoldering crisis or slow-burning crisis.

11.2.1 Sudden Crisis or Natural Crisis or Uncontrollable Crisis

Meaning: The sudden crisis is defined as 'a disruption in the company, business that occurs without warning and is likely to generate new coverage'. For example, business related accidents, natural disasters, sudden death or disability of a key person or workforce violence. Companies need to make sure that they prepare as best they can for sudden crisis.

Reasons: The following are the main reasons for sudden crisis.

1. Accidents and natural events.
2. Health and environmental disasters.
3. Technological breakdowns.
4. Economic and market forces.
5. Rogue employees.
6. Sudden death or disability of a key person.
7. Workplace violence.
8. Public resistance to an innovation.
9. Working from building, safety or health inspectors.
10. Rumours and suspicions.
11. Persistent customer companies etc.

How to overcome sudden crisis: Sudden crisis can be avoided by using the following measures:

1. Identify potential crisis.
2. Prioritizing potential crisis.
3. Avoiding the avoidable crisis.
4. Contingency planning through the following five steps:
    a) Organize a planning team
    b) Assess the scope of the problem

   c) Develop a plan
   d) Test the plan
   e) Keep the plan up-to-date.
5. Recognizing impending crisis.
6. Containment of crisis.
7. Relieving crisis stress.

11.2.2 Smoldering Crisis or Slow-burning Crisis or Continuous Business Crisis or Controllable Crisis or Seven Crisis

Smoldering crisis is defined as a serious business problems caused due to lake of management decisions or indecisions". For example, financial decisions, start decisions etc. It is after the slow-burning or smoldering crisis that caused the most damage to a company image and bottom line (Irvine). In short, they often are tough to detect and then to dissolve because they directly or indirectly involve management decisions and management has a tough time admitting errors because it reflects on their egos and abilities.

According to Dr. V.G. Patel the "Seven Crises" approach to business strategy is somewhat unconventional. The crisis referred to result from the manner in which the entrepreneur conceives, implements and runs his business.

The seven crisis are as follows:

1. Starting crisis
2. Cash crisis
3. Delegation crisis
4. Leadership crisis
5. Financial crisis
6. Prosperity crisis
7. Management succession crisis.

Each crisis has been explained in brief.

1. Starting Crisis

Meaning: Starting crisis is the outcome of the initial stage (starting) errors of the entrepreneur. Starting crisis may arise due to the following reasons:

Reasons:

1. Impulsive decision to start the business without thorough analysis of market potential for the product.
2. Lack of adequate managerial experience in the line of business the entrepreneur opted.
3. No proper maintenance of books of accounts and other records for taking managerial decisions.
4. Unable to make investment decisions. In other words, unable to estimate the capital requirement for the project and finally end up with insufficient funds.
5. Unaware of the availability of sources of funds available to the small and medium scale firms from government and non-government financial institutions and end up with investing own funds, which leads to inadequate funds.
6. Lack of thorough knowledge of provisions on tax matters like VAT, Customs Duty, Excise Duty etc., and its impact on his business.
7. Lack of support from family.
8. Lack of readiness to start the business. In other words, the entrepreneur is not fully competent to start the enterprise. (i.e., no proper education and training).

How to overcome the starting crisis?

Following are the suggestions to overcome the starting crisis of a business.

1. Take the advice of people who are interested in the venture like, bankers, consultants, future suppliers of materials, future directors, and check the viability of the new venture.
2. Conduct a through market research to find out market potential to the product or service. The market research can be done by the entrepreneur himself or it can be outsourced to marketing research organizations.
3. If the entrepreneur lack managerial and entrepreneurial competencies he has to undergo training from the EDI of India or any other organizations providing such training before the starts his business.
4. Learn the basic financial accounting, cost accounting and management accounting techniques like: breakeven analysis,

cost benefit analysis, ratio analysis capital budgeting etc. to take decisions at the beginning of the venture creation.

5. The entrepreneur should acquire the technical knowledge of production before he starts his business.
6. At the time of venture creation stage itself the entrepreneur must install the financial cost accounting and management accounting system. This will help the entrepreneur to ascertain the cost, sales, profit etc., in a systematic manner to generate the periodical reports for taking decisions.
7. Identify the institutional investors like, banks, SFC etc., who can help to obtain capital and additional funds at the right time as at right cost.
8. Before the commencement of venture the entrepreneur must find out the tax-laws applicable to his business and also the benefits he can avail by way of tax reliefs, tax holidays, subsidies and concessions from government.
9. Before the commencement of venture the entrepreneur has to estimate the investment in fixed capital like plant and machinery, land and building etc. Working capital and pre-operative expenses carefully. While estimating it must be more realistic.
10. The entrepreneur has to carefully think while deciding on selection of machinery.
11. Finally, take up more realistic and not over ambitions business venture.

2. Cash Crisis

Meaning: Cash is 'life blood' of any business therefore these must be availability of adequate cash. Cash crisis means inadequacy of cash, over stretch creditors, shrinking working capital and profit margins.

Reasons: The cash crisis may arise due the following reasons:

1. Cash crisis may arise due to the '**Credit Period**' given to the debtors (customers) on credit sales and creditors (suppliers) on credit purchases.
2. Unrealistic estimation of investment required for the business (project).
3. Cash crisis may arise due to heavy investment in fixed assets like, plant and machines, land and building etc. out of working capital.

4. When the entrepreneur fails to keep control over stock of goods or inventory.
5. When the entrepreneur unable to collect the money against bills recoverables.
6. Overtrading is another cause for cash crisis.

How to overcome cash crisis?

1. 'Credit Period' should not to long for the debtors (customers) an credit sales. If the credit period is long, it leads to locking-up to cash.
2. Working capital should not be used for the purchase of fixed assets.
3. Do not overstock raw-materials. It leads to locking-up of cash. If possible use Just-in-Time (JIT) inventory system (Japanese System).
4. Make proper arrangements to collect the dues from defaulting customers by outsourcing to the agencies.
5. Dispose the defective goods at a discount, sell worn-out machinery and other assets for cash.
6. Do not withdraw cash for personal purposes from the business frequently.
7. Use the short term idle cash efficiency by investing in high yield areas.
8. Think twice when you want to invest money on new product development.

3. Delegation Crisis

Meaning: When the level of operations becomes difficult to handle by owner entrepreneur he has to find out someone who can be delegated certain responsibilities so that he can look into important matters. But sometimes it may lead to some crisis.

Reasons:

1. The entrepreneur may perceive that delegation may lead to delegation of power and it may create problem between the two.
2. The delegation may lead to neglect of organizational prerequisites.

How to overcome the delegation crisis?

The following steps must be taken to overcome delegation crisis:

1. Appoint a qualified competent and effective person who can take the responsibility.
2. When it is difficult to handle the business independently. It is advisable to merge with another firm so that it will be cash to manage with more people.

4. Leadership Crisis

Meaning: It is the crisis which arises when the owner-manager cannot handle the task and responsibility when the strength of the firm's workforce. Leads a levels of about 150 to 280.

Reasons: Following are the reasons for leadership crisis:

a) When the single owner entrepreneur fail to manage the responsibility of a large company.
b) When the entrepreneur is unable to delegate the authority.
c) When the entrepreneur fails to adopt most effective management style.

How to overcome leadership crisis

1. To overcome leadership crisis, the entrepreneur must be an effective leader who has the vision and who can make the workers work effectively.
2. He must be a good communicator the responsibility rests with the entrepreneur to encourage open and authentic communication up down and across the organization.
3. Develop a conducive and effective communication system.
4. The entrepreneur must obtain training to learn management skills and styles to measures the company.
5. Develop a team of second line executives and give then sufficient authority create leadership qualities in them.

5. Financial Crisis

Meaning: When there is horizontal and vertical expansion of business if the entrepreneur fails to choose the right sources of fund, leads to financial crisis. The financial crisis may also arise when there is overambitious and unrealistic expansion plans using surplus funds.

Reasons:

1. Fail to choose right source of finance for expansions.
2. When there is unrealistic expansion plans
3. When company fails to go public etc.

How to overcome financial crisis?

1. Select the right source for finance from among different sources like, equity issue, loans from banks or financial institutions, public deposits, from suppliers and from leasing companies.
2. Consent monitoring of financial operators with good team work helps to avoid financial crisis.

6. Prosperity Crisis

Meaning: It is the crisis which arises due to overconfidence when there is prosperity in the business and intoxication of success.

Reasons:

1. When the entrepreneur becomes complacent after having crossed many hurdles and achieved success.
2. When the entrepreneur overestimates his own as well as his management team's capabilities.

How to overcome prosperity crisis?

1. Do not be overconfident and enter into an unknown projects.
2. Always be alert and cautions. Do not relax even in prosperity.
3. Because of success, do not remain passive. Be always aggressive.

7. Management Succession Crisis

Meaning: This crisis arises when the founder-owner of the firm dies or remains ill for a long period or sets incapacitated. This leads to problem viz., (a) who will look after the management of the firm, (b) split of voting right and control, (c) winning loyalty and trust from co-owners or shareholders, staff, employees and winning the confidence of financing agencies, clients and suppliers, (d) Tax and legal issues, (e) problems relating to estimating the worth of the business, (f) ownership rights, (g) no one groomed to takeover management responsibility, and (h) no second line authority to manage etc.

How to overcome this crisis?

a) Death in inevitable therefore, succession must be planned.
b) Selecting and grooming a management successor in advance is a must.
c) Develop a team to manage the activities.
d) The family members must know about key elements of your business like: assets, liabilities etc.
e) Have competent persons on the Board of Directors.

EXERCISES

Section A

1. What do you mean by Business Crisis?
2. Mention the Two Types of Crisis.
3. What is Sudden Crises?
4. Mention any four Reasons for Sudden Crisis.
5. What is Slow-burning Crisis?
6. Mention the 'Seven Crisis'.
7. What do you mean by Starting Crisis?
8. Mention any Two Reasons for Cash Crisis?
9. What do you mean by Delegation Crisis?
10. What do you mean by Leadership Crisis?
11. What do you mean by Financial Crisis?
12. What do you mean by Prosperity Crisis?
13. What do you mean by Management Succession Crisis?

Section B

14. What are the reasons for Starting Crisis?
15. What are the reasons for Cash Basis?
16. What are the reasons for Delegation Crisis?

17. What are the reasons for Leadership Crisis?
18. What are the reasons for Financial Crisis?
19. What are the reasons for Prosperity Crisis?
20. What are the reasons for Management Succession Crisis?

Section C

21. Discuss the reasons and how to overcome the Starting Crisis?
22. Discuss the reasons and how to overcome Cash Crisis?
23. Discuss the reasons and how to overcome Delegation Crisis?
24. Discuss the reasons and how to overcome Leadership Crisis?
25. Discuss the reasons and how to overcome Financial Crisis?
26. Discuss the reasons and how to overcome Prosperity Crisis?
27. Discuss the reasons and how to overcome Management Successation Crisis?
28. Discuss the reasons and how to overcome the Sudden Crisis?

SKILL DEVELOPMENT

1. Visit an enterprise which is in crisis and find out the reasons.

12

International Entrepreneurial Opportunities

STRUCTURE

12.1 Introduction
12.2 Meaning
12.3 Benefits of International Business Opportunities
12.4 Modes of International Business Opportunities
12.5 Export Procedures
12.6 Import Procedures
12.7 Financing International Business
12.8 International Finance

12.1 INTRODUCTION

Globalization makes the business environment increasingly global even for domestic firms. The major competition which many Indian firms encounter in the home market now, for instance, is from foreign firms. They now face a substantially growing competition from goods produced in India by MNCs and imports. The best answer for this global and capture the opportunities in developing and underdeveloped countries.

12.2 MEANING

International business obviously means 'Cross border business translations.' International business entails satisfying different needs or tastes or preferences of people in different countries. Thus, a very simple and common definition of international business is that "it is business across national borders." At includes exports and imports to goods and services or international sourcing of factors.

12.3 BENEFITS OF INTERNATIONAL BUSINESS OPPORTUNITIES

Competing in the global marketplace can provide many benefits, such as:

1. *Increased sales:* The entrepreneur will attract new buyers and widen the customer base. He may also import unique products that local customers can buy.
2. *Reduced cost:* The entrepreneur may set the goods at reduced price. Manufacturers in other countries can produce goods at a lower cost because of low labour cost or availability of raw-materials.
3. *Decreased dependence on current markets and suppliers:* When the economic conditions of a country suddenly workers, exports might help to sell the products and servicing abroad till the economy stabilize.
4. *Achieving higher rate of profit :* When the domestic market do not provide a higher rate of profits, the entrepreneur can expand the operations to foreign countries where there is higher rate of profit.
5. *Limited home market:* Due to the size of population or due to lower purchasing power of the people etc., size of the home market becomes limited. Under such circumstances entrepreneur has no option other than exports. Example European countries.
6. *Severe competition in the domestic market:* When there is severe competition from the other competitors in the domestic country, it may not be possible to survive for a long period. The best option is to enter the new markets of road.
7. *Availability of Technology and Managerial Competence:* When the availability of technology and managerial skills are lacking in some countries the entrepreneur prefers to so abroad to set that benefit.
8. *To increase market share:* To larger companies expand their business operation abroad to increase the market share. Example: Coca-cola, Pepsi, Unilever etc.

9. *Availability of raw-material:* One of the major reasons for attracting the companies from other countries is the availability of raw-material abundantly in a country. Example: Minerals, Petroleum etc.
10. *Availability of Quality Human Resources:* When there is quality human resource is available in a country at a lesser cost, the entrepreneur prefers to start the operations in that country. Example: Software industry.
11. *Tariffs and Import quotas:* Imports of products depends on the government's policies towards tariffs or duties and import quotas to reduce the competition to the domestic companies from foreign companies. Therefore, there is an opportunity to the entrepreneur the country where there is no such, restrictions.
12. *Political stability:* There is bright business opportunities in those countries where there is continuation of the same policies of the government, even there is change of political parties.

12.4 MODES OF INTERNATIONAL BUSINESS OPPORTUNITIES

International trade is one way the entrepreneur can become part of the global marketplace. This means he can export or import the products or services he sells or uses in his business. The different modes of international entrepreneurship opportunities are discussed below. (Fig. 12.1)

A. General Classification

1. Importing: According to Cyntnia L.G. "products and services that are brought in from another country to be sold are 'imports'. The main reason for entrepreneurs to import products is due to reasonable price and good quality. Some entrepreneur use imported products to make their own products."

2. Exporting: According to Cyntnia L.C. Greene, "products and services that are produced in one country and sent to another to sold are 'exports'. These products are shipped to countries all over the world.

Types of Exports: The following are the various ways an entrepreneur can become a player in international business:

A. General classification	B. Non-equity arrangements	C. Direct foreign investments	D. Extention to business	E. Using technology	F. Other modes
1. Importing	3. Licensing	6. Minority interest	10. Mergers and Acquisitions	11. Using the world wide web to export	12. Strategic alliance
2. Exporting	4. Turn-key projects	7. Majority interest			13. Third country-location
	5. Management contracts	8. 100% ownership			14. Counter trade
		9. Joint ventures			

Fig. 12.1: *Showing modes of international entrepreneurship opportunities.*

i) *Direct Exports:* Finding buyers or distributors in foreign markets and shipping the products to them is called 'Direct exporting'. For direct exporting the entrepreneur need to hire sales people who live in or travel to foreign countries.

ii) *Indirect Exports:* It is hard to make contact with buyers in other countries. Some businesses use commission agents, brokers, who find foreign buyers for their products or services. Thus, exporting by using commission agents is indirect exporting.

Modes of international entrepreneurship opportunities:

A. General Classification
   1. Importing
   2. Exporting

B. Non-equity Arrangements
   3. Licensing
   4. Turn-Key Project
   5. Management Contracts

C. Direct Foreign Investment
   6. Minority Interest
   7. Majority Interest
   8. 100% ownership
   9. Joint Ventures

D. 10. Mergers & Acquisitions
   Horizontal
   Vertical
   Product extension
   Diversified activity

E. 11. Using worldwide web

F. Other modes
   12. Strategic alliance
   13. Third country location
   14. Counter trade

B. Non-equity Arrangements

3. Licensing: Licensing is a business arrangement in which the manufacturer of a product or a firm (licenser) with property rights, trade mark, technology, production process grants permission to a foreign manufacturer or firm (licensee) against payment of a royalty. For example: Maruti Suzuki.

Advantages: Licensing arrangement is an excellent method for the entrepreneur to engage in international business because:

1. The process is low risk.
2. Need not make an extensive capital investment.
3. Can generate savings in tariffs and transportation cost.
4. Licensing is a more realistic means of expansion than exporting, particularly for the high-tech firm.
5. Access to the market is easier in comparison with equity investments.
6. Foreign governments are more likely to give their permission because technology is being brought into the country.
7. There is potential for the licensees to become partner and contributor in improving the 'learning curve' of technology.

Disadvantages:

1. It is possible the licensee will become a competitor after the contract expires. For example, Honda is a competitor of Kinetic.
2. To fit the licensee's market, the licenser must set the licensee to meet contractual obligations and adjust the products services.
3. Conflicts and misunderstanding may occur. Therefore the entrepreneur must manage the relationships.
4. There may be problem of integrity and independence of both the licenser and licensee.

4. Turn-key project: Under tern-key operations, the foreign entrepreneur builds the factory and other facility, train the workers to operate the equipment, train management to run the installations and hand it over to the owners once the operation is going.

In this arrangement the entrepreneur can gain some international experience without much risk and initial profits can be made.

Turn-key projects are common in the case of oil refineries, steel plants, cement and fertilizer plants.

5. Management contracts: It is a method for doing a specific international task. The management contract allows the purchasing country to gain foreign expertise without giving ownership of its resources to a foreigner. Under this arrangement the firm providing the management know-how may not have any equity stake in the firm being managed. Thus, many entrepreneurs have successfully entered international business by contracting their management techniques and managerial skills.

C. Direct foreign investments: Direct foreign investment can be an exciting venture for firms making efforts to increase their business and their competitive position in the market place. A direct foreign investment is "a domestically controlled foreign production facility. This does not mean the firm owns always a majority of the operations.

A firm can make a direct foreign investment by several methods: (a) by minority interest, (b) by majority interest, (c) 100% percent ownerships, and (d) joint ventures.

Thus, it is an arrangement to acquire an interest in an ongoing foreign operation.

6. Minority Interest: It is the minority equity position in foreign company, which will have enough influence on the management of operations. In some cases, less than 50 per cent ownership can constitute effective control because of stock ownership. A direct foreign investment typically involves ownership of 10 per cent to 25 per cent of the voting stock in a foreign enterprise.

7. Majority Interest: It is an arrangement to obtain majority interest in a foreign company. In this case the company becomes a subsidiary of the acquiring firm. In a technical sense, anything over 50 percent of the equity in a firm is majority interest.

8. 100 Per cent Ownership: It is the complete ownership and control in case of foreign investments when the entrepreneur has the capital, technology and marketing skills for successful entry into a foreign market.

9. Joint Venture: A joint venture happens only when two or more firms pool their resources and create a new entity to undertake productive economic activity. Under joint venture arrangement there will be sharing of assets, profits, risks and venture ownership with more than one firm (Derrick E. D'Souza).

Advantages

1. Firm would be able to gain an intimate knowledge of the local conditions and government where the facility is located.
2. It would be able to use the resources of the other firm.
3. It is possible to compensate the weakness of participating firms.
4. It is possible to reduce the capital outlay and risk.

Disadvantages

1. In joint venture there may be problem of fragmented control. Thus, joint venture arrangement can be a powerful tool for the international business.

D. Expansion of Business

10. Mergers and Acquisitions: In today's globalized economy, it is becoming evident that the current ways of doing business are not good enough to stay competitive in tomorrow's market. So organizations have to invent new ways of competing. Mergers and acquisitions have become universal tool to attain greater market share, acquire additional brand, cannibalize competing brands, realize improved infrastructure, create new synergies, capitalize on efficiencies and economies of scale and globalize in shorter span of time.

Normally, organizations do not depend on interval (business) growth alone. Growth and diversification is achieved both internally and externally. Internal growth and external growth (through mergers and acquisitions) are not considered to be mutually exclusive; they support and reinforce each other. Sometimes, internal growth is more adventurous at other times, external growth is more suitable. Organisations that want to grow faster, use various forms of mergers and acquisitions (M&As) based on the opportunities available to them under the given constraints in which they have to perform.

Benefits or Expectations of M&A

The factors which support the external growth and diversification through mergers and acquisitions include the following:

1. Faster achievement of goods and objectives.
2. Attainment of feasible market share with less risk, in shorter time and at lower cost.
3. Tax advantages.
4. Complementary capabilities etc.
5. Improved investment management capabilities after merger.
6. Helps to leverage current operating and asset management capabilities.
7. Saves cost i.e. M&As bring down the pre-policy expenses rates.
8. M&As also augment the competencies of a company as well as its product's portfolio.
9. Enhancement in the existing growth potential by way of expansion in the developing and under-developed markets.

Why Merger Fails?

It is very difficult to precisely define what makes a merger fail since its complex nature makes it impossible to fix a single answer fitting all situations. But one can certainly trace the road map that led to failures of a merger on the following lines:

1. Failure to anticipate a problem before the problem actually arises.
2. Failure to perceive the problem, when the problem does arrive.
3. Fail to attempt to solve the problem after perceiving it.
4. Tried but failed to solve the problem.

Types of Mergers: There are five basic types of mergers (according to Robert H. Isrish and Michael Peters)

1. **Horizontal Merger:** A horizontal merger is "the combination of two firms that produce one or more of the same or closely related products in the same geographical area to affect the economies of scale in marketing production or sales."
2. **Vertical Merger:** A vertical merger is "the combination of two or more firms in successive stages of production that often involve a buyer-seller relationship."
3. **Product Extension Merger:** A product extension merger occurs when acquiring and acquired companies have related production and/or distribution activities but do not have products that compete directly with each other. Example: Acquisition of Miller Brewing (Beer) by Philip Morris (Cigarettes)
4. **Market Extension Merger:** A market extension merger is "a combination of two firms producing the same products but selling them in different geographical markets." In this type of merger the acquiring firm can economically combine its management skills, production and marketing with the acquired firm.
5. **Diversified Activity Merger:** "It is the merger of two essentially unrelated firms." In this type of merger the acquiring firm is not interested in using its resources to expand the activity of the acquired company. For example, Hill Enbrand Industries (a furniture manufacturer) acquiring American Tourister (a luggage manufacturer).

E. 11. Using the World-wide web to Export

This is another type of exporting where the world-wide web (www) is used. The entrepreneurs create and modify their web sites to appeal to foreign customers.

F. Other Modes

12. Strategic Alliance: A strategic alliance is "an alliance with its competitors, existing or potential in critical areas, instead of competing with each others." The purpose of the kind of arrangement is to increase the flow of innovation, increase flexibility in responding to market and technological changes etc.

13. Third Country Location: When direct transactions between two nations are not permitted due to political or any other reason, the entrepreneur can enter the market through the third country base. For example: Taiwanese have successfully entered to China market through Hong Kong.

14. Counter Trade: Counter trade means the exports and imports are linked directly with each other. In this arrangement import of goods are paid for by export of goods, instead of cash payments. It is like barter system. There are several forms of counter trade.

12.5 EXPORT PROCEDURES

The export procedures are classified into five stages, namely,

1. Preliminaries
2. Inquiry, offer and receipt of confirmed order
3. Regulations regarding exports
4. Shipment
5. Payment Procedure.

1. Preliminaries

The activities in the preliminaries include the following:

a) **Importer-Exporter Code Number (ICE Number) :** The entrepreneurs intending to export and/or import goods and services must obtain an Importer - Exporter number from the regional licensing authorities. The ICE number is not required if the Director General of Foreign Trade (DGFT) exempts any specific business. (See Annexure 10.1) for model application for allotment of ICE number).

b) **Registration:** The exporters and importers have to register themselves with the export promotion councils (EPC), sales tax authorities etc.
c) **Membership in certain bodies:** The exporters and importers are highly benefited if the membership is obtained in export promotion councils, trade promotion organizations etc. This helps them getting information and for documentation.

2. Inquiry Offer and Receipt of Confirmed Order

Inquiry is the request made by a prospective importer regarding his wish to import certain goods.

Offer is a proposal submitted by an exporter expressing his intention to export specific goods at a specific price with specific terms and conditions. Exporters usually makes an offer in the form of a "Proforma Invoice" (See Annexure 10.2 for format of Proforma Invoice).

Receipt of Confirmed Order means the buyer sends the confirm order to the exporter by signing the duplicate copy of the invoice.

3. Regulations Regarding Exports

After obtaining a confirmed order the exporter must manufacture or procure the goods exactly as specified in the invoice and follow the procedures mentioned below:

a) **Packing and Marking:** After the manufacture or procurement of goods the exporter should arrange for packing and marking as per the international standards. While packing the exporter has to follow the instructions as per the Bureau of Indian Standards. Similarly, The British Standard Packing Code and Exporters Encyclopedia published in U.S.A.
b) **Quality Control and Pre-Shipment Inspection:** In order to ensure the quality of goods as indicated in the invoice, the exporter has to arrange for quality check and pre-shipment inspection.

If the goods to be exported are included under the compulsory quality control and pre-shipment scheme in accordance with the provisions of the export (quality control and inspection) Act, 1963, the export inspection council or other appropriate body conducts the quality control inspection.

c) **Excise Duty Rebates:** Government has exempted the goods meant for exports from excise duty. The exporters can claim for debate of excise duty or non-payment of excise duty. The rebate is provided under Rule 12 of the central excise rules, 1944. The exporter has to submit the following forms for rebate after the excise duty is paid: (i) Gate Pass, GP-1, (ii) AR-4 Form.

4. Shipment

Shipment here means transportation of goods either by ship or by air or by post or by land depending on the convenience.

Shipment by Ship

The exporter has to contact shipping companies for space, offer setting the confirmed order. The shipping company may issue **shipping advice** or **shipping order**, depending on the requirement of the exporter.

In case of shipping advice, the shipping company has no obligation to accept the cargo as the shipping advice is only providing information of availability of space at the time of issue of the acceptance. But in case of shipping order the shipping company has the obligation to accept the cargo.

Procedure for shipment: The exporter has to follow the procedures mention below:

i) **Customs Clearance:** The exporter has to set custom clearance of the goods before, they are loaded to the ship. Custom authorities accord their formal approved after scrutinizing complete set of shipping documents, copies of shipping bill etc. These documents include:

a) Proforma invoice in original and duplicate.
b) GR-I form (in duplicate).
c) AR-4 form (in original and duplicate).
d) Export licence (if required).
e) Letter of credit covering the export order, export contract or order in original.
f) Certificate of inspection (where necessary).
g) Form of declaration (in duplicate).

h) Shipping bill (five copies).
i) Quality control inspection certificate (if required).
j) Original contract wherever available.
k) Packing list.
l) Letter of registration certificate (if applicable).

ii) **Carting order:** Once the goods are ready for export and the shipping order is available, to exporter has to approach the superintendent of the concerned port trust for the latter's. permission to move the goods physically inside the port area. This order given by the superintendent is called *the carting order*.

iii) **Customs examination of cargo at docks:** The custom authorities after checking the documents check the goods to be exported at the docks. The customs appraiser after checking the consignment, will seal the package, after his satisfaction.

iv) **Let ship:** After setting the approval from the custom officials, the exporter arranges for loading the goods on the ship. Before loading takes place, the exporter's forwarding agent has to get the permission from the preventive officer of the customs department. This permission is called the '*Let ship order*'. Let-ship order authorities the shipping company to accept the cargo on board the vessel.

v) **Mate's receipt:** After the goods are loaded on the ship the captain of the ship furnishes a document to the post superintendent. This document is called '*Mate's Receipt*'. This certifies the loading of the cargo. This document provides the details of the goods, condition of the goods at the time of loading etc.

vi) **Port trust dues:** The port trust authorities after receiving the '*Mate's Receipt*', the 'Bill of lading' will be issued from the captain of the ship to the exporter.

vii) **Bill of lading:** The exporter's forwarding agent collects the *Mate's Receipt* and submits the same to the authorities and in turn collects the bill of lading from the port authorities.

The forward agent of exporter provides the following documents to the exporter at the final stage. They are:

a) A copy of the invoice duly attested by the customs.
b) Drawback copy of the shipping bill.
c) Export promotion copy of the shipping bill.

d) Full set of 'clean on board' bill of lading together with the non-negotiable copies.
e) The original letter of credit.
f) Customer's order or contract.
g) Duplicate copy of the AR-4 form.

Shipment by other Modes of Transport

1. **Shipment by Air:** Normally the perishable goods, goods of less weight and goods which are needed by the importer urgently are transported by air.
2. **Shipment by Post:** Certain goods of less weight are exported by post. Postal Notice No. 13 dated 3rd Dec. 1973 regulates the export trade by post.
3. **Shipment by Land:** Export of the exciseable goods to the nearby countries is similar to the one laid down for export by sea. AR-4 form is different for export by land. The exciseable goods are presented to the frontier customs officer/border examiner along with form 4 A.

Payment Procedure

After the goods are exported, the exporter is interested in setting payments for the exporter mode.

The exporter submits the relevant documents to his banker for settling the payment for the goods exported. Submission of relevant documents to the bank and the process of setting the payment from the bank is called "Negotiating the documents, through the bank". These documents are called 'Negotiable set of documents'. This set normally includes:

a) Bill of Lading
b) Commercial Invoice together with the packing ship and bill of exchange.
c) Certificate of origin
d) GR-I form (in duplicate)
e) Marine Insurance Policy (in duplicate)
f) Letter of credit (original) (Annexure 10.4 Provides a note of confirmed and irrecoverable letter of credit).

The letter of credit is opened by the importer through his bank authorities drawing a bill of exchange. Payment will be made against this bill of exchange by the importer bank. The exporter's bank realizes the export proceeds and pay to the exporter. (See Annexure 10.5 for Bank certificate of export and realization).

Export Incentives

Export incentives include:

a) **Duty Drawbacks:** Under this scheme, exporter is eligible to set back the excise duty and central excise paid on all raw-materials, components and consumables used in the production to goods exported.

b) **Excise Duty Refund:** The exporter is eligible for refund of excise duty after its export are if it is paid in the beginning.

12.6 IMPORT PROCEDURES

Importing refers to products and services that are brought in from another country to be sold in the home country.

The import-process consists of five stages viz.,

1. Preliminaries.
2. Enquiring and placing the indent.
3. Obtaining foreign exchanges.
4. Arrangement for payment.
5. Payment of customs duties and taking delivery of goods.

1. Preliminaries

a) *Licence and importer-exporter code number:* The importing firm or an individual has to obtain a licence and importer-exporter code number (See Annexure 10.1) from the controller of exporters and importers. The import licences are usually issued for a period of one year at a time.

b) *Enquiring and placing the indent:* After obtaining the import licence, the importer has to enquire with various exporters of other countries for goods and services he would like to import.

The importer at this stage asks to exporter to send the invoice. The importers may accept the invoice and send the indent directly to the exporter. Otherwise, they may send the indent through specialized intermediaries called "indent houses". They maintain close links with the foreign firms.

Indent may be open or closed. *Open indent* does not specify the price and other details of the goods and leaves them to the discretion of the exporter. *Closed Indent* specifies the brand, price, number, packing, shipping mode, insurance etc.

Indents incorporating the exact price is called 'Confirmatory indent'.

3. Obtaining Foreign Exchange

After sending the indent, the importer has to procure the required foreign exchange from the exchange control department of Reserve Bank of India. Entrepreneur has to produce the import licence and the prescribed forms for securing foreign exchange which is needed to pay for the import of goods.

RBI releases the foreign exchange based on the strength of the application, availability of foreign exchange and foreign exchange policy of the government.

4. Arrangement for Payment

The importer has to make arrangements for paying for importers after obtaining the foreign exchange.

5. Payment of Customs Duties and Taking Delivery of Goods

The importer has to pay for the custom duties on the basis of weight and size of the goods or based on the value of the goods. The custom duty may also be paid under the "Permanent Deposit System". Under this system, the importer maintains a running account with custom office and deposits money from time to time which is adjusted to the duty payable. The importer after all the above procedure set the delivery of goods.

12.7 FINANCING INTERNATIONAL BUSINESS

International business arrangements are concerned with special issues in addition to issues involved in domestic trade. They are:

1. Currency to be used.
2. Creditworthiness of the importer.
3. Acceptable methods of payment.
4. Arranging finance.

1. Currency to be used

Selection of currency to be used for setting the international business translations is an important issue in international finance. As such the hard currencies are the choice of exporter for setting the transaction in international business. Hence, the importers and struggle to earn hard currencies in order to meet their import bills. If the currency of the importing country is weak, the exporter prefers the payment in hard currencies like US dollars, UK pounds etc.

2. Creditworthiness of the importer

The exporter may ask the importer to send his credit rating done by an internationally reputed firm. Export-Import Bank of India, Export-Import Bank of USA etc., provide credit rating information to the exporters by collecting a fee. After evaluating the creditworthiness of the importer, the exporter and importer should come to an understanding regarding the method of payment. This process is required as there is an amount of risk involved in the payment of money by the importer.

3. Acceptable method of payment

After assessing the importer's creditworthiness, both the exporter and the importer should agree on a particular type of payment. Following are the methods of payments:

a) **Open Account:** Under this method the importer first receives the goods and then arranges for the payment. Hence, it is the safest form of payment to an importer. But is the element of risk involved to an exporter.

This method is suitable when the exporter has well established long-term relationship with the importer or when the importer's creditworthiness is certified by an authorized agency.

b) **Payment in Advance:** Under this method, the exporter prefers to set to advance payment from importer even before the shipment, as it involves no risk. This method is not suitable to an importer as it involves heavy risk in setting the delivery of the goods as per the order.

c) **Documentary Collection:** Due to the risk and problems involved in open account and advance payment, the banks and international financial institutions have developed a number of financial instruments. One of which is documentary collection.

Under this method commercial banks play an important role in the payment process. The exporter draws up a document called "Bill of Exchange", in which payment is demanded from the importer at a specified future date. There are two types of bills of exchange. These are:

i) *Sight Bill of Exchange:* Under sight bill of exchange the payment should be made immediately after the transfer of title of the goods to the importer by the exporter. The importer's bank after receiving the 'Bill of Lading' (i.e. after obtaining the title of the goods) and 'Sight Bill of Exchange' from the exporter's bank, asks the importer to arrange for the payment. After the payment is made by the importer, the bank gives the bill of lading to the importer.

ii) *Time Bill of Exchange:* Under this method, the time is given the importer to make payment against the bill of exchange, after receiving the possession of goods (i.e. Bill of Lading).

The importer writes, "Accepted" on the bill of exchange after obtaining to bill of lading. This document is called "Trade Acceptance". This is a negotiable debt instrument.

When the importer fails the make payment against the bill of exchange (i.e. documentary collection), the exporter can only sue in the court of law. Thus, there is involvement of risk in this method.

d) **Letter of Credit:** A Letter of Credit is an instrument issued by a bank wherein the bank promises the exporter to pay upon receiving the proof that the exporter completed all the necessary formalities specified in the document. The importer bank does this work by collecting after from the importer after obtaining a security to this effect. This guarantees the exporter regarding payment and hence, the payment is free from risk.

e) **Counter Trade:** It is the goods for goods deal. In other words, it is an arrangement to pay for import of goods and services with something other than cash.

f) **Credit Card:** Under this method the payments are made through credit cards issued by banks. Credit cards are used normally for small international business transaction by the market intermediaries like retailers and also by the customers.

4. Arranging for Finance / Export-Import Finance

The entrepreneur can arrange for the finance to do international business through banks and other financial institutions.

a) **Banks:** In the international business transaction the importer bank provides finance in the form of issuing a 'later of credit' to the exporter bank.

b) **Other financial institutions:** The important financial instruction which helps in arranging finance in the international business are Export Credit and Guarantee Corporation Ltd. (ECGC) and Export-Import Bank of India (EXIM).

i) Export-Import Bank of India (EXIM Bank)

EXIM Bank of India, set up in 1982 for the purpose of financing, facilitating and promoting foreign trade in India. It is the principal financial institution in the country and co-ordinates other institutions engaged in financing exports and imports. The bank offers a range of financing programmes at par with the industrialized countries and at the same time meets the special needs of a developing country.

The Bank is also involved in the promotion of two-way technology transfer through the establishment of joint ventures in India with the collaboration of foreign companies and also establishing joint ventures by Indian industrialists in other countries. The bank is a partner institution with European Union. This started helps the bank to promote European Joint Venture in India.

Functions

1. **Financial Assistance :** Provides financial assistance to the exporters under Foreign Exchange Management Act, 1999. It provides financial assistance for the following purposes:

a) Export of goods on deferred payment terms (e.g. export of machinery, equipment, manufactured products).
b) Turnkey projects (e.g. setting up of cement plant, sugar plant etc.)
c) Construction projects (e.g. Construction of roads, Bridge, Dams etc.)
d) Consultancy and Technical Services (e.g. Operations and Maintenance Controls)

2. **Advisory Services:** EXIM bank provides information and support services to Indian companies to improve their prospects for securing business in multilateral agencies, funded projects in the following ways:
a) Dissemination of business opportunities in funded projects.
b) Providing detailed information on project of interest.
c) Information on procurement guidelines, policies, practices of multilateral agencies.
d) Assistance for registration with multilateral agencies.
e) Advising Indian companies on preparation of expression of interest, capability profile.

3. **Promoting Indian Consultancy:** EXIM bank promotes Indian consultancy jointly with:
i) International finance corporation, Washington D.C., Africa project development facility, Africa Enterprise Fund, Technical Assistance and Trust Fund, Mekong project development facility.
ii) Eastern and Southern African Trade and Development Bank (PTA Bank).
iii) African Management Service Company (AMSCo.), Netherlands.

4. **Acts as consultant:** EXIM Bank acts as a consultancy in order to help the Indian exporters. Some of the consultancy service provided by the bank are:
i) Feasibility study for establishment of an export credit and guarantee facility for Gulf Co-operation Council Countries.
ii) Regional Co-operation in export finance and export credit guarantees for ESCAP.
iii) Study on promotion of international competitiveness and export of manufactured goods for ESCAP.

iv) Designing of export financing programmes – Turkey
v) Setting-up an EXIM bank in Malaysia.
vi) Design of export marketing seminars for SME's in Vietnam.
vii) Export development project – Ukraine
viii) Enterprise support fund – Armenia
ix) Establishing an export credit guarantee company in Zimbabwe – etc.

5. Knowledge Building : EXIM bank builds the knowledge necessary to the exporters for this purpose, the bank set-up 'Eximus centre for learning' at Bangalore in October, 1994 to organize seminars and workshops in areas like, international trade and investment, export marketing, quality, packaging, business opportunities in multilateral agencies funded agencies, sector and country specific programmes.

The Bank also conducts research studies on products, sectors, countries, macro- economic issues relevant to international trade and investment.

6. Promotional Programmes: EXIM bank promotes Indian consultancy at preparatory stages in projects overseas with potential of multilateral funding and down stream linkages for Indian exports. It conducts project feasibility studies, project formulation and related advisory services. For example: Railway, Sector study in Vietnam, Road Rehabilitation in Uzbekistan and Agriculture in Egypt etc.

ii) Export Credit and Guarantee Corporation Ltd.

ECGC is a company wholly owned by the government of India. This was set-up in order to provide export credit insurance support in Indian exporters. It functions under the administrative control of the Ministry of Commerce and is managed by a Board of Directors representing Government, Banking, Insurance, Trade, Industry etc.

Functions

1. ***Assistance to Banks:*** ECGC guarantees the export finance and credit facilities provided to exporters by bank. The guarantees assure the bank that, in the event of an exporter failing to discharge his liabilities to bank, ECGC would make good a major portion of the bank loss. Bank is required to be co-insurer to the

extent of the remaining loss. Various guarantees offered by ECGC to banks are:

a) Export Production Finance Guarantee
b) Packing Credit Guarantee
c) Post-Shipment Credit Guarantee
d) Export Finance Guarantee
e) Export Performance Guarantee
f) Export Finance (overseas lending) Guarantee.

2. ECGC guarantees banks which extend buyer's credit and line of credit to overseas buyers or overseas bank Institution or Government. Buyer's credit is a credit extended by a bank in India to an overseas buyer to pay for machinery or equipment that he may be importing from India for a specific project. A Line of credit is a credit extended by a bank in India to an overseas bank, institution or government for the purpose of facilitating import of a variety of listed goods from India into the overseas country.
3. **Shipment (comprehensive risk) Assistance:** ECGC covers risk in respect of goods exported on short-term credit, i.e. credit no exceeding 180 days. This policy covers both commercial and political risks from the date of shipment. It is issued to export turnover for the next 12 months is more than Rs. 50 lakh.
4. **Special Assistance to Supply Contracts:** ECGC provides insurance against political, commercial and other risk to contracts for exports of capital goods or turnkey projects or construction work or rendering services abroad which are not a repetitive nature and which involve medium or long-term credits.
5. **Insurance to Construction Contractors:** ECGC provides insurance facility to Indian Contractors executing a civil construction job in foreign countries.
6. **Special Services or Schemes:** ECGC assists the Indian companies, which have concluded contracts with foreign principal for providing them with technical or professional services. Three schemes are offered under special scheme are transfer guarantee, overseas investment insurance and exchange fluctuation risk cover.
7. **Assistance to Small Exporters:** ECGC assists the small exporters whose annual turnover does not exceed Rs. 50 lakh in order to encourage them to participate in the export trade.

12.8 INTERNATIONAL FINANCE

International finance includes the following:

1. Foreign Exchange.
2. Convertibility of the Rupee.
3. Balance of Trade and Payment.

1. Foreign Exchange

Definition

1. According to Dr. Paul Einzig "Foreign exchange is the system or process of converting one national currency into another and of transferring money from one country to another."
2. The Foreign Exchange Regulation Act, 1973(FERA) defines foreign exchange as "foreign currency and includes all deposits, credits and balance payable in any foreign currency and any drafts, traveller's cheques, letter of credits and bills of exchange, expressed or drawn in Indian currency, but payable in any foreign currency."

Functions of Foreign Exchange Market

The foreign exchange market is a market in which national currencies are bought and sold against one another. In other words, it is a market in which foreign exchange transactions take place.

A foreign exchange market performs three important functions:

1. *Transfer of Purchasing Power:* The primary function of a foreign exchange market is the transfer of purchasing power from one country to another and from one currency to another. The international clearing function performed by foreign exchange markets plays a very important role in facilitating international trade and capital movement.
2. *Provision of Credit:* International trade depends on credit facilities to exporters and importers. The exporters may set pre-shipment and post-shipment credit. Thus the credit function performed by foreign exchange market play an important role in the growth of foreign trade.
3. *Provision for Hedging Facilities:* Hedging refers to covering of export risk and it provides a mechanism to exporters and

importers to guard themselves against losses arising from fluctuations in exchange rate. This is an important function of a foreign exchange market.

Dealings in the Foreign Exchange Market

The important dealings which takes place in foreign exchange market has been given in brief.

1. ***Spot Exchange:*** It refers to the class of foreign exchange transaction which requires the immediate delivery or exchange of currencies on the spot. In practice, the settlement takes place within two days.

   Spot Rate and Spot Market: The rate of exchange effective for the spot transaction is known as the *spot rate* and the market for such transactions is known as the *spot market*.
2. ***Forward Exchange:*** The forward transaction is an agreement between two parties. Here, the delivery is made on a future date by one of the parties against payment in domestic currency by the other party. At the price agreed upon in the agreement.

   Forward Exchange Rate and Forward Market: The rate of exchange applicable to the forward contract is called the *forward exchange rate* and the market for forward transactions is known as the *forward market*.

   By entering into an appropriate forward exchange contract, the exporters and importers can cover risks arising out of exchange rate fluctuations. In India commercial banks are permitted to offer forward cover only with respect to genuine export and import transactions.

Forward Exchange Rates

The forward exchange rate is determined mostly by the demand for and supply of forward exchange. The forward rate may be at par discount or premium.

At Par: The forward exchange rate is said to be at par if the forward exchange rate quoted is exactly equivalent to the spot rate at the time of making the contract. When the supply is equivalent to the demand for forward exchange, the forward rate coil tend to be at par.

At Premium: Normally, when the demand for forward exchange exceeds its supply, the forward rate will be quoted at a premium. Say when, one dollar buys more units of another currency, say rupee in the forward then in the spot market, then forward exchange rate for a currency is said to be at premium.

At Discount: Normally, when the supply of forward exchange exceeds the demands for it, the forwards exchange rate will be quoted at discount. For example, when are dollar buys fewer rupees in the forward than in the spot market, the forward exchange rate for a currency is said to be at discount.

3. ***Futures:*** A futures contract is similar to a forward contract, but there are a few differences:

Forward contract	Futures contract
a) It is tailor-made for the client by his international bank	a) It is a standardized contract and can be traded only on an organized exchange and they are traded competitively
b) Margins are not required	b) Margins are required of all participants an initial margin must be deposited into a collateral account to establish a futures position.

4. ***Options:*** An option is a "contract of financial instrument that gives holder the '*right, but not the obligation*', to sell or buy a given quantity of an asset at a specified price at a specified future date."

Call Option: An option to buy the underlying asset is known as *Call option.*

Put Option: An option to sell the underlying asset is known as Put Option.

Exchanging the option: Buying or selling the underlying assets. via the option is known as exercising the option.

The Long and Short: The buyer of an option is known as the long and the seller of an option is known as the writer of the option or the short.

Premium: The price for the option is known as premium.

With reference to their exercise characteristics, there are two types of options, American and European.

American option: American option can be exercised at any time during the contract.

European option: A European option can be exercised only at the maturity of expiration date of the contract.

5. Swap Operation: Commercial banks who conduct forward exchange business may resort to a swap operations to adjust their fund position. The term swap means simultaneous sale of spot currency for the forward purchase of the same currency or the purchase of spot for the forward sale of the same currency. The spot is swapped against forward.

6. Arbitrage: Arbitrage is the simultaneous buying and selling of foreign currencies with the intention of making profit from the different between the exchange rate prevailing at the same time in different markets.

Exchange Rate Systems

There are two important exchange rate systems:

1. ***Fixed Exchange Rate System:*** Under fixed exchange system countries agree to keep their currencies at a fixed or stable exchange rate or pegged rate and to change their value only at fairly infrequent intervals, when the economic situation forces them to do so.
2. ***Flexible Exchange Rate System:*** Under the flexible exchange rate system, exchange rates ware freely determined in an open market primarily by private dealings and they like other market prices, vary from day to day.

2. Convertibility of the Rupee

Free convertibility of a currency means that the currency can be exchanged for any other convertible currency, without any restrictions at the market determined exchange rates. Convertibility of the rupee, thus means that the rupee can be freely converted into dollar, pound, sterling, Yen, Euro etc. and vice versa at the rates of exchange determined by the demand and supply forces.

Convertibility of the Rupee on Current Account

Convertibility of the rupee on current account is defined as "the freedom to buy or sell foreign exchange for the following international transactions.

a) All payments due in connection with foreign trade, other current business including services and normal short term banking and credit facilities.
b) Payments due as interest on loan and as net-income from other investments.
c) Payment of moderate amount of authorization of loans or for depreciation of direct investment.
d) Moderate remittances for family living expenses.

Thus, current account convertibility relates to the removal of restriction on payments relating to the imports and exports of goods, services and factors of income.

Capital Account Convertibility

Capital account convertibility refers to "the removal of the restrictions on payments relating to the transactions like inflow and outflow of short-term and long-term capital."

The Indian Government after introducing the full convertibility on current account is also contemplating convertibility on capital account also.

3. Balance of Trade and Payments

Balance of Trade

The balance of trade is a narrow term. It takes into account only merchandise exports and imports. Thus, balance of trade takes into account only the transactions arising out of the exports and imports of visible items. In other words, balance of trade does not take into account the exchange of invisible items like services of banking sector, insurance sector, transport sector, tourism sector, interest payment and divided payments and receipts etc.

Balance of Payment

The balance of payment takes into account the export and import of both the visible and invisible items. In other words, it takes into consideration, the export and import of goods of all kinds including consumer goods, consumer durables, fast moving consumer goods, capital goods, machinery, technical equipment and services like banking, insurance, tourism, transportation, payment of salaries, benefits, interest, dividends.

The balance of payment is a double entry system of all economic transactions between the residents of a country and the rest of the world carried out in a specific period. Therefore, balance of payments is a much wider term as compare to balance of trade. Balance of payment presents an account of comprehensive economic and financial transactions of a country with the rest of the world.

ANNEXURE–1

Application form for allotment of importer-exporter code (IEC) number and modification in particulars of an existing IEC No. holder.

(For Office use only)

File Number .... Date .... IEC No. allotted ....

1. Application for (please tick)
   a) Allotment of IEC No. ☐
   b) Modification in particulars of existing IEC No. holder ☐
2. Name and Address of the applicant
3. Address of all Branches/Divisions/Units/Factories located in India and abroad.
4. In case the application is for 1(B) give
   a) Existing IEC No. ....
   b) Nature of modification required and details thereof

      ....

      ....

(In case the application is for 1(B) information in S. No. 2 and 3 above will be as per pre-modified status)

5. Particulars of Fees Paid:
   (i) Bank Receipt / Demand Draft No. ....
   (ii) Amount (in Rs.) (In figures) ....
   (In words) ....
   (iii) Name of Bank & Branch of Issue ....
6. Permanent Account Number (PAN) of Income Tax ....
   Issuing Authority ....
   Date of Issue ....

DECLARATION/UNDERTAKING

1. I/We hereby declare that the particulars and the statements made in this application are true and correct to the best of my/our knowledge and belief and nothing has been concealed or held therefrom.
2. I/We fully understand that any information furnished in the application if proved incorrect or false will render me/us liable for any penal action or other consequences as may be prescribed in law or otherwise warranted.
3. I/We undertake to abide by the provisions of the Foreign Trade (Development and Regulation) Act, 1992, the Rules and Orders framed thereunder, the Export and Import Policy and the Handbook of Procedures.
4. I/We hereby declare that this application is made by me/us in the name of Registered/Head Office and I/We have not obtained or applied for Importer/Exporter Code Number previously in this name from any office of the DGFT (Not applicable for existing IEC No. holder)
5. I hereby certify that I am authorized to verify and sign this declaration as per Paragraph 3. of the Export and Import Policy.
6. I/We hereby certify that name of the Director/Partner/Proprietor/ Karta of the firm or company is a Director/Partner/Proprietor/ Karta of the Firm/Company which has come to the adverse notice of DGFT.

Signature of the Applicant : ....

Name : ....

Photo duly attested by bank

Designation : ....

Official Address : ....

Tel. No. : ....

Residential Address : ....

E-mail Address : ....

Place : ....

Date : ....

Source: M.I. Mahajan, "*A Guide on Export Policy, Procedure and Documentation*", Snow White Publications (P) Ltd., Mumbai, 2001 pp. 2.20 – 2.21.

ANNEXURE–2

PROFORMA INVOICE

Exporter	Pro-Inv. No. & Date	Exporter's Ref
	Buyers-Ref. No. & Date	
	Country of origin of goods	Country of final destination

Carriage by Sea/ Air/Multi Modal Transport	Place of Receipt by pre-carrier	Terms of Delivery and Payment
	Port of loading	
Port of discharge	Final destination	

Marks & Nos./ Container No.	Nos. kind of Pkgs	Description of goods	Quantity	Rate	Amount
Amount chargeable (in words)				Total	

Declaration : We declare that this proforma invoice shows the actual price of the goods described and that all particulars are true and correct.

Signature & Date

ANNEXURE–3

EXCHANGE CONTROL DECLARATION (GR) FORM

Exporter	Invoice No. & Date	SB No. & Date
Carriage	AR4/AR4A No. & Date	
Custom House Agent LIC No.	Q/Cert No. & Date	Import Export Code No R.B.I. Code No.

Pre carriage by	Place of Receipt by Pre-carrier	Export Trade Control	If export under Deferred credit [ ] Joint venture [ ] Rupee credit [ ] Others [ ] RBI's Approval/cir. No. & Date
Vessel/ Flight No.	Rotation No. Port of Loading		
		Nature of contract: CIF [ ]/CFR [ ]/FOR [ ] Others (specify)	
Port of discharge	Country of destination	Exchange Rate U/S 14 of CA	Currency of invoice

Sl. No.	Marks & Nos.	No & Kind of pkgs Container No.	Statistical code & Description of goods	Quality	Value FOB
Net Weight					
Gross Weight					
Total FOB value in words					

Analysis of export value	Currency	Rate	Amount	Full except value or where not as containable the value which exporter expects to receive on the sale of goods.
FOB value				
Freight				Currency
Insurance				
Commission				Amount
Discount				
Other deductions				

Contd....

Sl. No.	Export Tariff No.	Assessable Value under Sec. 14	Duty		Cess		Total Duty and Cesses	Duty Payment Particular
			Rate	Amount	Rate	Amount		
NOT APPLICABLE								

Declaration:

I/We declare that all particulars given here in are true and correct.

I/We also attach the declaration(s) under clause No.(s) ………..........................

Public Notice No. …….............……........……….. Dated ………………..........

Signature & Date

Is export under L/C arrangements? Yes [ ] No [ ] If YES, name of a advising bank in India	For customs Customs Assessable Value Rs. (Rupees ……….................…………….. Export value verified Customs Appraiser
Bank through which payment is to be received	
Whether payment is to be received through the ACU Yes/No	Date of Shipment Customs Appraiser

Declaration under Foreign Exchange Regulation Act : I/We hereby declare that I/We am/are the seller/consigner of the goods in respect of which this declaration in made & and that the particulars given above are true and that of the value as contracted with the buyers is the same as the full export value declared overleaf.

The full export under of the goods in not ascertainable at the time of export and that the value declared is that which I/We, having regard to the prevailing market conditions, expect to receive on the sale of goods in the overseas market.

I/We undertake that I/We will deliver to the bent named here in the foreign exchange representing the full export value of the goods on & before @ ………….. in the manner prescribed in Rule of the foreign exchange regulations rules, 1874. I/We further declare that I/We and are resident in India & I/We have on place of business in India. State Appropriate date of delivery which must be with 6 months from the date of export to ware houses established abroad with resume bank permission.

*Strike out whichever is not applicable

Date ………….. (Signature of exporter)

Space for use by Reserve Bank of India

ANNEXURE–4

Confirmed Irrevocable Letter of Credit

Name and Address of the Opening Bank

Messrs.

Date................

(Name and Address of Exporter)..

....

....

Confirmed Irrevocable Commercial Letter of Credit No. .... Without recourse of Drawers

THIS IS A CONFIRMATION OF DOCUMENTARY CREDIT OPENED BY CABLE UNDER TODAY'S DATE. IT IS ONLY AVAILABLE FOR SUCH AMOUNT AS HAS NOT ALREADY BEEN AVAILED OF UNDER SUCH ABLE ADVICE AND MAY NOT BE AVAILED OF AT ALL UNLESS ATTACHED TO AND AS PART OF OUR CORRESPONDENTS NOTIFICATION OF SUCH CABLE ADVICE THE TWO JOINTLY CONSTITUTING EVIDENCE OF THE OUTSTANDING AMOUNT OF THIS CREDIT.

Dear Sir,

At the request of M/s. (Name and address of the Importer) .... we hereby establish our CONFIRMED IRREVOCABLE LETTER OF CREDIT in your favour for the amount of .... Available by your draft(s) drawn on them at .... sight accompanied by the following documents marked (x) :

( ) Your signed Commercial INVOICE(S) in .... copies bearing the following clause: "We hereby certify that (a) this invoice is authentic (b) it is the only invoice issued by us for the goods described therein) it shows their exact value without deduction of any discount (d) their origin is ...."

( ) Full "CLEAN SHIPPED ON BOARD" Bill(s) of Lading drawn endorsed to the Order of (NAME AND ADDRESS OF THE OPENING BANK) ....
showing "FREIGHT PREPAID" and marked NOTIFY (THE OPENING BANK) ....
Branch and openers (the Importers).

( ) Airway Bill(s) Bearing this L/C Number drawn to our showing "FREIGHT ...." marked NOTIFY or Branch and Opener(s).

( ) Original Parcel Post RECEIPT(s) bearing this L/C Number showing postages paid and evidencing that the parcel(s) has been dispatched to our branch a/c, opener(s).

( ) Certificate of Origin from the Chamber of Commerce.

( ) INSURANCE POLICY / CERTIFICATE in duplicate, issued to your order and blank endorsed, covering the goods for the invoice(s) value plus .... % against WAR risks, S.R & C.C. as per Institute Clauses, and the following risks: (ALL RISKS) (W.A.) (F.P.A including short and non-delivery), (transshipment risk, if applicable) as per Institute Cargo Clauses, without any franchise. Claim if any payable in ....

( ) Insurance covered by openers. All shipments under this credit must be advised by you immediately after shipment direct to M/s .... (the importer) .... And to the openers referring to Cover Note No .... Giving full details of shipments. A copy of this advice to accompany each set of documents.

( ) Packing list .... copies.

( ) Marks and Numbers ....
Evidencing dispatch / shipment of the following Goods not later than .... by .... From Port .... To Port .... CIF, C&F, FOB.

( ) COMMODITY

Partial Shipments Permitted /not Permitted. Transshipment Allowed/Not Allowed

1. This credit is transmitted though (Name and Address of the Indian Bank) who are authorized to negotiate documents presented there against not later than ....
2. This credit is subject to Uniform Customs and Practice for the Documentary Credits (1993) Revision) of International Chamber of Commerce Publication No. 500.
3. Drafts must be marked "Drawn under (Name and Address of the Opening Bank) .... Credit No. ...." and amounts thereof endorsed on the reverse hereof by the negotiating bank.
4. We hereby agree with drawers, endorsers and *bona fide* holders of Draft(s) drawn under and in compliance with the terms of this credit that the same shall be dully honoured on due presentation.
5. Other conditions, if any. ....

(Authorised Signature of the Opening Bank)

Source : M.I. Mahajan, "*A Guide on Export Policy, Procedure and Documentation*", Snow White Publications (P) Ltd., Mumbai, 2001 pp. 2.34 – 2.35.

ANNEXURE–5

Bank Certificate of Export and Realisation
Form No. 1

To .... (Name and Address of Licensing Authority) We .... (Name and Address of Exporters) hereby declare that we have forwarded a documentary export Bill to .... (Name and Address of the bank i.e., Branch and City) for collection/negotiation/purchase as per particulars given hereunder.

Invoice		Export promotion copy of Shipping Bill duly authenticated by customs		Description of goods as given in the customs authenticated Shipping Bill	Bills of Ladings/ PP Receipt/ Airways Bill		Destination of goods Country	Bill Amount CIF/C&F FOB (in foreign exchange)	Freight amount as per Bill of lading/ freight memo
No.	Date	No.	Date		No.	Date	Name		
(1)	(2)	(3)	(4)	(5)	(6)	(7)	(8)	(9)	(10)

Insurance amount as per insurance company's bill/Receipt	Commission Discount paid/payable	Whether the export is in freely convertible currency or in India Rupees	FOB value/FOB value actually realized in free foreign exchange Rupees (9+10+11+12)	Date of realization of export proceeds	GR/PP Form No.	No. Date & Category of Duly Free License/ Imprest License, if any applicable
(11)	(12)	(13)	(14)	(15)	(16)	(17)

We further declare that the aforesaid particulars are correct. (Copies of invoices relevant to these exports and customs attested E.P. Copy of relevant Shipping Bil is attached for verification by the bank)

.... Signature of the Exporter

Place : .... Name in Block Letters

Date : .... Designation

.... Full Official Address

Official Seal/ Stamp .... Full Residential Address

Source : M.I. Mahajan, *Op.cit*, p. 2.59

EXERCISES

Section A

1. What do you mean by international business?
2. What do you mean by "Exporting'?
3. What do you mean by "Importing"?
4. What do you mean by turn-key projects?
5. What do you mean by Management contracts?
6. What do you mean by Minority Interest?
7. What do you mean by Majority Interest?
8. What do you mean by 100 percent ownership?
9. What do you mean by Mergers and Acquisitions?
10. What do you mean by Strategic Alliance?
11. What do you mean by Third country location?
12. What do you mean by Counter Trade?
13. What is Let Ship?
14. What is Bill of Lading?
15. What is Letter of credit?
16. Define Foreign Exchange.
17. What is 'Spot Exchange'?
18. What is 'Forward exchange'?
19. What is 'Futures'?
20. What is 'Options'?
21. What is 'Swap Operation'.
22. What is Arbitrate?

Section B

1. What are the advantages of Licensing?
2. What are the advantages and disadvantages of Joint Venture?
3. Why mergers fail?
4. What are the different types of mergers?
5. What are the functions of foreign exchange?
6. Write a note as 'convertibility of the rupee'.
7. Write a note on Balance of Trade and Payments.

Section C

1. Discuss the benefits of international business opportunities.
2. Discuss the different modes of international entrepreneurship opportunities, in brief.
3. Discuss the advantages and disadvantages of Licensing.
4. Discuss the benefits of M&A.
5. Discuss in brief the Export procedure.
6. Discuss in brief the Import procedures.
7. Discuss in brief the issues involved in financing international business.
8. What is EXIM bank? Discuss the functions of EXIM bank.
9. What is ECGC? Discuss its functions.
10. Discuss in brief dealings in Foreign Exchange Market.

SKILL DEVELOPMENT

1. Collect the application form for allotment of Importer-Exporter Code (IEC) & fill the form
2. Fill-up the proforma invoice.
3. Fill-up the 'Exchange Control declaration (GR) form.
4. Fill-up 'confirmed Irrevocable letter of credit'.
5. Fill-up 'Bank certificate of export and realization.
6. Visit Exporters and Importers Officer to know the procedures.

REFERENCES

1. Donald, F. Kuratko, Richard M. Hodgetts, Entrepreneurship – A contemporary Approach, The Dryden Press. Fourth edition.
2. Cynthia, Greene, Entrepreneurship Ideas in action: Thomson, South westeress; Second edition.
3. Robert D. Hisrish and Michael P. Peters; Tata McGrawHill, Fifth Edn.
4. W. Harynes; Entrepreneur Development, central book agency (P) Ltd.
5. CRISP; Entrepreneurship Development: Tata McGraw Hill Publishing Co. Ltd.
6. M.M.P. Akhouri, Entrepreneurship; Global Business Press New Delhi, 1992.
7. S. Anil Kumar, S.C. Poornima, Mini, K. Abrahim; Entrepreneurshop Development; New Age International Publishers New Delhi.
8. J.B. Patel and D.G. Allampalli; A manual on how to prepare a project report: EDII.
9. GEM India report 2001 to 2005 NSRCE, IIM-B.
10. Trainers manual; EDT of India.
11. Rakesh Mohan, Small scale industry policy in India – a critical evaluation; National Council of Applied Economic Research.
12. Bivek Debroy and Laveesh Bhandari; Small scale industry in India.
13. Lakshmi Mahesh; Small scale industry.
14. Proceeding of 3rd International Entrepreneurship forum confer 2003 – IIM – B – India
15. KSIC news: published by KSFG Bankers.
16. V.G. Patel, When the going gets tough: Tata McGraw-Hill Publishing Co. Ltd. New Delhi.

Index

A

Achievement motivation training (AMT), 110
Achievement motivation, 106
 definitions of, 107
 significance of, 107
 sources of development of, 109
Achievements motivation test, 94
Agro Industries Corporation (AIC), 273
Ancillary industrial undertaking, 141
Association of Women of Karnataka (AWAKE), 285
Azim Premji, 68

B

Business crisis,
 types of, 327
Business incubators, 200
Business plan, 219, 243
 and economic feasibility, 235
 benefits of, 220
 composition of, 223
 duration of, 222
 errors in, 237
 key questions of, 240
 precautions for, 239
 preparation of, 224
 social aspects of, 236

C

Capital account convertibility, 362
Cash crisis, 330
Cash expenditure estimate, 234
Central footwear training institutes (CFTIs), 260
Centre for Entrepreneurship development of Karnataka (CEDOK), 271
Communication skill, 128
Competencies,
 assessment of, 85
 types of, 77
Creative thinking process, 112
 phases of, 114
Crisis management, 326

D

Delegation crisis, 331
Deposit Insurance and Credit Guarantee Corporation (DICGC), 282
District industries centres (DICs), 269

E

Electronic Development Corporation (EDC), 272
Enterprises,
 types of, 6
Entrepreneur, innovation and, 119
Entrepreneur self-assessment profile guide, 97
Entrepreneur, 32, 56
 benefits of, 35, 56
 characteristics of, 39
 concept of, 33
 definitions of, 34
 functions of, 41
 importance of, 35
 problems of, 36
 qualities of, 36
 types of, 43

Entrepreneurial competencies test, 89, 92
Entrepreneurial competencies, 92
  components of, 73
  development of, 103
  meaning of, 73
Entrepreneurial function, 186
Entrepreneurial process, 14
Entrepreneurial qualities assessment, 86
Entrepreneurship development programme, 20, 21
Entrepreneurship development, 16
  objectives of, 17
  government policies on, 19
  process of, 18
Entrepreneurship motivation training (EMT), 104
  components of, 105
  objectives of, 104
Entrepreneurship,
  categories of, 13
  concept of, 3
  definitions of, 4
  importance of, 8
  India's potential for, 12
  need of, 8
Entrepreneurship,
  and Indian economy, 13
Export-import bank of India (EXIM Bank), 279
Export-oriented unit (EOU), 145

F
Financial crisis, 332
Foreign exchange market, 358, 359
Forward exchange rates, 359

G
General industrial estate, 300
Group entrepreneurship, 5
Gujarat Industrial Development Corporation, 303

H
Haryana State Industrial Development Corporation, 303
Hindu undivided family (HUF), 181
100% export oriented units, 291

I
Import procedures, 350
Industrial Area Development Board (IADB), 269
Industrial Credit and Investment Corporation of India (ICICI), 277
Industrial Development Bank of India (IDBI), 275
Industrial Development Corporation (IDC), 270
Industrial estate, 297
  definitions of, 298
  failure of, 302
  objectives of, 298
  types of, 300
Industrial Finance Corporation of India (IFCI), 274
Industrial Investment Corporation (IIC), 282
Industrial parks,
  scheme for, 304
Industrial policies of Govt. of India, 164
Industrial policy statement – 1948, 165
Industrial policy statement – 1956, 165
Industrial policy, August 2000, 166
Industrial policy–1977, 165
Industrial Reconstruction Bank of India (IRBI), 278
Industrial sickness,
  consequences of, 320
Industrial sickness,
  symptoms of, 316
Innovation process, 120
Innovation,
  principles of, 122
  sources of, 121
  types of, 120